THE WALL STREET WALTZ

The New York Stock Exchange on the corner of Wall Street and Broad Street at the turn of the century.

THE WALL STREET WALTZ

90 VISUAL PERSPECTIVES

ILLUSTRATED LESSONS FROM FINANCIAL CYCLES AND TRENDS

KENNETH L. FISHER

BUSINESS CLASSICS
A Division of Pacific Publishing Group, Inc.
Woodside, CA

ISBN: 0-931133-04-1
Originally published by Contemporary Books, Inc.

To my wife, Sherrilyn, who is my waltz partner in the dance of life, both emotionally and in our investment business, and particularly in our most important business—that of managing our most prized investments—Clayton, Nathan, and Jesse.

Contents

ACKNOWLEDGMENTS   1

INTRODUCTION   4

PART 1
STOCK MARKET VISUALIZATIONS   10

1
PRICE/EARNINGS RATIOS: THEN AND NOW
Dow Jones Industrials Price/Earnings Ratio, 1915–1986   15

2
IN CASE YOU DIDN'T GET IT THE FIRST TIME
The Stock Market vs. Its P/E Ratio, 1871–1937   17

3
EARNING A GOOD RETURN IN THE MARKET
The Long-Term Tie Between Earnings and Stock Prices,
1926–1971   19

4
EARNINGS YIELDS: STOCKS VERSUS BONDS
Earnings Yield on the S&P 500 vs. Yield on High-Grade
Corporate Bonds, 1946–1974   21

5
PRICE/DIVIDEND RATIOS PROVIDE
LONG-TERM VISION
Price/Dividend Ratios, 1920–1985   23

6
PRICE-TO-BOOK RATIOS: PLAYING IT BY THE BOOK
The Market's Price-to-Book Ratio, 1921–1986   25

7   vii
PRICE/CASH FLOW RATIOS: A HIDDEN TWIST
S&P 400 High Annual Price/Cash Flow Ratio, 1945–1986   27

8
AN ADVERTISEMENT FOR
SUPER STOCKS AND FORBES
Sears, Roebuck & Company's Stock Price, 1926–1955   29

9
MR. AND MRS. FINANCIAL—
REAL SPLIT PERSONALITIES
Railroad Stocks and Bonds, 1860–1935   31

10
NEVER A TIMER BE:
56 YEARS OF STOCKS AND INTEREST RATES
Short-Term Interest Rates vs. the Stock Market, 1919–1978   33

11
VALUE LINE INDUSTRIAL COMPOSITE:
ALL THE STATS THAT ARE FIT TO PRINT
Value Line Industrial Composite, 1970–1986   35

12
WEALTH INDEXES FOR CLASSES OF SECURITIES,
AND THE WINNER IS . . .
Wealth Indexes of Investments in the U.S. Capital Markets,
1925–1985   37

13
INVEST OVERSEAS AND DIVERSIFY?
British Stocks vs. Dow Jones Industrials, 1958–1977   39

14
STOCK PRICES ABROAD: SEVEN MORE MIRRORS
Stock Indexes in Seven Countries, 1970–1980   41

15
THE 51st ESTATE
Canadian vs. U.S. Stock Prices, 1962–1971   43

16
STOCK PRICES VERSUS GNP
Stock Market Indexes and Variations in GNP, 1955–1974   45

17
THE PREMIUM PRICE OF GROWTH
Price/Earnings Multiples of Emerging Growth Stocks as a
Percentage of the S&P 500 P/E, 1960–1986   47

18
GROWTH-STOCK GYRATIONS
Hambrecht & Quist Growth Index, Hambrecht & Quist
Technology Index, Standard & Poor's 400, January 1970 to
September 1986   49

19
"IPO" MEANS IT'S PROBABLY OVERPRICED
Number of Initial Public Offerings, 1969–1985   51

20
"WAKE UP, FOLKS"
Stocks vs. Five Investment Alternatives 1975–1985   53

21
TAKEOVER TACTICS IN RELATION TO ASSETS
Stocks, Inflation, and Merger and Acquisitions Activity,
1968–1984   55

22
THE SILENT CRASH NO ONE NOTICED
The Dow Jones Industrial Average as Adjusted for Inflation,
1920–1985   57

23
MOVING WITH THE MOVING AVERAGE
The 40-Week Moving Average of the Dow Jones Industrial
Average, 1965–1977   59

24
ALL THE NEWS THAT'S FIT TO PRINT
Stock Prices vs. News Items, 1949–1968   61

25
STOCK PRICES VERSUS RECESSIONS
Standard & Poor's Index of 500 Common Stocks and Cyclical
Declines in the Economy, 1948–1977   63

26
NINE MAJOR STOCK MARKET CYCLES
Long-Term DJIA Showing Bull and Bear Trendlines,
1929–1977   65

27
ROARING TWENTIES REVISITED?
Comparison of Dow Jones Industrials of the 1920s
vs. the 1980s   67

28
PRICE/EARNINGS RATIOS CAN BE DECEIVING
Price/Earnings Ratio, 1928–1929   69

29
A CLEAR WARNING
Stock Price Indexes, 1927–1929   71

30
THE BIG BOYS DON'T ALWAYS BUY CHEAP
Mergers Record, 1919–1928   73

31
PREFERRED STOCKS SHOULDN'T BE
Comparison of Industrial Common and Preferred Stocks,
1908–1932   75

32
THE 2 PERCENT RULE
The Panic of 1907   77

33
REMEMBER WHAT THE RICH MAN FORGOT
The Average Market Price of the 20 Leading Railroad and 12
Leading Industrial Stocks and of 5 Standard Bonds,
1896–1912   79

34
MONTHLY RAILROAD PRICES, 1843–1862
Indexes of Railroad-Stock Prices, Monthly, 1843–1862: Index
(8 Selected Stocks), 1843–1852; Index IIc (18 Selected Stocks),
1853–1862; and All-Inclusive Index, 1843–1862   81

35
FINANCIAL FLUCTUATIONS IN THE 18TH CENTURY?
YOU CAN BANK ON IT!
The Bank of England—Stock Prices, 1732–1846   83

36
CHARTING THE SOUTH SEAS
The South Seas Bubble, December 1719 to October 1720   85

37
190 YEARS OF STOCK MARKET MOVEMENTS
Annual Average Stock Prices, 1790–1980   87

38
DO YOU FIGURE THEY EARNED THEIR KEEP?
Annual Rates of Return on Common Stocks, 1925–1976   89

39
TWO WAYS TO MAKE A MILLION
Two Examples of the Power of Compound Interest   91

PART 2
INTEREST RATES, COMMODITY PRICES,
REAL ESTATE, AND INFLATION   92

40
THE INTEREST-RATE SHUFFLE
Long-Term vs. Short-Term Interest Rates, 1950–1975   97

41
LONG-TERM INTEREST RATES: FOUR COUNTRIES
IN THE WORLD ECONOMY
Long-Term Interest Rates in Selected Countries, 1960–1980   99

42
THERE SEEMS TO BE A BOND
BETWEEN THESE YIELDS
Bond Interest and Common Stock Yields of Four Countries,
1955–1965   101

43
THE SNAKE
AA Bond Rates Compared to the S&P 400 Earnings,
1960–1986   103

44
WHY THE INTEREST IN OIL?
Yield on 20-Year Treasuries and Price of Crude Oil,
1973–1986   105

45
HIGH INTEREST RATES HAVE BEEN A RECURRING
NIGHTMARE
U.S. Money Rates, Prime Commercial Paper, 1841–1918   107

46
125 YEARS OF THE COUNSEL OF THE CONSOLS
A Comparison of Yields on Consols and U.S. Railroad
Bonds, 1860–1980   109

47
THE SOURCE OF ENGLAND'S STIFF UPPER LIP
Long-Term Interest Rates, U.K., 1731–1970   111

48
WHEN HIGH IS LOW—AND VICE VERSA
Historical Record of Real Interest Rates, 1790–1980   113

49
COMPARING DOMESTIC AND ENGLISH
WHOLESALE PRICES
Wholesale Prices in England vs. the United States,
1782–1930   115

50
PRICES IN SOUTHERN ENGLAND
Price Index of Southern England, 1290–1950   117

51
WHOLESALE INFLATION
Wholesale Prices: All Commodities—Yearly Averages,
1749–1980   119

52
INFLATION—THE AMERICAN EXPERIENCE
United States Consumer Price Index, 1790–1985   121

53
GOLD: THE LITMUS TEST FOR COMMODITY PRICES
Prices, in Currency and Gold, of 40 Basic Commodities in
Different Countries, 1913–1936   123

54
PRICES IN THREE COUNTRIES
Retail Prices in Germany, England, and the United States,
1860–1910   125

55
A LESSON IN AVOIDING WARS
Effect of Wars on U.S. Wholesale Prices   127

56
NO PLACE TO GO BUT UP?
Commodity Prices, 1982–1986   129

57
LONG-TERM GOLD HOLDERS GET THE COLD
SHOULDER
200 Years of American Gold Prices, 1781–1981   131

58
THE LONG CYCLE IN REAL ESTATE ACTIVITY
Idealized 18 1/3-Year Real Estate Cycle, 1870–1955   133

59
RURAL REAL ESTATE: THE TRUE STORY
Change in Average Value of Farm Real Estate per Acre,
1981–1985   135

60
AND IT NEVER WAS, EITHER
Trend in U.S. Farm Real Estate Prices, 1919–1976   137

61
U.S. HOUSING PRICES
Single Family House Price Index, 1890–1980   139

PART 3
ANALYZING BUSINESS CYCLES, GOVERNMENT
FINANCE, AND QUACKERY   140

62
THE ONE MINUTE ECONOMIC CHEAT SHEET
American Business Activity, 1790–1986   145

63
WHAT DO YOU SEE IN THIS PATTERN?
Conspectus of Business Cycles in Various Countries,
1790–1925   147

64
UNEMPLOYMENT AND THE 1 PERCENT RULE
Unemployment Rate for Civilian Workers 1948–1983
(seasonally adjusted)   149

65
CARS CRASH, TOO!
New Auto Sales, Domestic Type (excluding imports),
1945–1983   151

66
HOUSING STARTS: AN INVERTED LOOK
Housing Starts and Real Residential Fixed Investment,
1950–1979   153

67
BREADLINES IN BRITAIN
English Unemployment, 1850–1914   155

68
A CAPITAL SPENDING MYTH
Expenditures for Business Plant and Equipment
as a Percentage of the Privately Produced
Gross National Product, 1900–1960   157

69
SOUTH AFRICA GOLD: HOW IMPORTANT?
Total World Gold Production, 1950–1983   159

70
IS LABOR REALLY OVERPAID?
Changes in the Equivalent of the Wage Rate of a Building
Craftsman Expressed in a Composite Physical Unit of
Consumables in Southern England, 1264–1954   161

71
ELECTRICITY USE AND ECONOMIC GROWTH
Kilowatt-Hour Sales of the Electric Industry vs.
Gross National Product or Expenditure   163

72
CRUDE OIL SUPPLY:
A TALE OF GOVERNMENT INVOLVEMENT
Domestic and Imported Crude Oil Supply, 1950–1979   165

73
TEXANS WEREN'T THE FIRST TO RIDE—
THE LEARNING CURVE
Accumulated Knowledge vs. Costs, Electric Utility Industry,
1896–1912   167

74
IN THE KNOW, OR HEAVILY SNOWED?
Net Public Debt as a Percentage of GNP, 1930–1986   169

75
TAXES: THE CUSTOMS OF OUR EVOLUTION
Sources of Federal Revenue, 1873–1940   171

76
GOVERNMENT GROWTH: THE BIG PICTURE
Public Finance, 1790–1953   173

77
STATE AND LOCAL TAXES ON A STEADY COURSE
State and Local Tax Sources, 1960–1979   175

78
THE STATES ARE REVOLTING
Federal and State-Local Expenditures, 1954–1983   177

79
YOU CAN'T PUT A NUMBER ON IT
The Laffer Curve   179

80
THE MYTH OF FEDERAL TAXES
Taxes and Spending and Their Relation to GNP, 1965–1987   181

81
BALANCING THE BUDGET WITH HOT AIR
Federal Income Tax Rates, 1909–1987   183

82
UNCLE "FAT CAT" SAM'S REAL ESTATE SCAM
Approximate Area of Federal Lands in the United States,
1781–1960   185

83
DEFENSE EXPENDITURES AND THE GNP
Defense Budget as a Percentage of GNP, 1945–1986   187

84
THE ECONOMIC CYCLE ECONOMISTS DENY
The Kondratieff Wave, 1780–1986 and Beyond   189

85
SUNSPOTS
Sunspots, 1755–1978   191

86
BEAR MARKETS VERSUS BARE KNEES
The Hemline Indicator, 1897–1986   193

87
DON'T BUY NUTTIN' WHAT EATS
Average Thoroughbred Yearling Prices Compared to
Dow Jones Industrials Yearly Close, 1970–1980   195

88
WALL STREET WITCH DOCTORS
Exponential Upsweep of Dow Industrials, 1926–1962+   197

89
FLUKES OF NATURE AND FINANCE
The 9.6-Year Cycle in Acreage of Wheat Harvested,
1860–1970   199

90
DON'T LOSE YOUR HIDE IN THE MARKET
Cycles of Hide and Leather Prices   201

CONCLUSION   202

APPENDIX: MYTHS TO FRIGHTEN CHILDREN   205

INDEX   207

Acknowledgments

This book came flowing out of the shower head at me one Sunday morning—all in a gush. With it came the realization that this book could be one that many people could enjoy. Also, as if by magic, from that first realization gushed forth enthusiastic volunteers to turn what they saw as a nifty idea into reality. Most of the old crowd of helpers who had helped with my last book came out from under cover to take up the charge, and with more zeal than the first time. Others joined in. Some of them had, over the years, joined me as full-time participants in our hidden little financial factory in the woods, 2,200 feet above the Bay Area—what we call Fisher Investments. Others who signed on were part of this project alone. All of them are appreciated.

Joseph Toms, one of our managing directors at Fisher Investments, provided the first feedback that suggested there might be interest in these charts and visualizations. After reading my first few attempts, he provided comments and suggestions that helped me hone the content and style. Chris Antonio and Ephran Younger arrived at Fisher Investments simultaneously, looking for work. Both had security industry backgrounds and were in the midst of career changes. And both of them bought the idea of working with me on *The Wall Street Waltz*. Chris and Ephran together drafted about forty of the stories herein. Ephran, who has become a key part of our securities research efforts, furthered the project by preparing on our computer system those few charts which are of our original creation (such as the South Seas Bubble chart). He was also instrumental in preparing and reworking the artwork on many of the other charts.

Arthur Frank set up the computerized chart-making capability for Ephran under the direction of Jeff Silk, a long-standing research analyst at Fisher Investments. Arthur also inputted much of the data involved. His sister, Mary Frank, photocopied for us until she was blue in the face, both at the library of Stanford's Jackson Graduate School of Business and at Fisher Investments for the many drafts we created en route to the finished manuscript. Once we decided to expand the scope of the project to the realm of the most interesting charts we could find, weeks and weeks had to be spent in libraries, primarily at Stanford and the San Francisco Business Library, searching for unusual and useful charts. Greg Crossfield, who handles much of our library research, took charge of this at Stanford, making great use of Charlie Brown, a student there, as well as Mary Frank, Jeff Silk, Ephran Younger, Sherrilyn Fisher (my wife), and my oldest son, Clayton.

Clayton put in the most hours of anyone, next to Charlie, marking charts with paper clips and putting them back on the shelf for future inspection by Greg or me. My younger sons, Nathan and Jesse, did much the same thing throughout our more limited company library.

Not only did Sherrilyn provide me wifely support and encouragement, but as Fisher Investments' office manager, she jumped headlong into the project, taking full responsibility for securing permissions from the copyright holders of the charts. Just locating the copyright holders on some specific charts was a gigantic task, involving finding the heirs of authors long

2 deceased. In some cases, despite thorough searching, we never could locate the appropriate copyright holders. We have run those few charts anyway, assuming that their appeal and validity make reprinting more in the public's good than any concern the copyright holder might have.

Sherri, with a background in art, also took responsibility for the touch-up and visual presentation of all the charts, working on many herself and overseeing Ephran Younger on the others. Finally, she and my three sons were all extremely patient with me through the whole process. Thank you.

Of course, this book would have been impossible without numerous copyright holders who granted us the right to use these charts in this work. They were patient with our requests and, for the most part, generous in allowing us use of these valuable charts.

Along the way, various outside readers made major contributions. The quantity and quality of commentary from these readers was particularly important in correcting errors, changing tone and emphasis, and suggesting previously unconsidered charts. Alfred P. Haft, Jr., of New York and Henry B. Roberts of Duluth, Minnesota, were particularly helpful in this regard. Each of them provided more than 20 pages of commentary and suggestions. Long-time friend Ken Koskella, of the Franklin mutual fund family, had few criticisms, but his explosively enthusiastic encouragement propelled me along. My father, Phil Fisher, corrected me on facts and, more importantly, on misimpressions of facts from his personal memory of the 1920s and 1930s financial markets. John and Ned Roscoe of The Customer Company raised serious philosophical questions regarding the validity of assuming a cycle is proved by only a few occurrences.

Dr. Frank Jewett, one of my former and most important economics professors, and now a financial planner at Ross & Jewett in Eureka, California, led me to strengthen my section introductions and analyses. Mike Brusin, another of my former economics professors, helped correct some historical errors, while providing some debate on the validity of comparing things long past to the present. Dr. Samuel B. Aronson actually graded each chart on its level of interest to him, showing me which needed to be reworked most. Tony Spare, Chief Investment Officer for the Bank of California, directed me to several charts I'd not previously considered and offered me pointed commentary of many charts. Early on, Jim Love of Kidder Peabody convinced me to eliminate one chart and rework others because the charts were overly technical.

Too many others provided assistance for me to be certain of covering them all, but other important readers and remarkers included Bill Gibson, Sutro & Co.; Don Romans, chief financial officer at Bally Manufacturing; Robert S. Haft, chief financial officer at Araca Petroleum; and Lennie Thompson, our firm's chief financial officer. Still others included Bruce Hannay, Merrill Lynch, Phoenix; Al Zick, director of pension and benefit assets, Staley Continental; James Palmer; and Monte M. Stern. All of your comments were appreciated and valuable. Thank you.

There were literally hundreds of charts we didn't use but

seriously considered. They ranged from Australian stock trends to U.S. liquor consumption per capita from 1900. Collectively, they should be acknowledged for their valuable contribution— that of leading me through a process of picking which charts were the best to include for your interest and education.

Finally, it is necessary to thank the creators of these charts themselves. The stories and credit lines tell you where the charts come from. But they cannot fully convey the labor and love that went into their creation. The collective financial and investment knowledge and wisdom of this group of chart buffs would dwarf that of any investment committee, advisory council, or faculty group in existence. Their efforts, spanning more than a century, cannot be acknowledged adequately. But to all these charters I am deeply indebted for their unique visual contributions.

Introduction

Did you know that price/earnings ratios were higher in early 1987 than in 1929? Or that in 1929 stocks collapsed at the same time all around the world? Or that double-digit interest rates dominated the 19th century? Do you care? Should you care? If you can't answer those questions, then do you really know what makes Wall Street waltz?

Maybe it will help if you consider that Arizona produced only 870,408 eggs in 1880, but its chickens laid fully 13,572,852 of them 10 years later. Doesn't help, huh? That little tidbit came from *The Abstract of the Eleventh Census: 1890*, which sits on my firm's library shelves along with lots of other obscure tomes stuffed with facts that nobody in his or her right mind would attempt to catalog. Lennie, our head trader, was mildly amused, but only mildly, when I blurted out those statistics—but then she came from Arizona.

Most of us couldn't care less. Every day we are so bombarded with "facts" that we haven't time to assimilate what's shoved at us, much less go out of our way to understand financial history and how it might relate to our lives. Most folks don't want to get a Ph.D. in finance or economic history. They just want to learn enough of the Wall Street Waltz that they can comfortably profit from the human race's second most awkward dance, without making fools of themselves on the waltz floor.

Most folks are afraid of the Wall Street Waltz. You might be—and probably should be, because most investors lose money on Wall Street. In fact, the way most folks end up with a million dollars in the stock market is to start out with two million.

That's even true of the pros. Why do folks lose out? One big reason is that there is so much misunderstood mythology floating around about investing that most of us never get to reality. We bandy the myths around as if they were fact. So this book came to be as a way to try to expose a myth.

Birth of an Idea, Birth of a Book

One weekend I was preparing for a client who was coming in on Monday. He had been babbling some end-of-the-world mythology about the country's debt load, and I was searching among old piles of files for a chart I'd stashed away years earlier. I hoped it would give the poor fellow some facts to help relieve his paranoia. The chart never showed up, which was a shame, because the guy never would take my word for it.

But several hours of searching did help me rediscover dozens and dozens of other charts that had also been filed away in dead storage. And the choicest ones were too good to put back. Collectively, they composed a mass of visual persuasion that spanned some of my best lessons from 15 years as a professional Wall Street waltzer, and before that from college. Our client-services guy has an Ibico binding machine for little booklets, and I bound the charts together.

On Monday the chart collection made a much bigger hit around the office than the 1890 census had. Everyone agreed that it would be a great aid for explaining to clients my sometimes bizarre-sounding views of reality. With a single chart and a few well-chosen phrases, I could get folks to see clearly phenomena they would never comprehend otherwise. A few days later, the charts were used to convey their first point to a client, and it worked. The next morning in the shower, it dawned on me that if I liked all these visualizations, and my staff liked them, and clients like them, that a lot of other folks might like them too—you, among others. The book was born.

It was born to explain at a glance, aided by a few paragraphs, financial phenomena that are unfathomable to most folks because they haven't been exposed to the raw facts in a sufficiently distilled, visual form. It was born to break down the Wall Street Waltz into its simplest and most understandable steps. This book contains my 90 all-time favorite charts and a brief explanation of each chart: what you should see in it, why it's important, and how it pertains to the present and the future. It's as close as you can get to a Wall Street picture book. Combining a chart and a brief story gives you a visualization.

So, here are 90 visualizations of financial reality that most folks couldn't see otherwise. Although you may have already been exposed to some of these visual perspectives in a less structured form, most will be new, even to most professional Wall Streeters.

About the Charts

Though I'm used to writing and most folks respect my qualifications to write a book like this, be careful not to let my verbiage get in the way of the charts. They're the important part. The words are intended simply as analysis to help you see.

These charts are authentic. They provide vivid visual perspective on how Wall Streeters have waltzed for centuries. If there is one thing I've learned in the financial world, it is that while events and curious phenomena enter and exit the scene almost daily, nothing really important has changed for hundreds of years. All those trendy new details that so excite the media and the menagerie aren't very important at all. The really important things aren't new and haven't changed, and very few folks ever discuss them. But by seeing how Wall Streeters have done their waltz before—right and wrong—you can gain perspective on doing it right, now and forever.

The charts themselves come from various sources—books, magazines, brokerage firm materials, newsletters, research services, and a few we designed ourselves. Some are quite old; others are rather new. The newest is one we constructed from some of the oldest data—dating back to 1720. All the charts are outstanding in their intellectual clarity and their rareness. None are easily located outside of this book without access to a good business library. In fact, as the book progressed, it dawned on me that I could provide you more than what was bound together that Sunday at my office. So, aided by associates, I spent weeks searching the stacks of the Jackson Library at Stanford's Graduate School of Business. We found dozens more, which were added to the set. I'm proud of this collection of charts. They say a lot.

5

Using This Book

How should you use the charts? The book is broken into three sections. In the first section, the visualizations are about the stock market. The second section examines interest rates, inflation, commodity pricing, and real estate. The third section covers general business conditions, the much-misunderstood realm of government finance, and my favorite quackery charts—ones that shouldn't be taken seriously, but from which you can still learn a lesson, and ones where something should be taken seriously that most folks won't consider because they think it's quackery.

Flip the book open anywhere. On the right-hand page is a chart. On the left-hand page is the story. Each visualization stands alone, so you can enjoy as many or as few as you have time for. Then put the book down and come back to it later—in a few minutes or a few years. Some of the charts are decades old and still wonderful, so they ought to be good for a few decades more. Every picture tells a story. Visualize them and learn the lessons.

If you don't agree with the conclusions I've drawn from the charts, that's OK. It's less important what you think about these things than that you *do* think about them. And it's going to be very hard for you to study these charts, read about them, and then come away unimpressed by the charts and what you learn from them—even if along the way you think I'm nuts.

At times you may see things in these charts that I've not commented upon. There's a lot there. You may also see what I've described and disagree with me violently. As you will see, many of history's most noted financial observers have screwed up terribly in their pronouncements. So, if you're sure I'm wrong about certain things, remember that I'm in very good company.

After all, despite an education in economics and history, 15 years as a professional Wall Street waltzer, authorship of a bestselling book about the stock market, and years of service as a regular *Forbes* columnist, I'm still regularly humbled by the intricate beauty of Wall Street's dance. At times it takes my breath away—sometimes by knocking the wind out of me.

This book is *not* about how to pick a winning stock or how to read financial statements. This book only covers—and it's a lot—the many lessons you can learn visually and in a hurry. It's a book about the Wall Street Waltz, the overview, the dance, all orchestrated by the interplay of human fear and greed, and choreographed by our own individual feeble psychologies. It is about the adrenalin rush we feel when we're confronted with the need to make a difficult decision that affects the economic well-being of our loved ones. It is about the many others who have gone before us doing the same stupid greedy and fearful steps, all in the name of money. And it's about how everyone is focusing on their feet rather than listening to the music.

The Electronic Pulse

What's with the music? Well, because the truly important things haven't changed in hundreds of years, the music hasn't changed much. But one thing that has changed can help you learn the rhythm: electronics. When I started into business, I used an electric adding machine and a slide rule. Today for about $30 you can buy a financial calculator, which costs less than the commission on a small stock purchase but lets you master the magic of compound interest—the rhythm to which Wall Street waltzes.

For example, you will learn in Chart 39 how simple it is to become a millionaire. You put just $2,000 a year into an IRA when you're between ages 25 and 30, and then generate 15 percent compounded annually. That little investment lets you retire at age 65 with a whopping $1.3 million. Does that seem too easy to be true? It is true! You can see it from Chart 39, but you can also confirm it yourself with a financial calcuator. It takes about 30 seconds. The devices even come with their own easy-to-understand instructions.

It always amazes me how many serious investors either don't know how to use a financial calculator, or don't keep one close by so they can check out the pervasive mythology all around us. For example, you'll learn in Chart 52 that inflation has boosted consumer prices about tenfold since 1900, but most folks are absolutely unable to figure out that a tenfold rise in 85 years averages 2.75 percent annually—not so much after all.

I calculated that, and I timed it. It took my Casio BF-100 calculator 8¼ seconds to figure it out to 10 decimal places. These days, a key to being a successful waltzer is the capability to determine compound rates of return, to understand the magic of compound interest, to know what is and isn't possible from reasonable investment results, to know what is and isn't reasonable.

It is amazing that in such a capitalistic society, so few people really understand the magic of compound interest and incorporate it into their daily thinking. If most people possessed that capability, we wouldn't have nearly the problems we have with supposedly bankrupt retirement systems, government deficits, and major Wall Street booms and busts. We probably wouldn't even have to worry about poor people. There wouldn't be many of them. But most people won't ever learn to get a calculator and plug it in—so you should. It will give you a real leg up on the others.

So, get a financial calculator, one that computes compound interest, and learn to use it. Time and again, I have verified something on a chart with my trusty calculator. Use your own calculator to check on my assertions. Being able to compute returns will make you much more confident of any financial phenomenon you encounter. It will also allow you to uncover the myths peddled by the world's many financial hucksters.

Who are those financial hucksters? Well, lots go by names like Senator, and Governor, and—yes—even Mr. President. Others are trying to take those people's jobs away from them. Others want to sell you something (for a sales commission). Some others are reporters who want a hot story, and still others have an ax they keep trying to grind, and, if you give them a chance, they will bury it in the back of your scalp. A thorough grounding in compound interest and the lessons in these visualizations should keep a lot of them away from you, or at least let you see them for what they are.

For example, the politicians want you to elect them so they can fix our economic ills. But you've got to wonder what's happening. We keep electing them, and they keep fixing them, and we seem to be stuck in a worse fix all the time. Why? Politicians can't fix things. They only make things worse. Because while most folks can't visualize it, we're all part of a worldwide financial economy. We always have been—for a few centuries, at least. And there isn't much government can do to make our results better than the worldwide trends.

Worldwide Finance

When the markets are rising here, they're rising in London and Brussels, and most likely even Malaysia. When interest rates are rising or falling here, they're almost certain to be doing the same thing soon in Paris, Tokyo, Toronto, the Antilles, and Brazil. For the most part, depressions and recessions are worldwide.

Of course, a single country can screw itself up, getting out of sync with the world. But its politicians can't improve its lot much, relative to the rest of us. Wall Street starts in Manhattan but dances nonstop, through the phone lines, all around the world. And, as you will learn throughout this book, Wall Street has waltzed worldwide since long before there were telephones—

since before there was even a Wall Street. So when politicians try some fancy maneuver, the financial world just waltzes around them. And when Wall Streeters want to party, all the politicians in the world can't stop them. Collectively, Wall Street is too powerful.

In upcoming pages you'll see the international nature of finance. You'll see that the dance is done the same way today that it was decades ago and centuries ago. You'll see that they danced in 1720 to the tune of "The South Seas Bubble" and "The Mississippi Scheme." Then in the the mid-19th century, they turned on "That Old Railroad Boom and Bust Blues." In the 1920s, and again just recently, "The Merger and Acquisition Bulge" was big. "The Snake" is popular still today. And, of course, tunes like "The Interest-Rate Shuffle" and "The Kondratieff Wave" have kept playing the whole time.

The waltz never stops. I hope it never will. It won't as long as capitalism is allowed to survive. Capitalism is the engine that has propelled our prosperity and emergence from feudalism into an amazing age of microcomputers (which bring "power to the people") and medicine (which lets us hang on to our lives).

Is there a real threat to capitalism? Is there any real risk that the waltz may die? Indeed! Your calculator and a copy of the U.S. budget will tell you the sorry truth. And it isn't about deficits or the federal debt, as you will learn with our governmental visualizations. But if government keeps expanding its size at the same higher growth rates relative to GNP that have prevailed over the last 20 years, it will take less than 100 more years for

Uncle Sam to have taken over everything. Everything including Wall Street and the waltz. Such is the power of relatively small differentials of compound interest. It is sad that everyone talks about federal deficits and debt, but no one talks about the real killer—the cancerlike growth of government.

But Wall Street probably won't pay too much attention. Because, as your financial calculator will allow you to see, the discounted cash value of anything 100 years down the road is essentially zero today. Wall Street won't let worries about governmental expropriation tone down its dance for decades to come. In the meantime, it will continue as it has—as it is described here, in the lessons in this book.

One Step at a Time

Each story stands on its own as a companion to its chart. Each chart seemed to deserve having its own story told, without having that story subordinated to some organized theme. The stories were all written with a focus on the chart alone. For example, several times conclusions appear to conflict with each other, because those conflicting conclusions are what appear to pop out at you from the pages of the chart.

Thus, this book on the Wall Street Waltz reflects the chaos and lack of overarching organization in the financial world. Compared to Wall Street, spread all around the globe and most of it almost totally structureless, this book is organized to a tee.

Probably this book will please you only if it helps you

profit. Since most of the crowd has lost money on Wall Street for centuries, they probably will continue doing so. Why shouldn't you, too? We can't all be Wall Street winners. The dance's psychological nature is that some of us must make fools of ourselves so that others can look like stars.

If it all seems too much for you, rest assured, the Wall Street Waltz really can be taken one easy step at a time. The key to Wall Street isn't making the fancy moves, but going through the dance simply and without losing your financial footing. You may never become the top stock market operator around, but if you will do what few of your peers will, and take the time to learn the lessons of the dance, you needn't fear making a fool of yourself on the dance floor.

PART 1
STOCK MARKET
VISUALIZATIONS

People who tell you they've got the stock market figured out, lock, stock, and barrel, are nuts. And anyone who tells you that any one stock market indicator is all-powerful in predicting the market's movements is doubly nuts. That's why this book has 90 visualizations covering a tremendous number of phenomena. But if there is any one stock market maxim you should hold in the highest regard, it is to avoid stocks when they're overpriced. Some folks overpay, and others hold onto well-bought stocks that have risen to become overpriced. The results are almost always sorry.

Perhaps the main reason people overpay and overstay is that they have little or no perspective on value. To gain some of that overview you could read dozens of books, take investment classes, and observe the world for years. Or, you could spend about an hour with the hundreds of years' worth of data in the first 11 visualizations in this part.

Stock Market Strategy

The first two charts give you the stock market's price/earnings ratio (P/E) for the last hundred years. You learn in a hurry that the market was always a good buy when average P/Es were below 10. You will also learn that when the market's P/E has been above the mid- to high teens, disappointment has usually followed. Were there exceptions to that rule? Of course! One of the beauties of the Wall Street Waltz is that every step has an exception.

That's where the other visualizations come into play. They collectively provide cross-checks to help keep you on track. For example, one exception is when P/Es soar sky-high in severe depressions such as the 1930s. The stocks dropped, but the earnings dropped a lot more. Those times were some of the best buying opportunities ever, but if you had focused just on P/Es you would have missed out. So you might conclude you shouldn't pay much attention to high P/Es.

But Charts 3 and 4 help put that in perspective. While earnings don't always drive the market in the short term, in the long term they sure do. Not only are stock prices and earnings closely correlated, but, as Chart 4 shows, if you invert P/Es and create E/Ps, the resultant E/P number is like a yield—an earnings yield—which has to compete favorably with (be higher than) long-term bond yields.

If you accept that earnings are important in the long term, how do you get a perspective of value in those unusual times when earnings vaporize, as they did in 1932? After all, how low is low? This is where you might try ratios of price to dividends, or to book value, or to cash flow, or to sales. Collectively these ratios won't allow you to get too far off the track. When the market sells for more than 28 times its dividends, 2 times book value, 10 times cash flow, and equal to sales, stock prices are too high and real scary.

Stocks are also scary when long-term interest rates are high and rising. After all, if E/P ratios have to compete with bond yields in the long term, then rising interest rates ought to be able to trigger declining stock prices. Charts 9 and 10 give you 2 visual perspectives of this issue spanning 115 years. Chart 9 shows that steeply rising long-term interest rates have often been the kiss of death for stocks, but in Chart 10 you will see that rising short-term interest rates are often less persuasive.

Beyond a sense of value, investors can benefit from other perspectives as well. For example, do you really understand the relative performance of stocks and bonds? Stocks have outperformed bonds, real estate, Treasury bills, gold, inflation, and just about every other investment since the mid-1920s. Since stocks rose spectacularly in the 20 years before that, and considering the data from other charts sprinkled throughout this book, we can safely assume that stocks' superior relative performance stretches back even further in history. You can see the last 60 years at a glance in Chart 12.

Wall Street: One Road Around the Globe

One of the popular myths that floats around Wall Street these days is that you can get greater returns with less risk by diversifying into overseas stocks. This is silly for several reasons. As the data in several of the charts from this section show, investing in the other major Western stock markets has provided virtually no real diversification effect. A true diversification effect exists only if the world's stock markets don't all rise and fall at the same time. But for the most part they do, and often in roughly comparable proportions. The English market tends to move closely with the U.S. market, and the Canadian market shows almost no divergence at all. Japan, Germany, France, the Netherlands, and Italy all tie very closely to the U.S. stock market.

This is just one of the ways you will see that Wall Street is the one road extending all around the globe. You *can* get a real diversification effect through foreign investing, but to do it, you have to enter the myriad of minor markets in places like Malaysia and Kenya. And how much real information can you get about what's going on in those places? Not much. We like to think that we're different, and to some extent we are. But you will see, not only in this section but throughout this book, that the U.S. economy is part of a global financial environment and always has been. Stock prices, other financial instruments, commodities, and inflation in general have moved together all around the world as long as capitalism has existed.

For example, many folks, in a self-centered way, think the 1929 crash was an American event. In Chart 29, you will see that it was a worldwide crash, which started in Europe. American investors who weren't so self-centered and watched European markets would have been warned of the coming disaster in 1929. In fact, the 1929–1932 debacle is so fascinating and there is so much misinformation and mythology floating around about it that it warrants several charts specially devoted to clearing the air on this disastrous decline that was unusual mainly in its magnitude—not in what signs you would have needed to avoid taking a beating. The scary part is the degree to which the

1928–1929 market bears similarity to the 1986–1987 market. Not only do both markets look similar in terms of price appreciation (see Chart 27) and P/Es, but both periods have seen similar merger-and-acquisition binges (see Charts 21 and 30).

Investment Lessons

In my 15 years as a professional investor, I've learned lots of lessons the hard way. One of them is to avoid initial public offerings (IPOs). Companies "go public" when it's a good deal for the company and existing shareholders—not when it's good for you. It's a way for the company to raise money through selling new stock, and they only do it if it's cheap money for them. IPOs sell on their sizzle and sex appeal. They're usually classified as high-risk growth stocks. But all stocks that are classified as growth stocks are high-risk.

I write the "Growth Stocks" column for *Forbes,* have for years, and I'm telling you point blank that any stock most folks think of as a "growth stock" is already too popular to be a good buy. A stock only has real potential if most folks think it has none at all. Then when investors later see that it does have potential, they're surprised, and the stock gets bid up as its popularity rises. If a stock is already extremely popular, the way stocks are when they're classified as "growth stocks," even with heady sales and earnings growth they only live up to expectations. They don't exceed expectations. If a popular company's performance is anything shy of spectacular, folks are disap-

pointed and the stock usually becomes a real dog.

For proof of this, look at Chart 18, where you will see that one of the best recognized growth-stock indexes has drastically underperformed the market. Ironically, you can use this phenomenon in reverse to get a handle on when stocks are cheap. Indexes of supposed growth stocks usually sell at much higher P/Es than the overall stock market. When they don't, but sell for about the same P/E multiple as the overall market, you know that the world isn't overly impressed with growth stocks. When folks won't pay up for a growth image, optimism is low, and that's a good time to buy almost all stocks, growth-oriented or not. In reverse, whenever growth stocks have had P/Es averaging 175 percent of the P/E of the overall market, investors have been too keen on growth, and stock prices in general have ended up being too high; then stocks are "good-byes."

This first part's visualizations contain other good lessons as well. You'll learn that news has much less impact on the stock market than most folks think. As you will see, Wall Street waltzes to a far stronger drummer than the strongest items flashed on the front pages. You will learn that it is impossible to outguess the stock market based on estimates of where the economy is headed, but that the stock market is a good forecaster of economic downturns. You'll see why I don't like preferred stocks—they don't perform. Whoever first named them "preferred" must not have seen a long-term chart of their financial results. You will learn that, over history, bull markets have averaged about three years in length and bear markets have averaged just shy of two years. And on average those busts have lost about 2 percent per month—not much less and not much more. You'll see it all in an easy-to-remember visual perspective.

The Old and the New

You will see some true antiquity and learn that all of this crazy Wall Street waltzing was going on long before Wall Street even existed. You will see how the stock price of the Bank of England fluctuated from 1732 to 1846. You will hear my favorite financial story of all time, the South Seas Bubble. You may have heard it before, but you've never seen an authentic chart of the phenomenon.

My telling of the tale is brief, so I hadn't room for the punch line, which is the international nature of 1720's financial boom-bust cycle. Economic historians often retell the parallel saga of John Law's French Mississippi Scheme. But what historians seem to have little regarded is that these two massively powerful speculative cycles built themselves over the years, side by side in England and France, and then climaxed and burst within days of each other in July 1720—but on opposite sides of the English Channel. This "coincidence" seems clear evidence of a semi-global financial world that existed long before most contemporary observers believe stocks were even traded.

On the more contemporary side, you will see 190 years of American stock prices at a glance, starting in 1790. But then you will also see detailed cameos of the railroad boom-bust cycle of the mid-1800s, the legendary Panic of 1907, the Rich Man's Panic, each of which teaches a lesson.

This part's final visualization (Chart 39) is among the most powerful anywhere. It shows the power of compound interest and how compounding can free anyone of financial worry. Becoming comfortably rich is a lot easier than most folks imagine, and it's not well understood. All you need to do is save a little as a young adult and invest it in something that does a bit better than average—like buying stocks that will do better than the stock market as a whole.

The stock market is tricky—one of our world's trickiest arenas—which is why books like this get written, to help explain it. Yet not much about its machinations is complex. If you learn the lessons of this part's visualizations, you won't know all the answers to what makes Wall Street waltz. You won't have all the moves, but you'll know more than most investors you'll ever meet with or have to compete with. You'll have perspective, which is something most folks get only with years of experience; some never get it at all.

1
Price/Earnings Ratios: Then and Now

I bet you'd bet that price/earnings ratios (P/Es) were sky-high in 1929. You lose. They were no higher than in the 1986–1987 stock market. That's scary. Why? When a stock price is high in relation to a company's earnings, the stock is usually overpriced. When all stocks are high-priced in relation to earnings, the market is usually ripe for a rip-roaring retreat. You know what happened after 1929. Almost every other time P/Es were this high, the market has done poorly too. With the Dow Jones Industrials averaging 19 times earnings in 1986, this graph was crying out a shrill warning from my dusty library shelves.

The graph came from a 1975 research report issued by the brokerage firm of Goldman Sachs. There is nothing unique about it except its simplicity. The Value Line graph (Chart 11) gives greater detail on P/Es, but is harder to draw conclusions from due to its added clutter. What you do see right off is that only a few times has the market sold at P/Es greater than 20, which is marked with a heavy horizontal line. Instead, most of the time, the market sold for less than 15 times earnings.

A great irony is that at the market's best buying points, before the rise in the 1920s and again before the rise coming out of the Great Depression, P/Es were sky-high—essentially infinite—because there weren't any earnings, as you can see on the accompanying chart. But it's rare, and it isn't the world we're facing as this book is coming to print.

Were P/Es sky-high in 1929 the way legend would lead you to believe? No way! That's part of why so many folks got fooled into holding their stocks going into the greatest slide ever—they didn't think stocks were too expensive. A most interesting point is that P/Es weren't any higher in 1929 than in 1986. If P/Es have usually been less than 15, this chart is an extreme warning sign for the current stock market.

Dow Jones Industrials Price/Earnings Ratio, 1915–1986

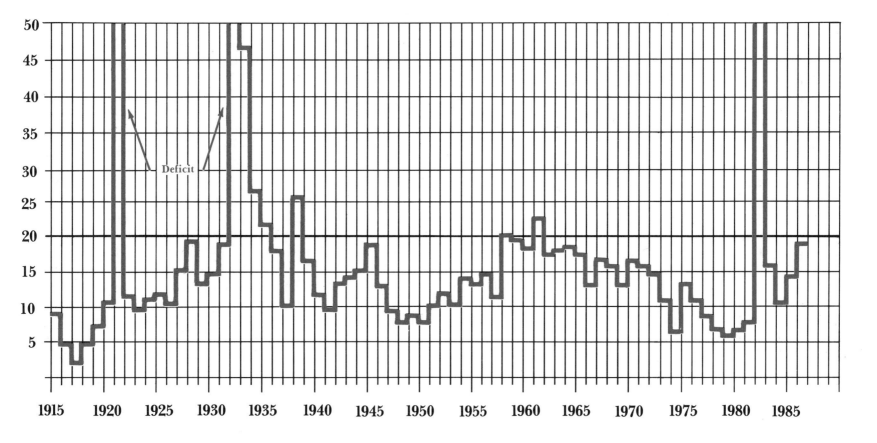

Source: 1915–1975, Goldman Sachs & Co., Gary Wenglowski; 1975–1986, data from Dow Jones & Co.

2
In Case You Didn't Get It the First Time

In case you're a skeptic and didn't believe it the first time, this chart gives you a glimpse of P/Es back further than any other chart I've ever seen. We constructed it at my office from Cowles Commission data (1930s Congressional investigation into securities and the causes of the Great Depression). It shows the P/E of the Cowles All Stock Index from 1871 to 1936, which overlaps the preceding graph by 21 years. The chart is a little different in the period from 1915 to 1936 than what you've already seen, but only because the index is a little different—broader and perhaps a bit less volatile than the Dow Jones Industrials. Still, both charts reinforce much the same idea.

First, note that as the market sold above 20 times earnings on only five occasions between 1915 and 1976 (see Chart 1), this chart shows it above 20 times earnings on only four occasions. One was when the earnings disappeared in the 1930s. The market fell, but the vanishing earnings boosted the P/E. (This rare phenomenon also happened in 1982, when the Dow Jones Industrials' earnings vaporized temporarily, and the market, which had plummeted, sold at a whopping P/E of 100 anyway.) This also happened, but to a lesser degree in 1893 and 1894, as shown on this chart, when the P/E peaked at 28. The index fell 22 percent in those years, from 43.5 down to 33.9.

That came as part of what was known as the Panic of 1893, which was part of a worldwide depression (as shown in Chart 63), which caused earnings to fall even more—57 percent, from 2.74 to 1.19—and which produced the higher P/E of 28. In the next 10 years the market doubled, so it must have been cheap.

This rare phenomenon of 1893, 1921, 1932, 1937, and 1982 is historically when P/Es have gotten to their highest levels, and is also when the market has been absolutely cheapest, and is about the only time when a high P/E has proved to be cheap. And it's also why I don't put too much faith in P/Es alone (see discussion for Chart 8).

Most of the time, the market's P/E averaged a little below 15. It rarely got much lower than that. It broke below 10 only during World War I and a few times during the years shown in Chart 1. So you shouldn't expect a repeat anytime soon of the ultralow P/Es that you saw prevailing during the 1970s. Ironically, the P/E hit its all-time low in 1917, at 5, but that didn't produce an immediate resounding bull market. The Cowles All Stock Index was at 55 in 1917, rose to 71 in 1919, and fell back to 55 in 1920. Of course, the P/E, at 7, was low even then, as measured by either this chart or Chart 1. And then the fireworks really began as the market started its Roaring Twenties ascent, proving that the market was cheap then.

But most important is that the market's P/E was rarely as high in the last 115 years as in 1986 and 1987. And the only times when a high P/E has been bullish have been when the market has been falling but earnings have temporarily fallen even more. This chart reinforces the warning from Chart 1, which says stocks may have rough sledding ahead. (For a theoretical explanation of why P/Es and the market should be related this way, skip ahead to Chart 4.)

The Stock Market vs. Its P/E Ratio, 1871–1937

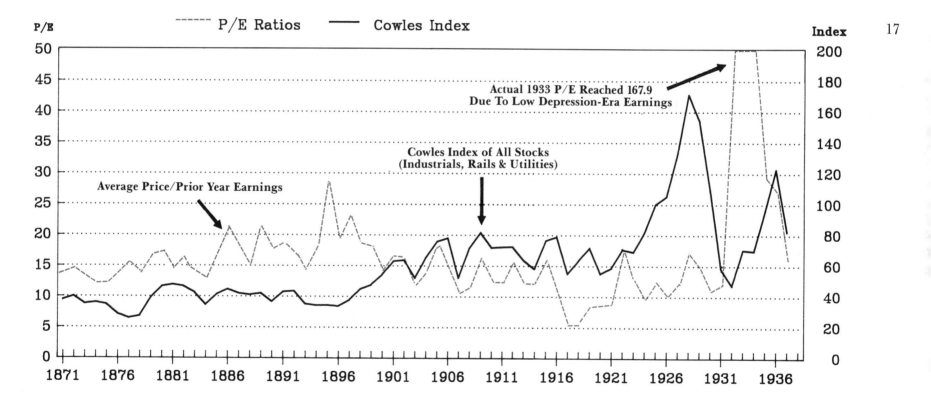

Source: Cowles Commission All Stock Index.

3
Earning a Good Return in the Market

"Well, if earnings can be misleading, why does everyone focus on them so much and, particularly, why do you do so in this book?" (see Charts 1, 4, 17, 28, and 43). Earnings are often misleading *in the short term*. But in the long term, as this chart depicts, earnings control the market's direction. This chart shows a 44-year span where the Standard & Poor's (S&P) index of 425 industrial stocks is stacked up against the earnings of the underlying companies. Between 1945 and 1958, there is a wide discrepancy between the two lines, as earnings were high relative to stock prices. But for most of this chart's time span, the long-term fit between earnings and stock prices is compelling.

Earnings and stock prices are tightly correlated in the long term because of one of the aspects of stock ownership that you get with virtually no other form of investment. As a stockowner, you are a part owner in a business—a nonbiological, but almost living, entity with the capacity to adapt and prosper as economic conditions change. Let's say costs rise for car makers. If people want to buy cars, they will have to pay higher prices. The car maker can respond through better marketing to convince customers why they should want cars at higher prices, or respond through cost-reduction efforts to get back to square 1, or diversify into new areas where costs may be low. The possibilities are limited merely by the limits of management's combined creative imagination.

But shouldn't interest-rate fluctuations drastically affect the price/earnings relationship? In the short term that can certainly be true, which is one of the many reasons price/earnings ratios can be misleading in the short term, but in the long term interest is just another cost of business—the cost of money. Interest is an important cost, but as a percentage of sales certainly less important for most industrial outfits than labor, inventories, or even taxes.

When interest costs rise, profits fall in the short term. But in the long term, a business has the potential to evolve and adapt to meet the changed cost conditions. If business collectively can respond in profitable ways, it will and will earn money over time that compensates for the high interest rates. If business can't respond in profitable ways, it will cut back, and interest rates will fall. This is a further expansion of the lesson of the Snake (see Chart 43). High growth rates in earnings tend to correlate with rising corporate bond rates, and falling bond rates tend to correlate with vanishing earnings growth. This is why over a period of a few years, or even five to ten years, stock prices may have very high or very low P/Es, but in time they come back to the middle of their historic range.

The lesson? Look down the road a few years and consider whether the market is reasonable, or much too high or low. Given reasonable future profit margins, mild growth, and P/Es in the middle of their historic range (see Chart 1), where might the market be in five years, and what kind of a return might you get if you buy now? Based on those considerations, the market is a bit on the pricy side in early 1987.

The Long-Term Tie Between Earnings and Stock Prices, 1926–1971

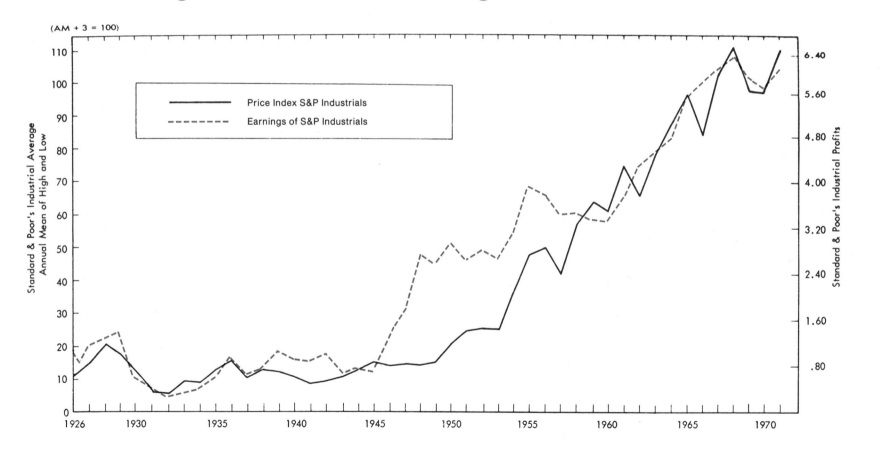

(AM + 3 = 100)

Price Index S&P Industrials

Earnings of S&P Industrials

Standard & Poor's Industrial Average Annual Mean of High and Low

Standard & Poor's Industrial Profits

Source: Standard & Poor's.
   *Based on 425 stocks.

4
Earnings Yields: Stocks Versus Bonds

Is there really a meaningful relationship between interest rates and stock valuations? You bet. This chart is another visual perspective of that love affair. It highlights a most fundamental concept of investment management. For stocks to perform well, their earnings yield has to compete favorably with the interest rate achievable with bonds. Let's see how and why.

The chart shows two lines. The red line is the yield from high-grade corporate bonds from 1946–1974. The black line is the earnings yield from the S&P 500. An earnings yield is an inverted P/E ratio, or the earnings divided by the price paid to get those earnings (see Chart 43). It is expressed as a percentage, which is directly comparable to a bond yield. For example, a P/E of 20 is an E/P, or earnings yield, of 5 percent (1/20 = 0.05). The chart shows that for 20 years the earnings yield on stocks was always greater than the interest yield from bonds.

Investors normally demand a higher earnings yield from stocks than from bonds for two reasons. First, owning stocks is fundamentally riskier. Earnings can decline, hurting the stock-holder's future earnings yield. But bondholders keep getting paid unless the company goes belly-up. Second, while the company may be earning plenty, you may not get much in dividends because management probably plows lots of the earnings back into the business for future growth. But the bond's income you get right away—and you know the old saying: A bird in the hand is worth two in the bush.

Formerly, that bird-in-the-hand business was mitigated a bit by the favorable tax status given to capital gains. If a company retained its earnings rather than paying dividends and used that cash to fund growth and higher future earnings, resulting in a higher stock price, taxable investors (individuals rather than pension plans or foundations) got a big tax break on their capital gain compared to what their taxes would have been if they had received that same cash flow as dividends or bond income. The 1981 tax law provided the greatest incentives for investment in decades by reducing capital gains tax rates from 35 percent to 20 percent. Along the way, it also created enough tax incentive to induce the first sustained period of earnings yields less than bond yields.

But with the 1986 tax law, reduced capital gains rates are dead and gone, and all income is treated equally. Now, both because of the reduced tax incentives and the mass of historical evidence, the relationship is likely to revert to bond yields lower than the earnings yields of stocks. This could be a real negative for stock prices in the immediate future. As described in Chart 43, it would take a dramatic interest-rate decline and steeply rising earnings from mid-1986 levels to justify current stock prices, much less fuel the fires of a hot stock market.

Earnings Yield on the S&P 500 vs. Yield on High-Grade Corporate Bonds, 1946–1974

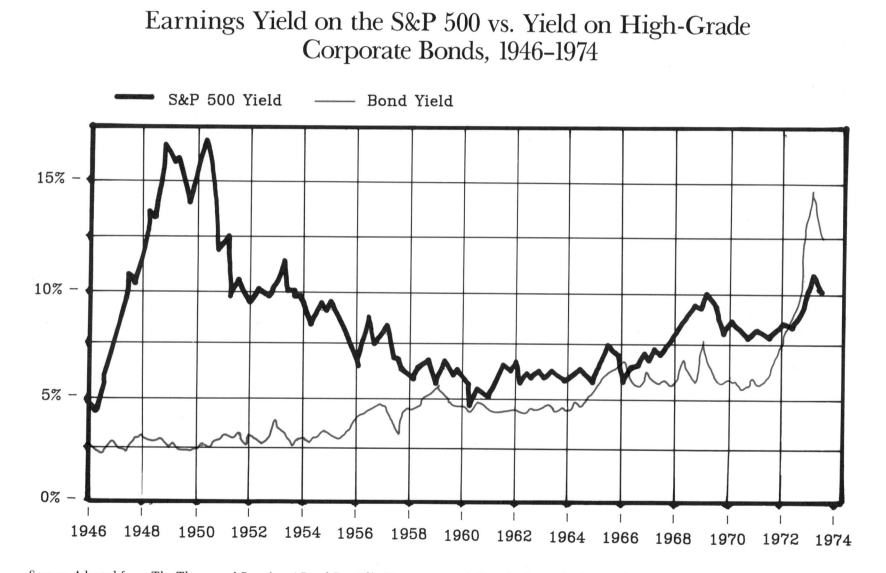

Source: Adapted from *The Theory and Practice of Bond Portfolio Management*, ed. Peter L. Bernstein, New York: Institutional Investor Books, 1977.

5
Price/Dividend Ratios Provide Long-Term Vision

22   This chart shows the single most powerful indicator of long-term stock market direction I've seen. It's so simple, but inexplicably powerful. It doesn't say if the market is headed up or down right now, but its predictive record of what's a few years down the pike is stunning. Chart A is the background—the Dow Jones Industrials since 1920. The solid line delineates the Dow's latest 12-month dividends multiplied by a price/dividend ratio of 22.7. Notice that the line follows the Dow quite closely. This shows that for the past 65 years, the Dow Jones Industrials sold for an average of roughly 22.7 times their dividends.

Chart B holds the predictive power. It illustrates the Dow's price/dividend ratio for the same 65-year period. It is merely the price of the Dow divided by its last four total quarterly dividends. If the Dow is at 1,800, and the Dow stocks paid a total of $90 of dividends in the last year, then the price/dividend ratio is exactly 20. (The total Dow dividends appear regularly in *Barron's* if you want to track this yourself.)

There are three horizontal dotted lines on this graph. The middle one is the aforementioned 22.7 average. The high and low dotted lines are the most telling market forecasters. The lower line represents 17 times dividends. When the market has sold close to or below 17 times dividends, a major bull market has almost always started soon. By contrast, the top line represents 28 times the market's dividends, and when the market has sold that high—like in 1928 and 1929—it has almost always led quickly either to steeply falling stock prices or, as in 1937 or 1945, to mildly falling prices that didn't recover for years.

Connecting the charts with arrows shows the power of this valuation model. The price/dividend ratio indicates how over- or undervalued the market is. Follow the bulleted lines to see how remarkably accurate this indicator has been in calling market turning points. Whenever price/dividend ratios are far below the norm, say at 17, stocks have appeared very cheap in retrospect. By the same token, the fact that the market sold at 32 times its dividends when I wrote these words does not speak well for the stock market of 1987–1988.

To make more sense of all this, it may help to realize that the price/dividend ratio is just an inverted dividend yield. If the Dow's dividend yield is 5 percent, its price/dividend ratio is 20 (1 divided by 0.05 equals 20). Hence, when price/dividend ratios are high, dividend yields are low.

These charts came from a 1985 article in *Barron's* by Craig Corcoran. At the time, the ratio stood at 22, and Mr. Corcoran was using the model to correctly imply the potential for higher prices. A year later, by his own logic he would have to conclude that at 32, the market had become too high. Unfortunately, that advice never made it into *Barron's*.

Price/Dividend Ratios, 1920–1985

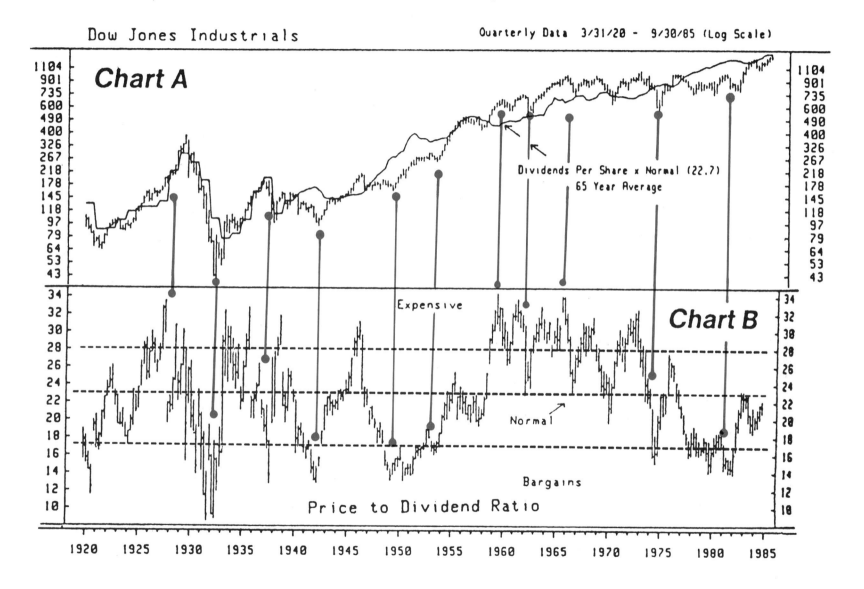

Dow Jones Industrials   Quarterly Data 3/31/20 – 9/30/85 (Log Scale)

Chart A

Dividends Per Share x Normal (22.7)
65 Year Average

Chart B

Expensive

Normal

Bargains

Price to Dividend Ratio

Source: Craig Corcoran, "All Systems Go," *Barron's*, November 18, 1985.

23

6
Price-to-Book Ratios: Playing It by the Book

24 Can the Dow Jones Industrials, as some writers suggest, soon hit 3,000? It's possible, but historic valuations say it's unlikely. Proponents predict that prices will triple from the 1982 1,000-plus level because stocks more than tripled in other major bull markets such as the 1920s and 1950s. These analysts cite internal fundamentals: Earnings and dividends doubled since the mid-1960s, but the market remained in a 20-year trading range between 700 and 1,000—presumably prices got too cheap, particularly adjusting for inflation. Fans of the idea note that rising earnings raised book values too—through retained earnings plowed back into the businesses. Supposedly these rising book values (i.e., shareholders' equity, or the value of assets minus all liabilities) understate the Dow's real value, since accounting shows assets at their cost rather than their value after inflation. So, inflation should build pent-up pressure for a big boom.

But slow down. This chart shows the Dow divided by its prior year's book value—commonly known as the price-to-book ratio. Most bull markets start from low price-to-book ratios. The great bull market since 1982 started from an exceptionally low 1.10 price-to-book ratio. Since 1934, the Dow fell as low as book value only once, in 1979. In early 1987, the Dow's price-to-book was historically high—2.02—close to the 52-year high of 2.36 reached in 1965. This says there is little upside room left.

Compare this chart with the market's wiggles (see Chart 26). Stocks have performed poorly when the price-to-book has gotten high. The higher this ratio, the worse the subsequent results. If the Dow were to reach 3,000 it would be at 3 times its current 944.97 book value—a figure never achieved in the last 55 years. The price-to-book did get that high in 1928 and 1929 (peaking at 4.5), but you know what happened next. What about possible growth in book value? Between 1927 and 1929 book value grew, but only about 20 percent. Sadly, the Dow's book value was about 3 percent higher 5 years ago than today. Rapid growth in book value is anything but certain.

Could recent inflation make this ratio obsolete—and a 3,000 Dow likely? Yes, but here's a hitch: The Dow's earnings aren't inflated, they're current. Hence, at their present level of $115, a 3,000 Dow means a P/E ratio of 26—much higher than 1986's average P/E of 18—and sky-high compared to the history of P/Es illustrated in Charts 1 and 2. P/Es that high have happened only when earnings disappeared (1921, 1932, and 1982). While possible, P/Es that high aren't historically likely. Here's another hitch: Price/dividend ratios are also nearing record levels of 32, clearly in the range signaling market peaks (see Chart 5).

So, while folks may predict a 3,000 Dow, and that may be possible, most valuation methods point out that it isn't likely—and that if it does occur, it would be so high in relation to the history we've known as to suggest an enormous bust immediately thereafter.

The Market's Price-to-Book Ratio, 1921–1986

Ratio

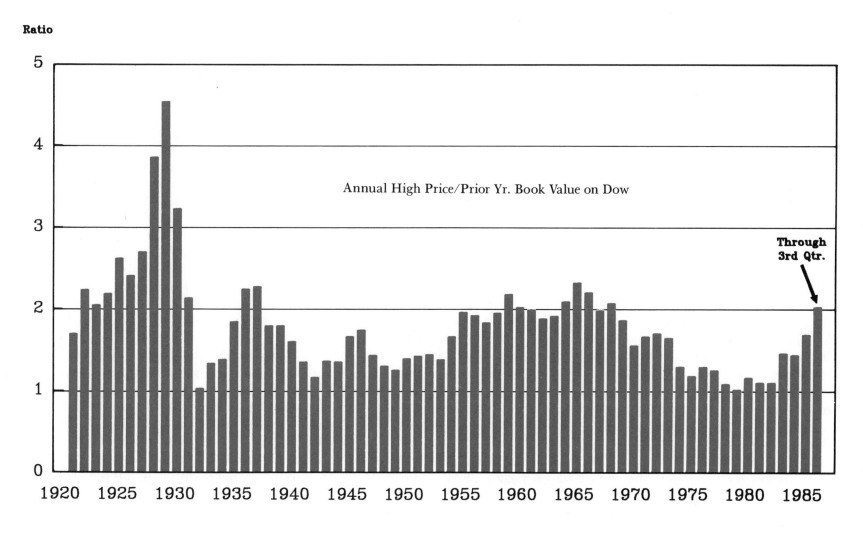

Annual High Price/Prior Yr. Book Value on Dow

Through 3rd Qtr.

25

Source: The above chart is reprinted from "Investment Strategy Quarterly" by permission of Merrill Lynch, Pierce, Fenner & Smith Incorporated. Copyright 1986 Merrill Lynch, Pierce, Fenner & Smith Incorporated.

7
Price/Cash Flow Ratios: A Hidden Twist

26 Do all stock market valuation measures indicate that stocks are currently drastically overpriced? Almost, but one that says there still may be room to rise is the ratio of the market's price to its cash flow. Cash flow is the sum of earnings plus depreciation. Depreciation comes from amortizing capital expenditures for plant and capacity over their estimated useful lives. Business has been pumping money into capital expenditures at record levels lately—contrary to public perceptions (see Chart 68)—so depreciation and cash flow also have been rising more than the public thinks.

This chart shows the price/cash flow ratio going back to 1945. While the market is far from bargain-basement levels by this standard, it's at levels that haven't always kept stocks from rising a lot further. Currently the market, this time measured by the S&P 400, is selling at 10 times its cash flow. The last time it sold at this price/cash flow ratio was in 1972 and 1973: from there the market was a disaster, losing 47 percent of its value in a year and a half. But going back further in history shows a different picture.

In 1948 the market sold at record lows of only five times cash flow. This low level indicated the market was ultracheap, and the market immediately began one of its biggest bull markets ever, rising threefold by 1958. As prices rose, so did the ratio—steadily—until 1961, where it hit an all-time peak of 12.5, far above the 1986 level of 10. But anyone who sold out in 1958, when the ratio first got above 10, would have been sorely upset as stock prices doubled again in the next 10 years. After 1961, the ratio fell back and plateaued for a few years as price rises mirrored cash flow increases, which were fueled by rising earnings and depreciation. Finally, starting in 1968, as prices fell, so did the ratio.

The market is currently well above the kind of supercheap levels that existed both in 1948 and before the current bull market began in the 1975–1982 period. But the pattern that began in the late 1970s looks a lot like the pattern that began in 1948. So clearly there is in this relationship a historical precedent for prices to rise far above where they are. This is particularly interesting in light of the media and the public's almost total lack of awareness that capital expenditures have been so high and, therefore, that depreciation and cash flow have boomed relative to corporate earnings.

Often what moves the market most is the thing folks aren't looking at. Since a lot more people look at P/Es and price-to-book ratios (see Charts 1 and 6) than at price/cash flow ratios, and since there is a hidden bullish twist to cash flow that few folks see, this chart represents a big part of the backbone of the case for a continued bull market that takes prices higher. If high levels of capital expenditures boost cash flow by 20 percent in the next few years, even with flat earnings, and if the price/cash flow ratio rises to 11, the market could move up another 30 percent and still be within the bounds of history.

S&P 400 High Annual Price/Cash Flow Ratio, 1945–1986

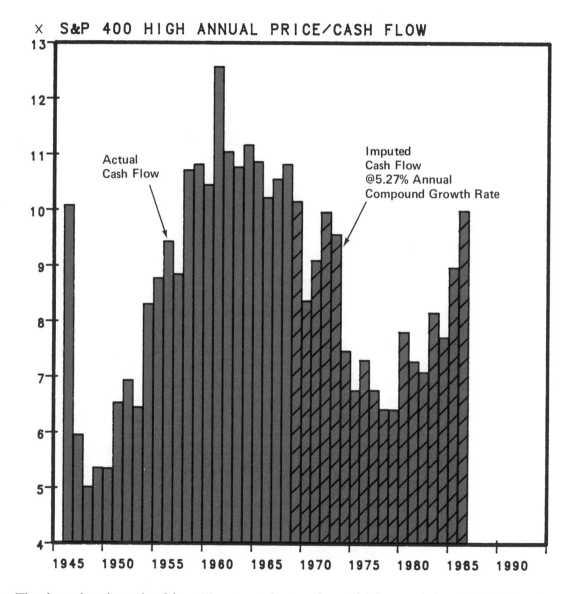

X **S&P 400 HIGH ANNUAL PRICE/CASH FLOW**

Actual
Cash Flow

Imputed
Cash Flow
@5.27% Annual
Compound Growth Rate

Source: The above chart is reprinted from "Investment Strategy Quarterly" by permission of Merrill Lynch, Pierce, Fenner & Smith Incorporated. Copyright 1986 Merrill Lynch, Pierce, Fenner & Smith Incorporated.

8
An Advertisement for *Super Stocks* and *Forbes*

How do you know when a stock is really cheap? Most people use price/earnings ratios. What if the company isn't making money, so it doesn't have a P/E? Then try price/sales ratios (PSRs), which are just like P/Es but use the company's annual sales where the P/E uses the company's earnings. PSRs are effective in valuing stocks, particularly at the very times when P/Es won't work. I made my name in the investment world by doing research into and publicizing the results of using PSRs, so they are dear to my heart. This chart shows a classic example of how PSRs pay off when the more conventional use of P/Es won't.

You should never buy a big company's stock unless the company's total stock market value is less than 40 percent of the company's annual revenues—preferably much less. That means the stock's PSR is less than 0.40 (40 percent equals 0.40). So, if a company had $10 billion in annual sales, its stock market value must be less than $4 billion to be considered. If it had 100 million shares and its stock were 35, it would be OK ($3.5 billion market value), but if the stock were 45, it then would be too high.

This chart starts before Sears's big 1927–1928 run-up. Sears peaked in 1928 and fell most of 1929—so you might have thought it was cheap—particularly when its price fell enough to lower its P/E ratio to just 12 in mid-1929. Most folks think a P/E of 12 is rather cheap. It often is. But P/Es are often misleading too, and while no one knew it, the earnings of Sears were about to collapse. Heaven help you if you had held on. From its 1929 low, Sears lost another 90 percent of its value in 3 years. That's where PSRs come in. They keep you out of situations where unsustain-ably high earnings mask an overpriced stock, and they help you value the company once the earnings and stock collapse.

In 1929 Sears's PSR varied between 1.05 and 2.37; its total stock market value was never less than 105 percent of its annual revenues and started out at 237 percent—always too high by my rules. By relying on PSRs, you would have been forced out of Sears and wouldn't have had to suffer any of that soon-to-come 90 percent drop. You would have sat on the sidelines until 1932. For most of 1932, Sears's PSR was far less than 0.40. You could have bought it and profited nicely in the next five years. At its 1932 low point, Sears PSR was a bargain-basement 0.15. Of course, it was very cheap, but it had no profits. So, if you were using P/Es, you would have been foiled again.

This chart is just to show you that low P/Es don't ensure success the way some folks claim these days. Before I came along, no one wrote about PSRs, and there still isn't much. If you want to learn more about them, read my book *Super Stocks*, my monthly *Forbes* columns of the last few years, and my upcoming columns in future issues. Remember, when you're hunting, you don't shoot the same type of arrow at a bird as at an elephant. When you're hunting stock profits, you want to have the right arrow in your quiver for every type of target imaginable. PSRs are one of the most powerful arrows available. They knock 'em dead.

Sears, Roebuck & Company's Stock Price, 1926–1955

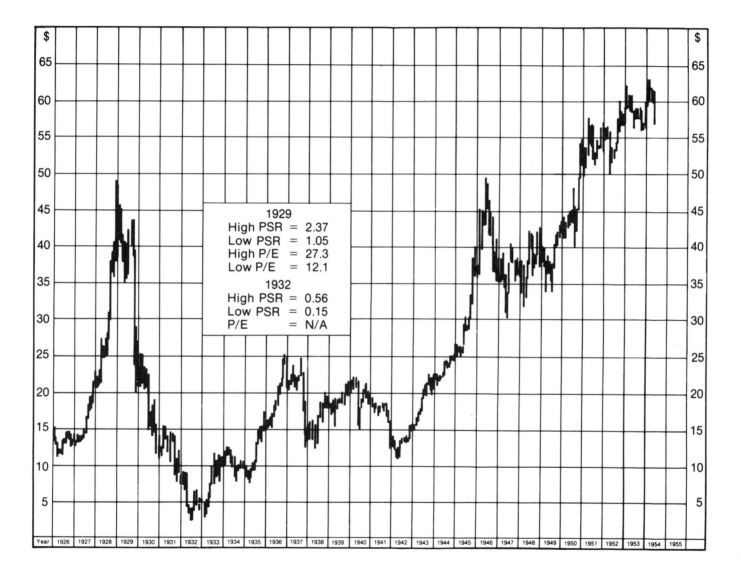

1929
High PSR = 2.37
Low PSR = 1.05
High P/E = 27.3
Low P/E = 12.1

1932
High PSR = 0.56
Low PSR = 0.15
P/E = N/A

Source: M. C. Horsey & Company, Inc., P.O. Box H, Salisbury, MD 21801, as adapted in Kenneth L. Fisher, *Super Stocks*, Homewood, IL: Dow Jones-Irwin, 1984.

9
Mr. and Mrs. Financial—Real Split Personalities

Some folks think rising long-term interest rates won't hurt stocks, because they think that corporate earnings will rise even faster. As this chart shows, stocks do at times bulge through a wall of rising interest rates, but it's a rare day in paradise. This chart not only gives you an 80-year perspective on the timing of movements of the stock market, as measured by railroad stocks (the upper chart), but it also compares those movements to interest rates.

Seeing the interest rates is a tad tough because they're shown on an inverted basis—as the *price* of railroad bonds (the lower chart). As interest rates rise, bond prices fall. When rates fall, bond prices rise. It's a mechanical, arithmetic function (study Chart 33). So, on the chart's vertical axis you see two scales. The inner one is for stock prices, and the outer one is for inverted interest rates. So, for example, the chart shows you that in 1899 and 1935, yields hit long-term lows at 3 percent.

Why look at railroad stocks versus railroad bonds? The first reason is to compare securities of the same entities—apples to apples, not oranges. Second, during most of this chart's duration, railroad securities were the blue chips of the day. These were the securities folks were most interested in then. Third, you can see that while rising interest rates (falling bond prices) don't always ensure a stock market decline, they seem to be a real drag on stock prices. There have been precious few times when stocks made big moves up while bonds were making a big bust.

Take a look. Bonds had two major moves: a big upsweep in price from the 1860s through 1899 and then a big plunge,

dropping steadily until 1920 as interest rates rose. But within those broad sweeps, look at the times when bond prices started falling (meaning that interest rates started rising) to see what happened with stocks then. As shown in Chart 33, it is common for stock market peaks to be foreshadowed by a few months of rising interest rates. But in going through these bond-price declines one by one, you find only 4 times when stocks rose out of the 21 times when bonds fell.

When did those anomalies occur? Briefly in 1863. Then stocks inched up in 1868 and 1869, again in 1900–1902, and finally in 1928 and 1929. Of course, if you had sold in mid-1928 when you realized rates were rising, you would have been very glad indeed by 1930. So, in a way, there were really just three exceptions. Three out of 21 isn't much. The odds are much better betting that stocks will fall as interest rates rise. For example, parallel declines in stock and bond prices started in 1860, 1864, 1866, 1881, 1888, 1892, 1895, 1902, 1906, 1909, 1916, 1919, and 1922.

Of course, falling interest rates don't assure rising stock prices. Between 1873 and 1877, stocks fell while bond prices boomed. Ditto from 1887 through 1889. And from 1893 through 1895, interest rates fell and stocks went basically nowhere. So, despite a few exceptions, this chart makes it painfully obvious that rising long-term interest rates are the stock investor's enemy. Lately interest rates have been falling, which is good, but should they start bouncing back up, back off.

Railroad Stocks and Bonds, 1860–1935

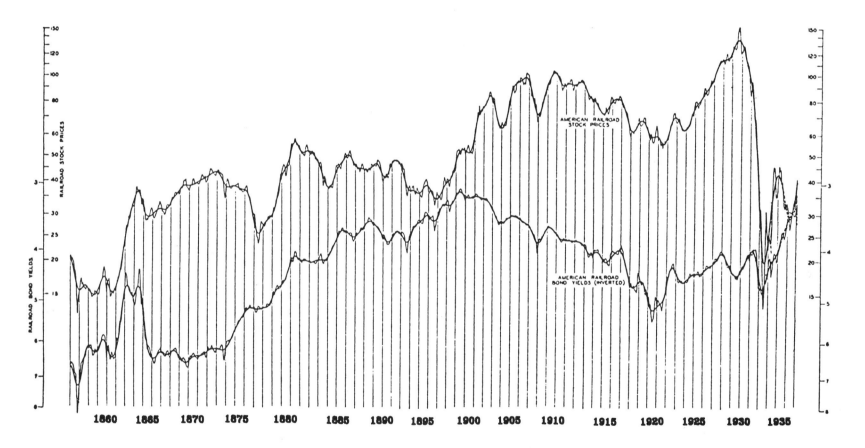

Source: Frederick R. Macaulay, *Some Theoretical Problems Suggested by the Movements of Interest Rates, Bond Yields and Stock Prices in the United States Since 1856*, National Bureau of Economic Research, New York, 1938.

10
Never a Timer Be:
56 Years of Stocks and Interest Rates

32

Trying to outguess the stock market is futile, but folks keep at it. Ironically, most people think that if they could forecast interest rates they would be able to forecast stock prices. But it works that way just enough to get you into trouble.

It's natural to assume that interest rates drive stock prices, and sometimes they seem to. Lower interest rates are thought to stimulate economic activity. Increased economic activity leads to higher sales, lower borrowing costs, and therefore stronger corporate earnings. Falling rates make the returns from alternative investments seem more attractive than they had been before the rates fell. When rates rise, the process should, by all logic, work in reverse. Higher rates should simultaneously cripple corporate earnings and make the return from those earnings seem less appealing by comparison.

But somehow it doesn't always work out. This chart shows 56 years of the Dow Jones Industrial Average (DJIA) and two key interest rates. The discount rate is the interest rate charged by the Federal Reserve (F.R.) System to troubled member banks for borrowed funds. This rate, and the rate for prime commercial paper (see Chart 45) provide a good proxy for short-term interest rates over this time period. If you study the other interest-rate examples in this book, it won't surprise you that the two rates move in tandem. While reviewing this chart, don't be confused where the lines representing the interest rates are split. They are separated to keep the DJIA index intact and to fit all the data into a more compact area.

Point A shows two locations on the charts where short-term

interest rates did the expected—falling rates coincide with rising stock prices. But point B pinpoints two times the rates and prices didn't behave as expected. Rates fell from 1929 through 1932—right along with stocks—and 1958 was a classic example of rapidly rising interest rates living happily hand-in-hand with a major bull market in stocks. Examining this and other interest rate charts uncovers plenty of examples where stock prices move up when interest rates fall, down when they fall, down when they rise, and up when they rise. Those are all the possibilities.

Despite the myths and the snake-oil salespeople who want to sell you their newsletters based on interest-rate forecasts, there is no consistent relationship between short-term interest-rate movements and the stock market. Don't buy stocks or sell stocks because of someone's forecast as to where short-term interest rates are going. Even if the forecaster is right, it may be meaningless. So far, to my knowledge, no one has ever consistently predicted the direction of markets—interest rates or no—year in and year out over the decades. Rates have fallen since 1983, and stocks have risen in a bullish trend consistent with the myth of interest rate–stock price correlation. But the whole thing could *bear* out just as easily.

Short-Term Interest Rates vs. the Stock Market, 1919–1978

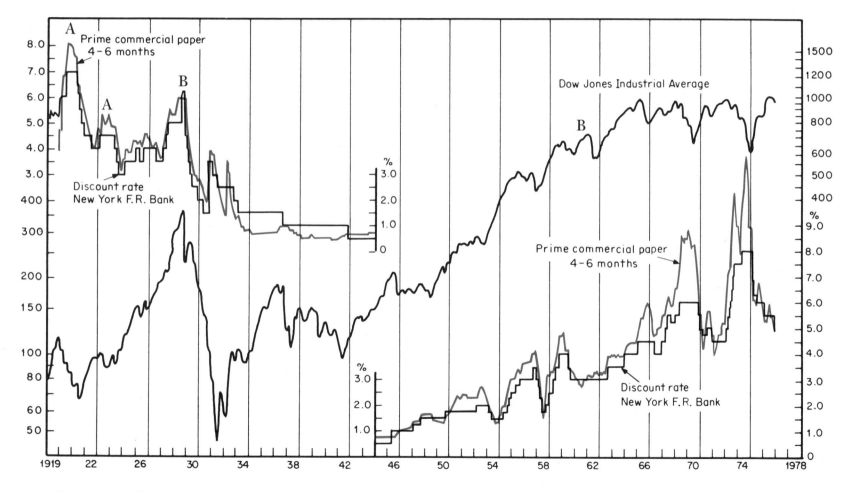

Source: The Bank Credit Analyst.

11

Value Line Industrial Composite: All the Stats that Are Fit to Print

If I could include only 10 charts in this book, instead of 90, this one would be right at the head of the pack. It lets you discern more about the market and its valuation characteristics than any other chart I've seen. You can compare a single stock or group of stocks to the broad market's characteristics. In essence it gives you a complete 15-year statistical snapshot of the market as if it were agglomerated into one big stock of a single big company, plus a projection for next year—all of which you can use either to help determine whether the market is too high or low or to compare individual stocks with the overall market.

You get a price history of the Value Line Industrial Composite (VIC), which both in the timing of its movements and their approximate magnitude closely mirrors other broad market indexes such as the S&P 500 or the Dow Jones Industrials. On the right-hand side of the chart are added row numbers from 1 through 24. Consider row 9. It shows you VIC's average annual P/E, which was 19 in 1972 before the market bust. But you can also see that anyone who bought VIC at a P/E less than 10 and held for a few years did fine.

Then you can go on from there to be a real student of the market. For example, at the top of the page, right under the title, "Industrial Composite," are the annual high and low prices for VIC. It shows you that in 1978 VIC ranged from $14½ to $19½. You can compare that price range to the prior year's earnings (row 4), book value (row 7), cash flow per share (row 3), and on and on. You can then compare those average stock market characteristics to the stocks you own.

Why look at the prior year's numbers? Because in any given year investors can see only historical valuation data for any stock—the current year's numbers aren't reported until after the year is over and the books are closed and audited.

You can compare financial strength. Row 19 divided by row 20 gives you Wall Street's sacred debt/equity ratio. The lower the better! How do your companies compare with VIC's 1986 ratio of 45 percent? How do your stocks' net profit margins compare with VIC's 4.2 percent (row 17)? You can compare how much of VIC's cash flow comes from earnings versus depreciation (row 14 divided by row 15) and compare that to your stocks. On the left-hand side of the chart, at the location marked "A," you see the makeup of current assets and liabilities, which you can use to analyze industry's basic liquidity. A good introductory tutorial to balance-sheet analysis such as this is in Louis Engel's classic book, *How to Buy Stocks.*

I got started in the investment world by using charts like this to compare many years of stock price ranges to the prior year's total revenues. Maybe you will see some important relationship missed by others like me.

Value Line Industrial Composite, 1970–1986

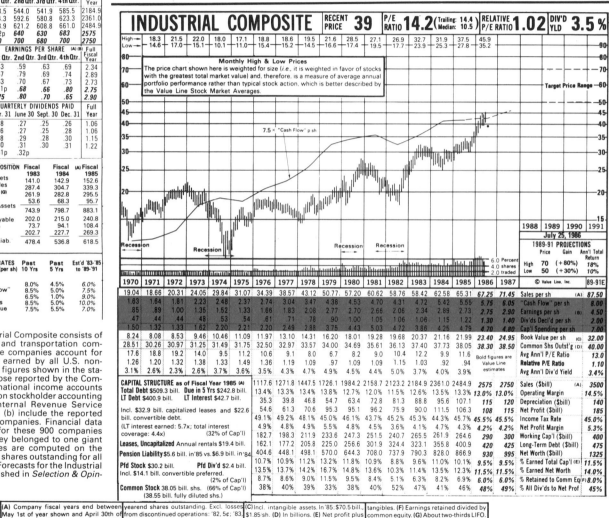

Left-side statistical tables:

Fiscal Year Begins	QUARTERLY SALES ($bill.)				(A) Full Fiscal Year
	1st Qtr.	2nd Qtr.	3rd Qtr.	4th Qtr.	
1983	513.5	544.0	541.9	585.5	2184.9
1984	564.3	592.6	580.8	623.3	2361.0
1985	593.9	621.2	608.8	661.0	2484.9
1986	622p	640	630	683	2575
1987	670	700	680	700	2750

Fiscal Year Begins	EARNINGS PER SHARE (A)(B)				Full Fiscal Year
	1st Qtr.	2nd Qtr.	3rd Qtr.	4th Qtr.	
1983	.43	.59	.63	.69	2.34
1984	.67	.79	.69	.74	2.89
1985	.63	.70	.67	.73	2.73
1986	.61p	.68	.66	.80	2.75
1987	.75	.80	.70	.65	2.90

Calendar	QUARTERLY DIVIDENDS PAID				Full Year
	Mar. 31	June 30	Sept. 30	Dec. 31	
1982	.28	.27	.25	.26	1.06
1983	.26	.27	.25	.28	1.06
1984	.28	.29	.28	.30	1.15
1985	.30	.31	.30	.31	1.22
1986	.31p	.32p			

CURRENT POSITION ($BILL.)	Fiscal 1983	Fiscal 1984	(A) Fiscal 1985
Cash Assets	141.0	142.9	152.6
Receivables	287.4	304.7	339.3
Inventory (G)	261.9	282.8	295.5
Other	53.6	68.3	95.7
Current Assets	743.9	798.7	883.1
Accts Payable	202.0	215.0	240.8
Debt Due	73.7	94.1	108.4
Other	202.7	227.7	269.3
Current Liab.	478.4	536.8	618.5

ANNUAL RATES of change (per sh)	Past 10 Yrs	Past 5 Yrs	Est'd '83-'85 to '89-'91
Sales	8.0%	4.5%	6.0%
"Cash Flow"	8.5%	5.0%	7.5%
Earnings	6.5%	1.0%	9.0%
Dividends	8.5%	5.0%	10.0%
Book Value	7.5%	5.5%	7.0%

EXPLANATION: The Industrial Composite consists of over 900 industrial, retail and transportation companies (except rails). These companies account for about 80% of the income earned by all U.S. nonfinancial corporations. The figures shown in the statistical array differ from those reported by the Commerce Department in the national income accounts because they (a) are based on stockholder accounting techniques rather than Internal Revenue Service bookkeeping methods and (b) include the reported results of just the larger companies. Financial data and stock market values for these 900 companies have been pooled, as if they belonged to one giant company. Per-share figures are computed on the basis of the total number of shares outstanding for all the companies at yearend. Forecasts for the Industrial Composite have been published in *Selection & Opinion* since July 11, 1975.

Main chart header:

INDUSTRIAL COMPOSITE	RECENT PRICE 39	P/E RATIO 14.2 (Trailing: 14.4 / Median: 10.5)	RELATIVE P/E RATIO 1.02	DIV'D YLD 3.5%

| High | 18.3 | 21.5 | 22.0 | 18.0 | 17.1 | 18.8 | 18.6 | 19.5 | 21.6 | 28.5 | 27.1 | 26.9 | 32.7 | 31.9 | 37.5 | 45.9 |
| Low | 14.6 | 17.0 | 15.1 | 10.1 | 11.0 | 15.4 | 15.2 | 17.4 | 19.5 | 17.7 | 23.9 | 25.3 | 27.8 | 35.2 | | |

Monthly High & Low Prices

The price chart shown here is weighted for size (*i.e.*, it is weighted in favor of stocks with the greatest total market value) and, therefore, is a measure of average annual portfolio performance rather than typical stock action, which is better described by the Value Line Stock Market Averages.

7.5 × "Cash Flow" p sh

Target Price Range

| | 1988 | 1989 | 1990 | 1991 |
| July 25, 1986 | | | | |

1989-91 PROJECTIONS

	Price	Gain	Ann'l Total Return
High	70	(+80%)	18%
Low	50	(+30%)	10%

© Value Line, Inc.

6.0 Percent shares traded 4.0 / 2.0

Main statistical array:

1970	1971	1972	1973	1974	1975	1976	1977	1978	1979	1980	1981	1982	1983	1984	1985	1986	1987		89-91E
19.04	18.66	20.31	24.05	29.84	31.07	34.39	38.57	43.12	50.77	57.20	60.62	58.76	58.42	62.58	65.31	67.25	71.45	Sales per sh (A)	87.50
1.63	1.64	1.81	2.23	2.48	2.37	2.74	3.04	3.47	4.38	4.53	4.70	4.31	4.72	5.42	5.55	5.75	6.05	"Cash Flow" per sh	8.00
.85	.89	1.00	1.35	1.52	1.33	1.66	1.83	2.08	2.77	2.70	2.66	2.06	2.34	2.89	2.73	2.75	2.90	Earnings per sh (B)	4.50
.47	.44	.44	48	.53	.54	.61	.71	.78	.90	1.00	1.05	1.06	1.06	1.15	1.22	1.30	1.40	Div'ds Decl'd per sh	2.00
1.50	1.32	1.33	1.62	2.20	2.21	2.20	2.49	2.88	3.75	4.43	5.03	4.72	3.86	4.25	4.79	4.70	4.80	Cap'l Spending per sh	7.00
8.24	8.08	8.53	9.46	10.46	11.09	11.97	13.10	14.31	16.20	18.01	19.28	19.68	20.37	21.16	21.99	23.40	24.95	Book Value per sh (C)	32.00
28.51	30.26	30.97	31.25	31.49	31.75	32.50	32.97	33.57	34.00	34.69	35.61	36.13	37.40	37.73	38.05	38.30	38.50	Common Shs Outst'g (D)	40.00
17.6	18.8	19.2	14.0	9.5	11.2	10.6	9.1	8.0	6.7	8.2	9.0	10.4	12.2	9.9	11.6	Bold figures are Value Line estimates		Avg Ann'l P/E Ratio	13.0
1.26	1.20	1.32	1.38	1.33	1.49	1.36	1.19	1.09	.97	1.09	1.09	1.15	1.03	.92	.94			Relative P/E Ratio	1.10
3.1%	2.6%	2.3%	2.6%	3.7%	3.6%	3.5%	4.3%	4.7%	4.9%	4.5%	4.4%	5.0%	3.7%	4.0%	3.9%			Avg Ann'l Div'd Yield	3.4%

CAPITAL STRUCTURE as of Fiscal Year 1985 (A)
Total Debt $509.3 bill.   Due in 5 Yrs $242.8 bill.
LT Debt $400.9 bill.   LT Interest $42.7 bill.
Incl. $32.9 bill. capitalized leases and $22.6 bill. convertible debt.
(LT interest earned: 5.7x; total interest coverage: 4.4x)   (32% of Cap'l)

Leases, Uncapitalized Annual rentals $19.4 bill.

Pension Liability $5.6 bill. in '85 vs. $6.9 bill. in '84

Pfd Stock $30.2 bill.   Pfd Div'd $2.4 bill.
Incl. $14.1 bill. convertible preferred.
(2% of Cap'l)

Common Stock 38.05 bill. shs.   (66% of Cap'l)
(38.55 bill. fully diluted shs.)

1117.6	1271.8	1447.5	1726.1	1984.2	2158.7	2123.2	2184.9	2361.0	2484.9	2575	2750	Sales ($bill) (A)	3500
13.4%	13.3%	13.4%	13.8%	12.7%	12.0%	11.5%	12.6%	13.5%	13.3%	13.0%	13.0%	Operating Margin	14.5%
35.3	39.8	46.8	54.7	63.4	72.8	81.3	88.8	95.6	107.1	115	120	Depreciation ($bill)	140
54.6	61.3	70.6	95.3	95.1	96.2	75.9	90.0	111.5	106.3	108	115	Net Profit ($bill)	185
49.1%	49.2%	48.1%	45.0%	46.1%	43.7%	45.2%	45.3%	44.3%	45.7%	45.5%	45.5%	Income Tax Rate	45.0%
4.9%	4.8%	4.9%	5.5%	4.8%	4.5%	3.6%	4.1%	4.7%	4.3%	4.2%	4.2%	Net Profit Margin	5.3%
182.7	198.3	211.9	233.6	247.3	251.5	240.7	265.5	261.9	264.6	290	300	Working Cap'l ($bill)	400
162.1	177.2	205.8	225.0	256.6	301.9	324.4	323.1	355.8	400.9	420	425	Long-Term Debt ($bill)	475
404.6	448.1	498.1	570.0	644.3	708.0	737.9	790.3	828.0	866.9	930	995	Net Worth ($bill)	1325
10.7%	10.9%	11.2%	13.2%	11.8%	10.9%	8.8%	9.6%	11.0%	10.1%	9.5%	9.5%	% Earned Total Cap'l	11.5%
13.5%	13.7%	14.2%	16.7%	14.8%	13.6%	10.3%	11.4%	13.5%	12.3%	11.5%	11.5%	% Earned Net Worth	14.0%
8.7%	8.6%	9.0%	11.5%	9.5%	8.4%	5.1%	6.3%	8.2%	6.9%	6.0%	6.0%	% Retained to Comm Eq (F)	8.0%
38%	40%	39%	33%	38%	40%	52%	47%	41%	46%	48%	49%	% All Div'ds to Net Prof	45%

Footnotes:

(A) Company fiscal years end between May 1st of year shown and April 30th of following year. Fiscal years for about 80% of companies end Dec. 31st. (B) Based on yearend shares outstanding. Excl. losses from discontinued operations: '82, 5¢; '83, 8¢; '84, 8¢; '85, 11¢. Excl. net nonrecurring losses: '82, 4¢; '83, 4¢; '84, 2¢; '85, 34¢. (C) Incl. intangible assets. In '85: $70.5 bill.; $1.85/sh. (D) In billions. (E) Net profit plus ½ long-term interest paid, divided by long-term debt plus net worth including intangibles. (F) Earnings retained divided by common equity. (G) About two-thirds LIFO. p: preliminary.

Factual material is obtained from sources believed to be reliable but the statistics and comments published herein cannot be guaranteed as to accuracy or completeness.

Source: *Value Line Selection and Opinion*, July 25, 1986, p. 953.

12
Wealth Indexes for Classes of Securities, and the Winner Is...

Stocks or bonds—which is better? While gentlemen prefer bonds, stocks have been the best buy. Will it always be so? For an answer, consider this classic chart. It comes from the well-known Ibbotson/Sinquefield study published by the Financial Analysts Research Foundation (available in most libraries). The study measured rates of return provided by classes of securities. This study, along with the equally well-known Fisher/Lorie study, proved that stocks have done better than the other investments.

Starting in 1926, which eliminates any temporary distortions from the Great Depression, the study showed that a dollar invested in the average of all New York Stock Exchange (NYSE) stocks in 1926, including appreciation and dividends, would have become $211.20 by 1985—a 9.3 percent annual rate of return. This return is far higher than the 3 percent average annual inflation rate. But the return generated by T-bills and long-term government bonds just matched inflation. Even more interesting, they found a phenomenal 12.2 percent average annual return from so-called small stocks. This is now well documented and called the "small-firm effect." Interestingly, it isn't about small firms—just ones that aren't worth much in the market. Small stocks are defined as the 20 percent from the NYSE that each year have the smallest total market value (price times total existing shares of stock). These "small stocks" did much worse than everything else during the Great Depression but later made up for it, plus a lot more.

Why did stocks do better than bonds, and small stocks better than stocks in general? There are conflicting views. Folks who are partial to bonds think inflation played a key role, which may no longer be true if inflation stays dormant. Others think the favorable capital gains rate on appreciation of stock prices was important. This will vanish with the 1986 tax legislation.

Folks like me, who like stocks, see businesses as people—who are inherently flexible in the long-term and able to adjust to changes in the world as they develop—and thereby provide improving profits and better potential returns. Why did the small stocks do so well? Smaller companies may be more flexible and even better able to adjust to the world than bigger companies. And bigger companies whose total stock market values are low (probably because they've had troubles and the stock has been flattened) have almost certainly felt severe pressure to adjust and may, after the problems, be able to adjust better than their less troubled brethren.

If you believe in businesses as groups of problem-solving people, you'll take this chart's lesson to heart and be a life-long holder of stocks from the market's lesser names (not necessarily the most speculative stocks—remember, all the stocks studied here were on the NYSE). But skeptics can take heart from other, longer charts (see Chart 51) and conclude that many trends lasting 55 years and longer finally turn and dust their previous beneficiaries. Maybe in the next 55 years stocks won't adjust so well.

Wealth Indexes of Investments in the U.S. Capital Markets, 1925–1985

YEAR–END 1925 = 1.00

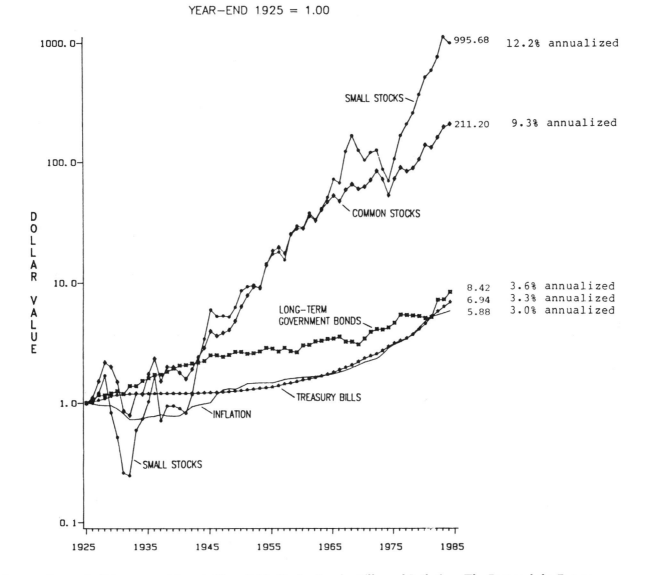

Source: Roger G. Ibbotson and Rex A. Sinqefield, *Stocks, Bonds, Bills, and Inflation: The Past and the Future,*
1985 Edition, Monograph Number 15, The Financial Analysts Research Foundation, University of Virginia.

13
Invest Overseas and Diversify?

You can reduce your risks and maximize profits by investing globally, right? Balderdash! While overseas investing is quite the rage these days, and has also been successful recently (that's why it's quite the rage), there is a lot less diversification and safety in overseas investing than the marketers of these products (mutual funds?) want you to believe.

Why? As this book shows with varying charts, the world's nations are far more economically linked and stock market linked than most folks believe—tremendously so. While all the ocean's waves don't match perfectly, as any California coastal kid knows, when the surf's up, it's up. This chart compares the U.S. market with the London market from 1958 through 1977. Note how closely the two indexes correlate. Note in 1960–1962 and 1972–1975 where a pronounced movement in the United States was perfectly mirrored in England for bull and bear markets. Most often, when the U.S. market is in a major upswing or decline, within a few jiggles of a hair's breadth most of the world's markets will be too. It's been that way for decades. Perhaps the all-time classic example was the 1929 correlation in England, France, Germany, and the United States (see Chart 29).

Why then do we hear so much about diversifying overseas lately? Even though the United States makes up half the world's stock market—and adding in Japan and England gives 80 percent—that other 20 percent has risen in price far more than U.S. stocks have since the 1981–1983 worldwide recession. Since 1981 the U.S. market increased at about a 12.5 percent average annual rate through mid-1986. But that other 20 percent of the world rose about 18 percent per year.

Doesn't that confirm the wisdom of overseas investing? Not really. It merely shows that at a time when the trends were simultaneously bullish, the smaller and perhaps riskier overseas markets went up more—much as U.S. over-the-counter markets often rise and fall more in bull and bear markets than does the New York Stock Exchange. In a bear market these smaller foreign markets will be apt to go down more too. That isn't much of a real diversification effect—just an opportunity to take a flier on Hong Kong, Italy, or South Africa.

The problem is compounded by the difficulty in understanding the oblique variations in accounting and customs in the less familiar countries. Also, the big companies overseas are often small by U.S. standards, and it is harder to get information. Do you recognize Endesa, the seventh-highest-valued stock in Spain? Maybe you confused it with Astra, the sixth-largest from Sweden? Or Fraser & Neave, number 7 in Singapore?

This isn't to say that some folks won't regularly make good money overseas. Some professionals will because they know what they're doing. But the average investor won't, and he or she won't know enough about it to tell the pros who do from the pros who have just been lucky in this recent spectacular foreign bull market. If you know what you're doing in the United States, you can do just fine. And if you don't know what you're doing in the United States, how in the devil are you going to know enough to do better wheeling and dealing in Malaysia?

British Stocks vs. Dow Jones Industrials, 1958–1977

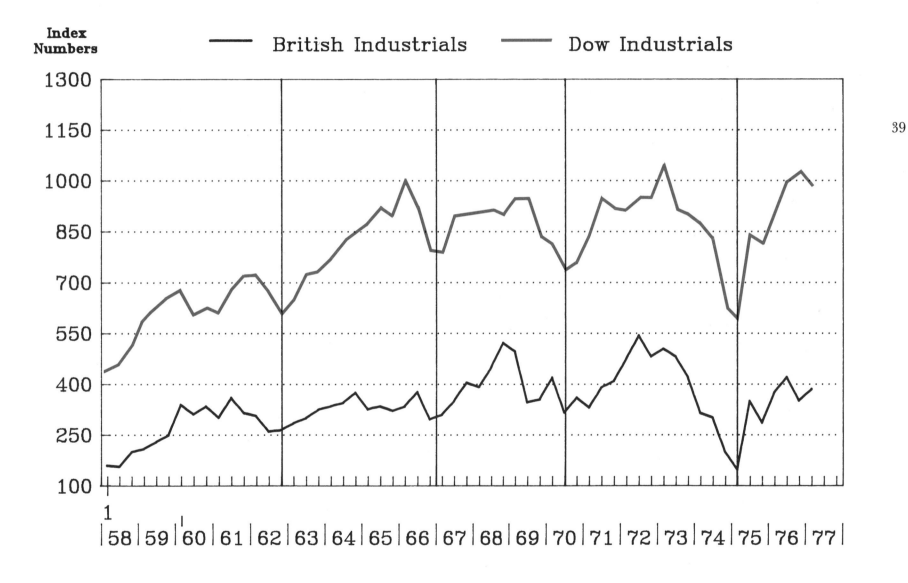

Index Numbers — British Industrials ——— Dow Industrials

39

Sources: *The London Daily Mail, Financial Times,* and Dow Jones & Company.

14
Stock Prices Abroad: Seven More Market Mirrors

How often can you find a stock that rises in a falling market? Lots of folks hope to, but few do. When the market falls in a big way, so do almost all the stocks. So do almost all the stocks in all the countries. This chart shows another way to look at the stock market's global nature, as described in Chart 13. It shows the amazing correlation between these seven major countries' stock markets. The vertical lines running through all the charts reflect high and low time periods for the U.S. market. While each country has its own jiggles, Canada, France, Germany, and the United Kingdom match the American action within months, often within weeks. Japan and Italy vary a bit more but show many similarities.

Take for example the major decline that ended in late 1974. It rippled through all these countries, and, except for Italy, each country's stock market reached a bottom within months of when market troughs developed in the other countries. Walk your way through the declines in the United States, Japan, West Germany, France, and the United Kingdom. They all started and ended within months of each other. Sure, France and Japan appear to have bottomed out about a month earlier than the others, but they were all awfully close together.

Then there was the American stock market's bull phase that ended at year-end 1972. It was perfectly coincident with Japan's peak, a temporary Canadian peak, and it happened just before Germany's peak, just before France's, and just after the United Kingdom's. Again, only Italy was out of phase.

Now consider the American trough that developed at year-end 1977. This time Canada, France, Italy, and the United Kingdom mirrored the U.S. decline very closely. Japan and Germany didn't go down, but they didn't move up right then either.

The world's different markets can't mirror each other perfectly any more than different stocks mirror each other's action perfectly. But the world's markets do ripple into each other and usually reflect the same general worldwide trends. If stocks are much cheaper in one country than in another, that is, the earnings yields (see Chart 43) are higher in the "cheaper" country, money is apt to flow to the cheaper country's stocks.

So if you accept the interrelationship of the world's stock markets, how do you profit by it? You can use other countries' markets as a limited warning signal. Some few of the major Western nations usually turn down before the others. Take the year-end 1972 peak. Germany and the United Kingdom turned south before the United States did. In 1976, France, the United Kingdom, and Germany all took a dive before U.S. stocks. And as mentioned, France, Germany, and Japan started heading up a little before the United States as they entered the great 1975 bull market. These early "leaders" provided a warning. To see how this would have helped you avoid the 1929 debacle, see Chart 29. Look for divergence between what's going on in the United States, and what's going on overseas. And when the others start to buck the U.S. trend, prepare to see your bucks follow theirs.

Stock Indexes in Seven Countries, 1970–1980

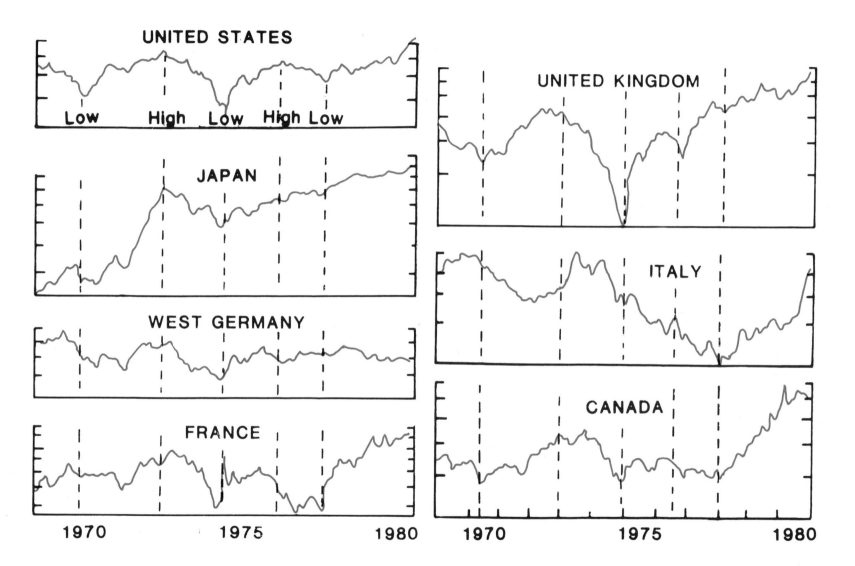

41

Source: *Business Conditions Digest*, Department of Commerce, December 1980, p. 59.

15
The 51st Estate

While markets tend to move simultaneously all around the Western world, some places move more simultaneously than others. For example, for all intents and purposes, Canada is the financial 51st state of the United States or, perhaps, in investment terms the 51st estate. This chart shows how closely the Canadian market was tied to the U.S. market from 1961 until 1969. As you can see, the two markets moved together almost perfectly, not only in timing, but also in magnitude.

While other charts throughout this book show the commonalities between financial markets in differing countries, looking at Canada, the dissimilarities are so small as to be immaterial. For example, look at 1965 and 1966. There is no measurable difference between the movements for the two indexes. Chart 14 aims at a different point and is in a different format, but it shows you that the similarities continue during 1969–1981.

Why does the Canadian market move so closely with the U.S. market? Simple—their economy as a whole lock-steps with the U.S. economy. Financially, whatever happens in the United States happens in Canada with almost no difference. Yes, there are business differences, but they aren't terribly important. For example, Canada is resource-rich, making the country relatively mining oriented, producing products like potash-based fertilizer. Potash (potassium chloride) is one of the three principal fertilizers, all three of which are necessary for all plants. Canada has the world's richest reserves and is the largest exporter. Because the United States has relatively little potash, it buys most of Canada's. As U.S. agriculture swings up and down, so does demand for potash.

It is almost as if the Canadian government's policies are totally unimportant. While Canadians would bridle at that notion, it is clear from this chart how tough it is for them to set any policy that takes them out from under the shadow of the U.S. economy. While it would be socially impossible, and I'm not suggesting such a thing, it would probably be more economically efficient if Canada eliminated the duplicate efforts of its independent government and became part of the United States. It would merely formalize what happens informally anyway.

What is the lesson here? First, when you see some mutual fund claiming to diversify your money by investing in Canada, beware: There really isn't a diversification effect by moving your money into the 51st estate. There are just that many more stocks to add to your menu to choose from. That's good, but not critical, since there are already more than 5,000 actively traded stocks in the United States and another 7,000 that are publicly traded (even if illiquid and relatively thinly traded—meaning you can't buy and hope to be able to sell it when you want).

The good news is that Canadian stocks are that many more stocks to choose from, because you can use all your senses regarding what's going on in the United States to buy stocks in Canadian businesses. Whereas it is awfully tough for U.S. investors to make sense out of most of the world's many foreign stock markets, buying Canadian stocks is just like visiting next door.

Canadian vs. U.S. Stock Prices, 1962–1971

43

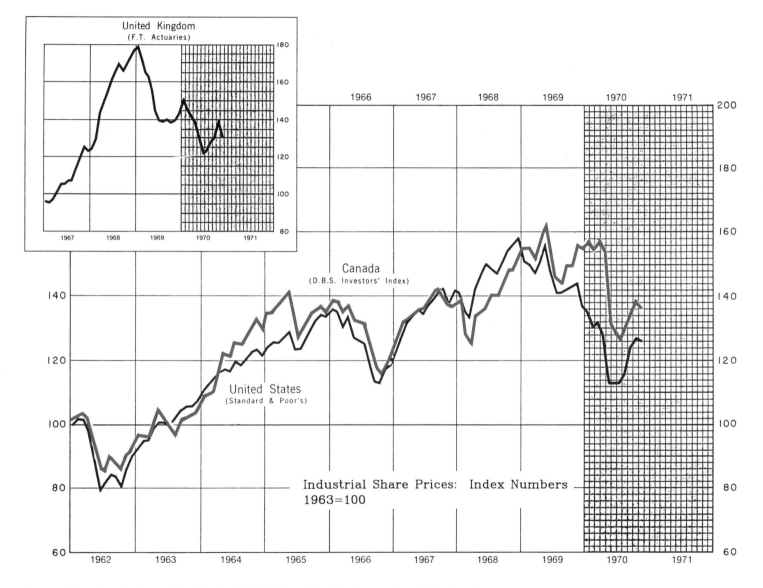

Source: *Canadian Business Chartbook,* 1971 Edition, The Conference Board in Canada.

16
Stock Prices Versus GNP

Have you ever heard of the old rule of thumb that in-the-know investors have often used to measure stocks as an inflation hedge? It is the ratio of the Dow Jones Industrials to GNP. The theory says that as inflation pushes GNP higher, stocks should follow too—eventually. So, when stocks sell at historical lows relative to GNP, they're good buys. At historical highs they're bye-byes. Supposedly stock values should keep pace with GNP because the business of the companies is a key and steady part of GNP.

It sounds good, but be skeptical. These charts show stock indexes versus GNP from 1955-1971 in England, France, Germany, Japan, The Netherlands, and the United States. Each stock index was adjusted to match it one-for-one to that country's 1955 GNP. Only France saw a major long-term variance between stock prices and GNP. Elsewhere folks did well throughout this time period if they sold when the stock index was more than 130 percent of GNP and bought when the index fell below GNP.

How so? Well, in 1965, the Dow Jones Industrials peaked just below 1,000. GNP was $725 billion. Divide 1,000 by 725—the result is 138 percent of GNP. By this theory, that would be a good time to sell. It was. Later, after 1972, stocks collapsed and ushered in a decade of the lowest levels relative to GNP since the 1930s. But GNP kept rising, fueled by an expanding economy and inflation. GNP is now $4 trillion—5½ times higher. According to this theory, to keep pace with the economy, the Dow Jones Industrials should not only have doubled in recent years, as it did, but more than double again to 4,000. So, if you believe this theory, you're a superbull.

But you might just be bull-headed. Here's why. These charts cover a unique time period of worldwide low interest rates, so stocks sold at historically high levels. Interest rates are lots higher now. So, all things being equal, stocks should sell lower relative to GNP than they did back then (see Chart 43 on earnings versus interest rates).

Furthermore, the Dow Jones Industrial Average should sell lower relative to GNP than it did—for three reasons. First, business is slowly losing its share of GNP as Uncle Sam annually boosts its share (see Charts 76 and 80). In the last 20 years, Uncle Sam expropriated 6 percent of GNP—and business lost it. So businesses' stock value should fall enough to compensate for this lower portion of GNP. At the same time, Uncle Sam's efficiency is poor. As its share of GNP rises, overall GNP growth should fall. In a slower-growth economy, stocks should be worth less. Finally, Dow Jones–type companies lose their share of GNP to new, more innovative companies, and so do their stocks.

In the United States today, economic growth comes mainly from small, innovative outfits, not the big bureaucratic monsters the Dow Average comprises. For example, Digital Equipment Corporation grew from zip to $8 billion in sales in the last 25 years. Intel, Apple Computer, Price Club, and Federal Express—none existed 20 years ago. More fledglings are emerging now. They, not the big guys, provide most of our growth, so the Dow's market value shrinks relative to GNP as the fledglings boost their share.

How much lower should the Dow sell for, relative to GNP? I haven't the foggiest idea; it's too hard to figure. But I'm sure of one thing: This old stand-by should be put on stand-by.

Stock Market Indexes and Variations in GNP, 1955–1974

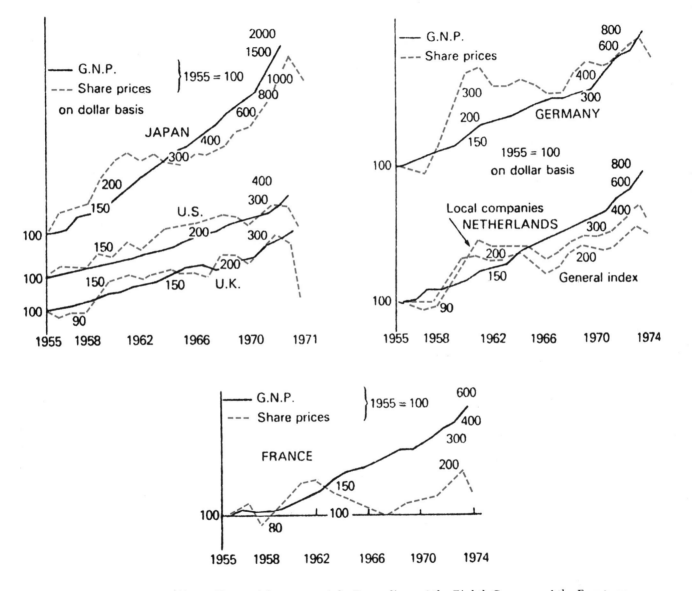

45

Source: *The Evaluation of Ordinary Shares; A Summary of the Proceedings of the Eighth Congress of the European Federation of Financial Analysts Societies*, ed. Felix Rosenfeld, Dunod, 1974.

17
The Premium Price of Growth

One tricky and effective way to outfox the market is to buy growth-oriented stocks when these companies are selling at a historically low P/E in relation to the overall market. A P/E is a stock's price divided by its earnings per share. It is the most standard measure of value on Wall Street. This chart shows the P/E multiple of emerging growth stocks as a percentage of the average P/E for the Standard & Poor's 500.

As a general rule, you make good money buying growth stocks when they are selling at average P/Es of 125 percent of the P/E for the overall market—or less. That's because normally P/Es are much higher for rapidly growing companies than the market as a whole, because folks will pay for an exciting company's rosy prospects.

But when Wall Street won't pay up for growth, you can buy a quality growth company for little or no more than you would have to pay for a big stodgy lump of a company that isn't going anywhere. Which would you rather buy? In time everyone catches on and bids up the growth stocks—yours too, if you bought in time.

The 1977–1978 period may have been the best time in the last 50 years to buy growth stocks. The average valuation multiple for growth companies, as measured by the Hambrecht and Quist Technology Universe, rose sixfold between 1978 and 1983. Folks made big bucks with growth companies starting in 1962–1964 and again in 1970. But all the opportunities have not gone by.

This graph speaks well for the prospects for growth stocks in 1987 and 1988, because the graph now shows a movement back down to the "buy" level. Even though the overall market may seem high by some standards, this graph says growth stocks should do well, at least over the next few years.

Originally this chart appeared in a quarterly report from the T. Rowe Price New Horizons Fund, and is based on the data from their fund. It now appears in each of their quarterly reports, so you can update yourself on it there.

Price/Earnings Multiples of Emerging Growth Stocks
as a Percentage of the S&P 500 P/E, 1960–1986

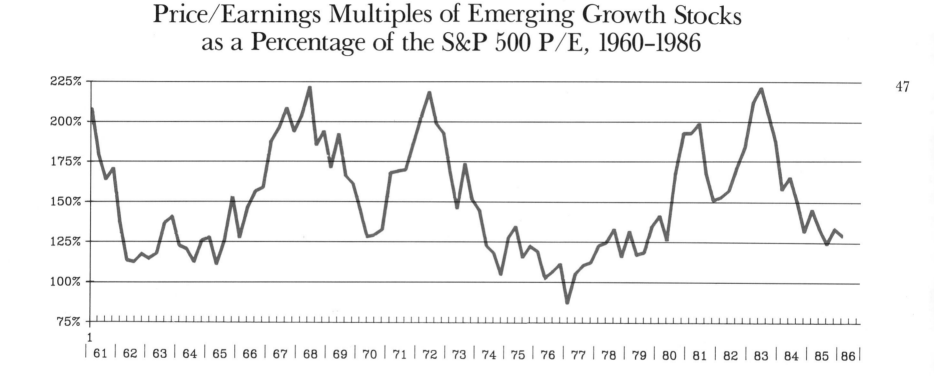

Source: Dennis Sherva, Director of Research, Morgan Stanley.

18
Growth-Stock Gyrations

This chart teaches several lessons. First, looks can be deceiving. It looks like the Hambrecht & Quist Growth Index did phenomenally and left the Standard & Poor's 400 in the dust. Then, too, it looks like the Technology Index matched the market (as represented by the S&P 400). None of these conclusions is true. For example, on the seeming standoff of the S&P 400 and the Technology Index, the chart doesn't include the S&P 400's dividend yields of more than 5 percent annually—the Technology Index paid virtually nothing. The best lesson from these charts is to get a financial calculator that allows you to figure compound rates of return. Then use it to look behind the numbers to the real, and often hidden, meaning.

The Growth Index was about 195 in 1971. It flopped steadily to 80 in 1978. Then it rose irregularly to a peak of about 1,020 in 1983 before ending up at about 680. The upshot? The 1971–1978 period turned in returns of –12 percent per year. Ouch! But during 1978–1983 the compound return was a spectacular 66 percent per year. After 1983 the return was again a –12 percent per year. So much for the value of a big upward move surrounded by poor results—the overall 15-year return for 1971–1986 was a paltry 8.7 percent. By contrast, the dowdy-looking S&P 400 grew almost as fast (from a lower beginning level) at 7.6 percent per year over those 15 years. But don't forget that the S&P gave you another 5 percent each year in dividends, which don't show.

So, adding in dividends over this entire time period, the S&P 400 did better than either H&Q index—and a lot better than the Technology Index. To make money with the H&Q stocks, you would have had to know how and when to sell. Why didn't growth bail out the growth stocks? Stocks that society broadly considers to be growth stocks are usually overvalued.

As a kid, I learned from my father what moves stocks: It's the difference between what a company is and what the financial world thinks it is—i.e., relative expectations. The best long-term performers are unpopular stocks of what end up being good companies. Folks get pleasantly surprised and won't sell. Others will want to buy. But a widely hailed "growth stock" is already popular, so even if it's a great company it won't go up, because no one's expectations will be exceeded. When you understand that, you've got the real key to making money. It's better to buy underloved value than overloved growth.

There's a final lesson here too. Whenever anything has been going straight up for a few months or longer, it won't be long until it peaks and falls. A prolonged straight-up move is unsustainable and is the one and only place where stop-loss orders make sense. Straight-up moves almost always end up forming a perfect cone. As prices skyrocket, maintaining a stop-loss 10 percent below each new high is just about your only chance to get to the top without having to ski down the other side.

Hambrecht & Quist Growth Index, Hambrecht & Quist Technology Index, Standard & Poor's 400, January 1970 to September 1986

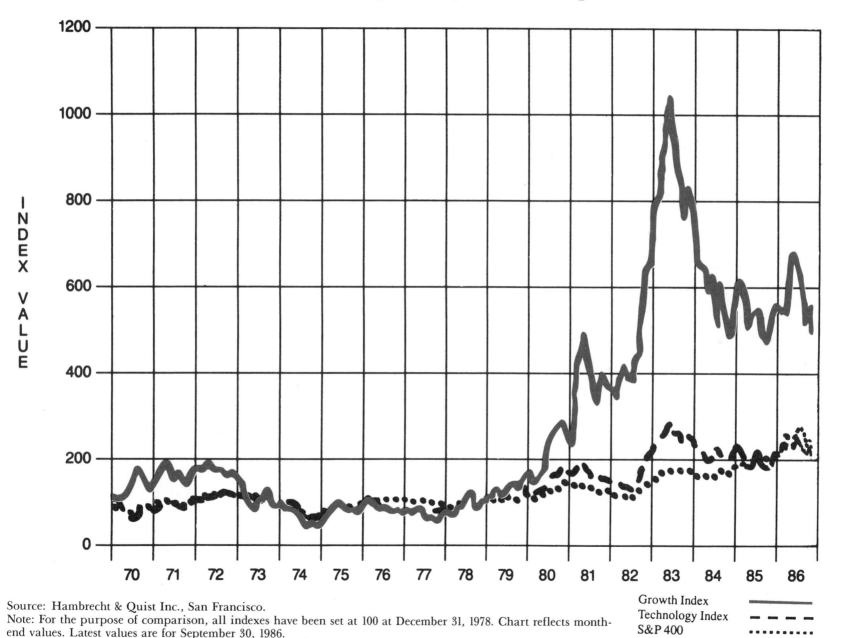

Source: Hambrecht & Quist Inc., San Francisco.
Note: For the purpose of comparison, all indexes have been set at 100 at December 31, 1978. Chart reflects month-end values. Latest values are for September 30, 1986.

Growth Index ——————
Technology Index — — — —
S&P 400 ·············

19
"IPO" Means It's Probably Overpriced

Don't waste your time. When a company "goes public"—an initial public offering (IPO)—lots of folks rush in, hoping to get in on the next Apple Computer or Intel. They could get more at the bank. Nine IPOs out of 10 are money losers within two years. Even the few long-term winners, like Apple, rarely do well compared to the very best stocks. If you don't believe it, see how few recent IPOs appear in *Forbes*'s annual review of the top-performing stocks (in February).

IPO stocks often rise immediately, because the brokers selling them are getting sales commissions of several percent for their hype, so they create lots of mindless momentum around these issues. Investors get suckered in by the excitement and by dreams of a big hit. And they usually get hit, because companies raise money through stock offerings only when the price is great for them—which is too high on average to be a good deal for buyers. Soon the hype wears off and the stocks get clobbered. Many of 1983's crop of new issues have since lost most of their value—like blue-ribbon Diasonics, which was once worth hundreds of millions and then the stock fell from $30 to $3. A good chunk are bankrupt now, too—like Victor Technologies, which was also a blue-blood issue.

But here's the real kicker: Not only do IPOs usually perform poorly, but as a group they can be used effectively as an indicator of when the market is overheated or underbought.

This chart shows the total number of IPOs each year from 1969 through 1985. When the number of IPOs was high, it was a good time to sell. When it was low, it was a good time to buy.

What's high and what's low? Just remember, sell whenever IPOs are at measurably high levels in relation to the prior few years. Following this rule, you would have sold in 1972, in 1980 or 1981 (depending on how itchy you were), and in 1983. Those years were the best years to sell during this era, and that strategy would have put you at the top of the heap of all investment pros.

In contrast, if you bought after the number of IPOs had fallen from the prior year's level or whenever the number of IPOs hadn't risen from the prior year's level, you would have done very well then, too. You could have bought in 1982 and ridden the phenomenal 1982–1983 bull market. Or you could have bought in 1984 or 1985 and caught what has since been a spectacular rise. Or you could have bought anytime in the mid- to later 1970s and done well. Only in 1973 would this indicator have given you a bum steer, causing you to buy and then letting you suffer the big decline of the 1974 bear market. But you're not going to find any single perfect indicator to teach you all the steps to the Wall Street Waltz. They keep changing the music.

In 1986 IPOs were again setting records, which didn't speak well for 1987 and perhaps 1988. But who knows, maybe this will be the second time when the indicator will fail. When hundreds of companies are finding that stock prices are high enough to make selling stock the cheapest way to raise capital, it's a good idea to remember that whenever there is a buyer and a seller, somebody is wrong. Make sure it's not you.

Number of Initial Public Offerings, 1969–1985

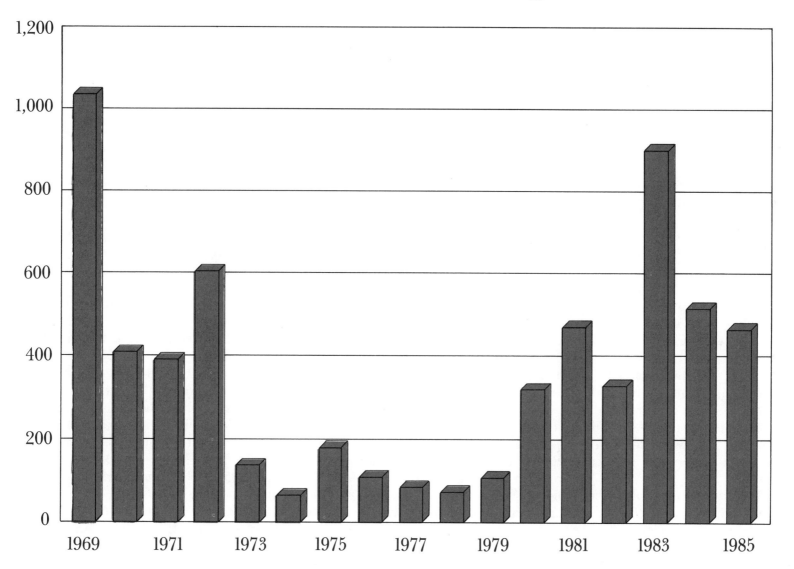

Source: Going Public (IPO Reporter).

20
"Wake Up, Folks"

My competition said that—well, sort of. My *Forbes* columns are in every other issue of the magazine. When I'm not in, David Dreman is; when he's not, I am. David's financial commentary is among the most insightful and thought-provoking anywhere. This chart came from his March 11, 1985, column, in which he urged folks to "wake up" and notice the bull market, which he successfully predicted would continue despite having already had a 10-year run. The chart's implications and David's wisdom in analyzing it are worth noting. The chart compares the 1975 to 1984 performance of stocks against antiques, bonds, U.S. Treasury bills, gold, and copper.

It probably doesn't surprise you that stocks did better than bonds and T-bills. As Chart 10 shows, stocks have done better than fixed-income alternatives for decades. But it's rare to see stocks compared with "hard-money" alternatives. David railed at the doom-and-gloomers who sold millions of books and newsletters during these 10 years based on buying gold and other hard-money inflation hedges. As he pointed out, unless you were among the 1 in 1,000 who sold at the top, gold would have earned you only 4.8 percent per year—less than your bank account. But if you've seen Chart 57, you probably aren't surprised. Throughout most of history, gold has left investors short. Copper did worse. Interestingly, fine art, as shown here by Sotheby's Composite Art Index, is the one hard-money asset that came close to matching the performance of stocks, rising more than 12.5 percent annually.

Of course, there are difficulties in investing in art, which may outweigh its investment merits. First, to buy quality pieces, you need big bucks per unit. And when you buy 100 shares of IBM you don't have to worry about forged certificates, but you must have art authenticated. You also need to store your art, which might be a joy for you, your living room wall, and your neighborhood thief. Finally, one of the big advantages of stocks is that you can sell them quickly, whenever you want, with commissions that through a discount broker run less than 0.75 percent of the value traded. With art, the transaction costs would run many times that.

Some folks might say that David fudged the results by starting the comparison in early 1975—at the beginning of a major bull market for stocks. Certainly the test starts at a favorable time for stocks. But 1984 was a bad time for stocks to end the test. If David had ended the test two years later, using 1986's higher prices, stocks would have left the others much further in the dust, regardless of when the analysis started.

The whole point of David's article was to urge folks to hang on to stocks, or buy them, during those next few years—despite the market's prior 10-year bull phase. In that, David was vindicated completely by the 1985–1986 50 percent rise in the stock market. But a broader lesson from this chart is an extension of Chart 10. Stocks are about the best investment going in the long term. Adjusting for dividends and taking into account liquidity and lack of management or maintenance responsibilities—and despite getting periodically bear-beaten—you can't beat the long-term returns provided by American stocks.

Stocks vs. Five Investment Alternatives 1975–1985

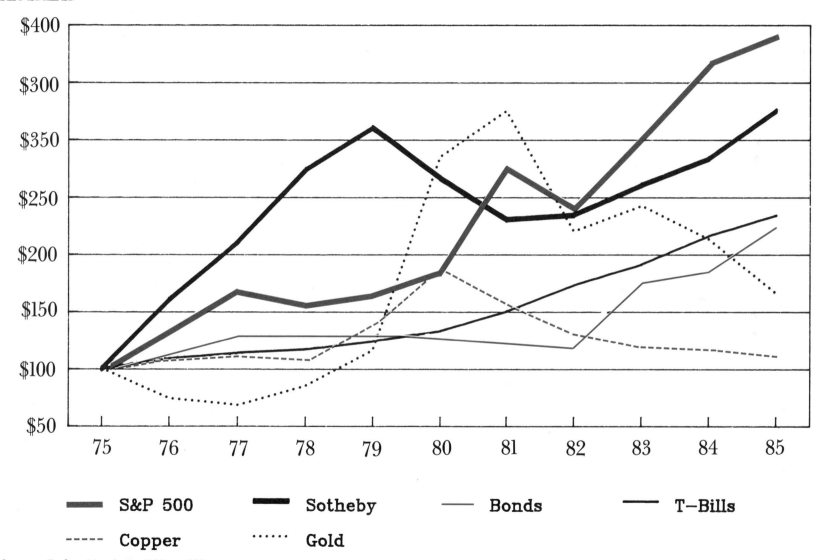

53

Source: *Forbes*, March 11, 1985, p. 222.

21
Takeover Tactics in Relation to Assets

With the Dow Jones Industrials setting record highs and most measures of stock market value at the top of their historic range, you can see that stocks are still cheap by considering their replacement cost, right? Not according to the first chart here. It shows the ratio of total stock market value of all stocks (price times total shares of stock) to the replacement cost for the underlying assets of these industrial companies.

In 1968, with stocks selling at levels averaging 1.5 times the value of the companies' assets, stocks were clearly overpriced by this or any other measure. And, sure enough, they fell for the next 15 years. Along the way, stocks became steadily cheaper in relation to the replacement cost of their assets, both because stock prices fell and because replacement costs rose under inflationary pressures. By 1980 stocks were selling for less than 70 percent of the replacement cost of their underlying assets.

Another way to look at this is through the eyes of takeover artists. The 1960s wheeler-dealer conglomerators bought companies fast and furiously, as shown by the second chart. But these fast-trackers knew that their own stocks were overpriced, so when they made acquisitions, they bought small companies and paid for them with overvalued stock (the wheeler-dealers'). By 1980, with those vastly reduced prices in relation to replacement cost, stocks were cheap, which made them even more buyable. But the 1980s takeover turks wouldn't want to use their cheap stock to finance the takeovers. Now, they kept their stock and hocked the shop to do fewer but bigger deals—financed by floating junk bonds. As the second chart shows, the inflation-adjusted value of takeovers rose back to the 1968 level for the first time in 1984. In nominal dollars (not adjusted for inflation), the 1984 takeover level was 300 percent higher than in 1968.

Accounting records assets at cost, not at current value or at what it would cost to rebuy those assets today. When stocks are low relative to replacement costs, it is cheaper to take over firms than to start them from scratch. That's why the current takeover binge has bulged. If you wanted to expand in a given industry, it was cheaper to go out and buy an existing company than to build plant and capacity from scratch. Drexel Burnham responded by developing the junk-bond phenomenon to finance this frenzy.

So, doesn't that mean stocks are still cheap after all? Hardly! As 1968 proved, or as the 1920s proved (see Chart 30), merger manias are often the warning sign of an overpriced market and rarely speak well for stock prices over the following five to ten years. Since 1982, stock prices have risen 150 percent, which would raise the ratio from 0.69 back up to 1.7—except that the denominator has been rising too. Inflation has boosted the denominator by about 20 percent since 1982. Dividing the 1.7 by 1.2 brings the overall ratio back down to 1.4, which is lower than in 1968, but not by much. Beware!

Stocks, Inflation, and Merger and Acquisitions Activity, 1968–1984

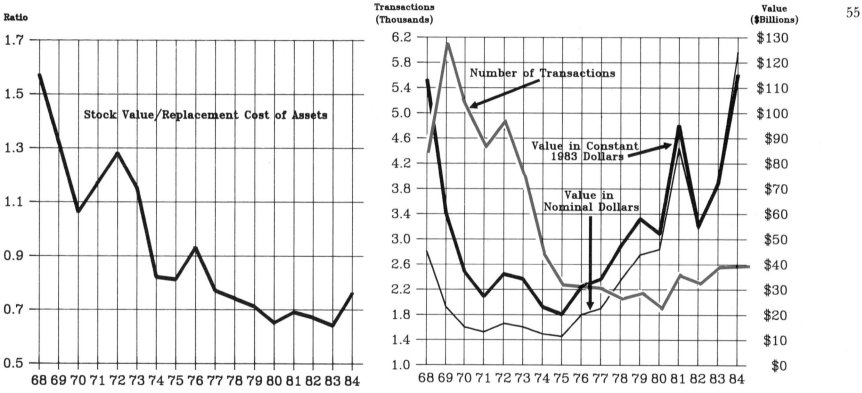

Source: Allan Sloan, "Why Is No One Safe?" *Forbes,* March 11, 1985.

22
The Silent Crash No One Noticed

Everyone knows the market is up, but adjusted for inflation it's still cheaper than in the 1960s—right or wrong? It turns out that's right. Of course it was high in the 1960s, but who's counting? The top half of this chart shows the Dow Jones Industrial Average from 1915 to 1984. Its fancy footwork should be old hat to avid market watchers. But the chart's bottom half adjusts the Dow for inflation—a different story. Between the two stock market charts lies a single line representing inflation, via the Consumer Price Index.

First, note the chart's earliest years. Stock prices, adjusted for inflation, dropped sharply from 1915 through 1921. As you can see in Chart 53, there was tremendous inflation throughout the Western world during this period. Since stock prices weren't going anywhere (see Chart 27), they were declining on an inflation-adjusted basis. If stocks don't increase while inflation rages, then they're falling in "real" value. This created the bargains that set the stage for the 1920s.

Interestingly, the 1920s superbull market was larger on an inflation-adjusted basis than on a nominal basis, because consumer prices fell slightly from 1921 to 1929. The Dow Averages increased 5.97 times in value, from 63.9 in 1921 to 381.17 in 1929, but on an inflation-adjusted basis they increased 6.4 times from 33.83 to 216.33. And, while of little consolation to investors, the decline after 1929 was only 86 percent adjusted for inflation, rather than the Dow's actual 89 percent drop—again, because consumer prices dropped.

From there, inflation continually beat the market's real

return downward, so that when the Dow couldn't quite kiss 1,000 in 1965, its value adjusted for inflation was less than one-third that level—only 306. Now for the interesting part: The market listlessly zig-zagged, with no real direction for 17 years, while inflation raged. In 1982, the Dow Averages stumbled through to a cyclical low of 769.98, but as this chart shows, its inflation-adjusted value was then less than 85. That means that during those 17 years the market had lost almost as much of its real purchasing power as it did in the years after the Great Crash of 1929—72 percent versus 86 percent in 1929.

Of course, this chart is two years old. The market has since risen about 62 percent to an early 1987 peak of 2,200. The consumer price index has increased about 11 percent from 1984 to early 1987. This puts the early 1987 inflation-adjusted Dow at about 180.9 (123.95 times 1.62 divided by 1.11).

Since the real, inflation-adjusted value of the market is lower than 20 years ago, some folks think this proves stocks aren't a good inflation hedge and no place to invest. Others say this chart proves the current market isn't as high as some other charts in this book imply, so maybe the market is a good place to invest after all. Those same people also argue that a 1929-like crash isn't ahead of us; they say we already came through it, with the sound of the thundering crash muffled by the 17-year hiss of inflation. When historians someday hiss about those recent 17 years, they may refer to them as the Crash that was neither seen nor heard—just devalued.

The Dow Jones Industrial Average as Adjusted for Inflation, 1920–1985

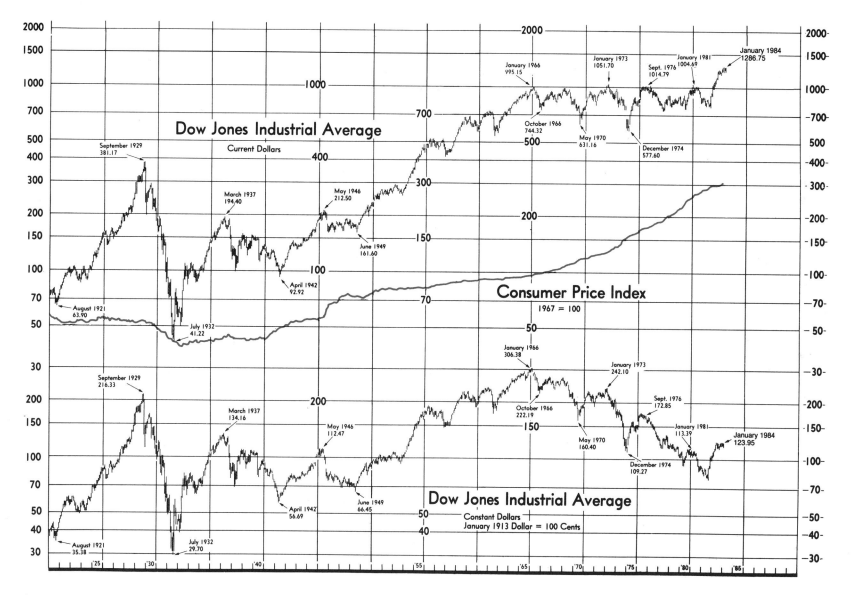

Dow Jones Industrial Average
Current Dollars

September 1929
381.17

August 1921
63.90

July 1932
41.22

March 1937
194.40

April 1942
92.92

May 1946
212.50

June 1949
161.60

January 1966
995.15

October 1966
744.32

January 1973
1051.70

May 1970
631.16

Sept. 1976
1014.79

December 1974
577.60

January 1981
1004.69

January 1984
1286.75

Consumer Price Index
1967 = 100

September 1929
216.33

August 1921
35.38

July 1932
29.70

March 1937
134.16

April 1942
56.69

May 1946
112.47

June 1949
66.45

January 1966
306.38

October 1966
222.19

January 1973
242.10

May 1970
160.40

Sept. 1976
172.85

December 1974
109.27

January 1981
113.39

January 1984
123.95

Dow Jones Industrial Average
Constant Dollars
January 1913 Dollar = 100 Cents

57

Source: Media General Financial Weekly, Richmond, Virginia.

23
Moving with the Moving Average

An amazing contradiction lies in the battle between two major schools of investment analysis—technical versus fundamental. Technical analysis looks at the past action of a stock, the market, interest rates, or some related event and bases forecasts on that information. Fundamentalists base forecasts on valuations like P/Es or book value, coupled with analyzing future trends for the economy, industries, or single businesses.

There are plenty of adherents to each style, but the fundamental folks dominate for two main reasons. First, all the legendary players who've repeatedly made big bundles decade after decade came from the fundamental side—not a technician in the bunch. Second, there has never been a serious academic study demonstrating that a security's prior price action has anything to do with its future price action. So, most pros consider themselves fundamental analysts—your author included.

Ironically, all the great fundamentalists I've known or read about used a few disguised technical tools with their overriding fundamentals. Why? Some things seem to work—at least a bit. Consider the amazing success of the simple 40-week moving average, which starts with the sum of the closing price for the last 40 weeks divided by 40. Then, each week you do the same thing, adding the new week's price and dropping off the first week's. When the market is above its moving average, it's thought to be bullish. When it's below its average, it's bearish.

This chart shows the market versus its moving average for 1966–1978. They mirror each other closely. But if you had bought every time the market first exceeded its average and sold when it next dropped below its average, you would have stayed on the market's "right" side amazingly often. For two examples, see "A." The first was mid-1969, when the market broke below the moving average. If you sold then, you would have avoided the next 200-point free fall. Then in mid-1970 the DJIA again surpassed its average. If you bought then, you would have banked the next 150-point rise.

Moving averages don't predict market turns—they imperfectly confirm them after the fact. For example, point B shows the market resuming an upward trend long before the 1975 market exceeded its moving average. And sometimes you get "whipsawed" this way; "C" shows several times when the market traded within a narrow range and this tool would have taken you into and out of the market without success. But, as you can see by examining the cases, when you got whipsawed it would have cost you little relative to the savings gained at other times.

I've never used moving averages as a strict buy/sell rule, but instead to warn when I need to be especially concerned that things may not be going as I've expected them to. Ironically, my results would have been much better had I used them more absolutely at times. And, there is nothing magical about 40 weeks. Moving averages can be 39, 41, 2, or 2,002 weeks. But shorter periods whipsaw you much more often. Longer periods seldom give a signal. Forty weeks seems good because it sends relatively few signals that aren't worth pause for thought.

The 40-Week Moving Average of the Dow Jones Industrial Average, 1965–1977

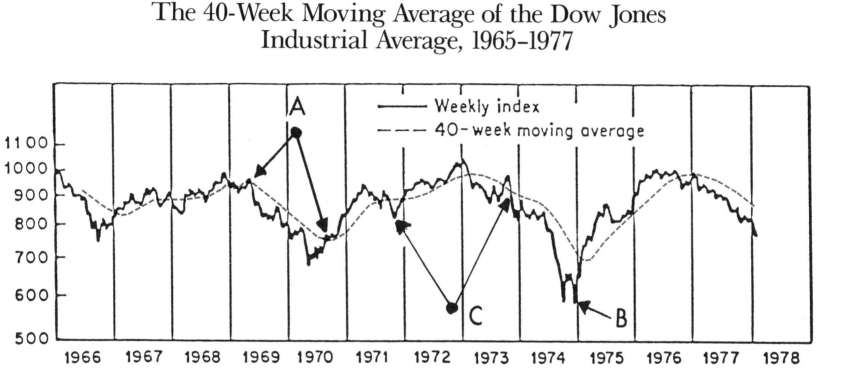

Source: Martin J. Pring, *Technical Analysis Explained*, 1st Edition, New York: McGraw-Hill Book Company, 1979.

24
All the News That's Fit to Print

"The president has been shot. Quick, sell everything!" It isn't hard envisioning such lines. They left lots of lips when Kennedy died on November 22, 1963. But not learned lips. That Friday, when the news hit, the Dow Industrials buckled 28 points (3.8 percent), but they made it all up and more on Monday. As you see here, the bull market kept right on booming—uninterrupted for the next two years. So much for the market's view of the most beloved president since FDR. Ditto for Ike's 1955 heart attack.

This chart shows that the headlines that strike terror in our hearts rarely even cause the market heartburn. It shows the major news shocks from 1949 to 1969. The lesson? News that seems awfully important usually has little market impact. For instance, the communist showdown in Korea—its beginning hardly rippled the market. Maybe you're one of those antibusiness hardliners who believes wars are probusiness, maybe even caused by Wall Street. To prove that wars influence the market, you cite the market's big rise in those three Korean War years— about 28 percent. But if that's so, why did the market rise another 66 percent in the three years after the war ended? Major news has very little market impact.

The market didn't care when Fidel Castro stopped being a closet communist. Or when Russia beat the United States into space with Sputnik. Or when they threw out Nikita Khrushchev. What would have happened if they gave the power to push the button to a Godzilla? Apparently the market wasn't too concerned. The Tonkin Gulf crisis or the Suez? Never a ripple. Eugene McCarthy upset Johnson in the 1968 New Hampshire presidential primary, and LBJ announced he wouldn't seek reelection. Again, the market yawned.

Yes, it's true that the market seemed to react poorly when Kennedy "jawboned" steel prices down in 1962, but maybe the market was ready for a rest anyway. IPO activity was at record levels (for a discussion on IPOs and overpricing, see the text with Chart 19), and the market had risen 250 percent in the prior 13 years—without even a 15 percent hiccup. What about in other eras? The same phenomenon persists. There was a small drop in the market after San Francisco's 1906 fire and earthquake. But it actually started days earlier, dried up, and the market rose above its prequake levels before the real drop (see Chart 32). What about the two World Wars? You can't detect a major break—up or down—in the weeks before or after the major news items tied to those wars. Interestingly, the market bottomed and soared just after the 1942 announcement of price controls. Then it bottomed and soared again when they were ended in 1946. Make what you will of it.

News seems to occur at random relative to the market; it doesn't move the market. There is an old Wall Street saying, "The market knows," which means the market already knew it was going to happen, as if via a direct link to God. But it may be more realistic to think that the market doesn't care. We're egotistically human-centered, so we love news. But the market knows that no one person or event reshapes the overall economic scheme.

Stock Prices vs. News Items, 1949–1968

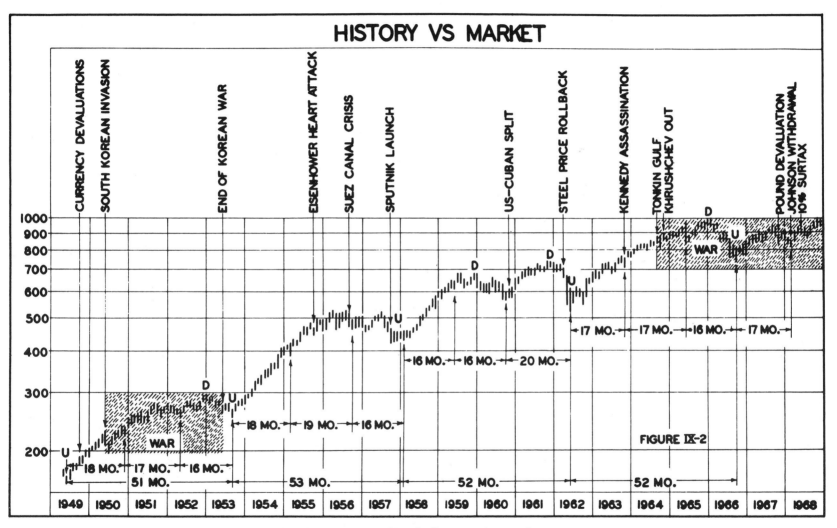

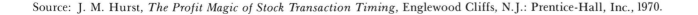

How History Does Not Influence The Market!

Source: J. M. Hurst, *The Profit Magic of Stock Transaction Timing*, Englewood Cliffs, N.J.: Prentice-Hall, Inc., 1970.

25
Stock Prices Versus Recessions

Oh, my God! Everyone says we're in a recession, so I'd better sell my stocks fast. Right? Probably not. It turns out that you can do a pretty good job of predicting the economy using prior changes in stock prices, but predicting stock prices from economic forecasts works almost not at all.

Here's why: The stock market is almost magical, because it always leads the economy. It goes down long before the economy drops and then heads higher long before the economy rebounds. It always has.

This classic chart plots the S&P 500 from 1948 to 1976, but does so on a background that is shaded during periods of economic recession. The white areas are times when the economy was expanding. The beginning of a shaded area represents when the expansion first turned into a recession. The end of a shaded area denotes when the recession ended and the next business expansion resumed. For example, note 1970. The shading tells you that the economy started declining just before the year began and dropped without interruption until year-end. It also lets you see that the economy then expanded throughout 1971, 1972, and most of 1973.

Now note the relationship between the shaded, recessionary years and the stock market. Stocks drop for many months before the economy sours—often for a year or more. And stock prices always head higher long before the worst depths of a recession's decline. For example, consider that 1970 recession. Stock prices peaked out in 1968, more than a year before the economic decline started. Then stock prices bottomed out halfway through the recession, while the economy kept skidding lower. So just at the economy's darkest hour, when things are at their economic worst and your pants are scared off you, stock prices are already long on their way upward.

To most people it is inexplicable. According to the National Bureau of Economic Research, the stock market is the single most successful predictor among the components of their index of "leading" economic indicators—almost perfect. This chart shows that declines in stock prices foretold the coming of every single recession, and only had one major drop that wasn't followed by a recession (1962).

Since economists are notoriously poor at predicting the economy's behavior even a few months in advance, you see the futility of predicting stock market peaks and troughs based off economic predictions. The economists would have to be able to time the economy's peak and trough at least a year before events unfolded. Most of the time, most economists are too optimistic, and most normal folks don't know a recession has started until months after we're into it. So when you see stock prices falling, expect the economy to weaken in six to twelve months. But when you see a recession, look for stock prices to be headed higher soon, even as the economy spirals seemingly ever lower. Yes, the market is perverse but, bless her, beautifully so.

Standard & Poor's Index of 500 Common Stocks and Cyclical Declines in the Economy, 1948–1977

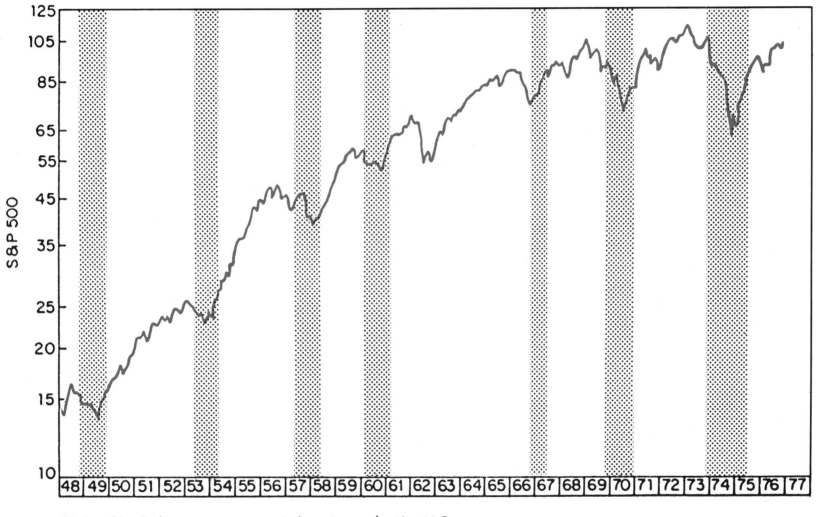

Note: Shaded areas represent downturns in the U.S. economy.

Source: Richard Crowell, *Stock Market Strategy*, Boston: McGraw-Hill, 1977.

26
Nine Major Stock Market Cycles

Have you ever wondered how often bull markets come around? How about bear markets? These two charts tell it all in a very simple fashion. They come from Martin J. Pring's book *Technical Analysis Explained: An Illustrated Guide for the Investor*, which is a great source of charts. What you see is that between 1929 and 1977 there were nine major bull market trends and nine major bear markets. That means that over the 48 years shown, a full boom/bust cycle has occurred about every 5.3 years (48 divided by 9 is 5.3).

This chart also describes the relative length of the major bull market and bear market trends. A quick glance shows that the 1929 decline lasted about two and a half years. The 1937–1942 downtrend was the longest at a monstrous five years. The 1946–1949 decline lasted three years, and the 1953 decline only one year. The 1956–1957 decline, while more of a plateau than a bust, lasted two years. The 1962 and 1966 declines each lasted just one year. The 1968–1970 decline was about one and a half years, and the 1973–1974 decline was two years.

When you tally them, you see that out of 48 years only about 19 years were periods of major downtrends, or about 40 percent of the time. Those 9 bear market trends lasted a little more than 2 years each on average (19 divided by 9 equals 2.1).

Interestingly, if you disregarded the exceptionally long 1937–1942 decline, the result wouldn't be much different. There would then be 14 years representing 8 major downtrends, and the average downtrend would have lasted 1.75 years (14 divided by 8).

So anyway you figure it, bear markets averaged just about 2 years per bust.

By contrast, the bull markets averaged about three years apiece. The 1932–1937 market rose for five years, and the 1938–1939 not quite two years. The 1942–1946 market lasted four years. The market rose two and a half years from mid-1949 through 1951 and two years from 1954 through 1955. The 1958–1962 bull market lasted four years, the 1962–1966 market three and a half years, the 1970–1973 market two and a half years, and the 1974–1976 market two years. That is a total of 27½ years, which means the average bull market lasted 3 years. The market was in a major bull market trend almost 60 percent of the time. Again, throwing out the superlong 1932–1937 bull market, as you did for the comparable bear market, the average would still be 2.8 years (22.5 divided by 8 equals 2.81).

Conclusions? The historical odds are stacked against pessimists, but not overwhelmingly. You can expect that the market will be rising about 60 percent of the time and falling 40 percent of the time. Note that the 1987 bull market, which started rising in August 1982, is a full four years old at the time of this writing—quite old by historical standards. Only three of these nine bulls lasted as long. None lasted still another year. That indicates caution.

Long-Term DJIA Showing Bull and Bear Trendlines, 1929–1977

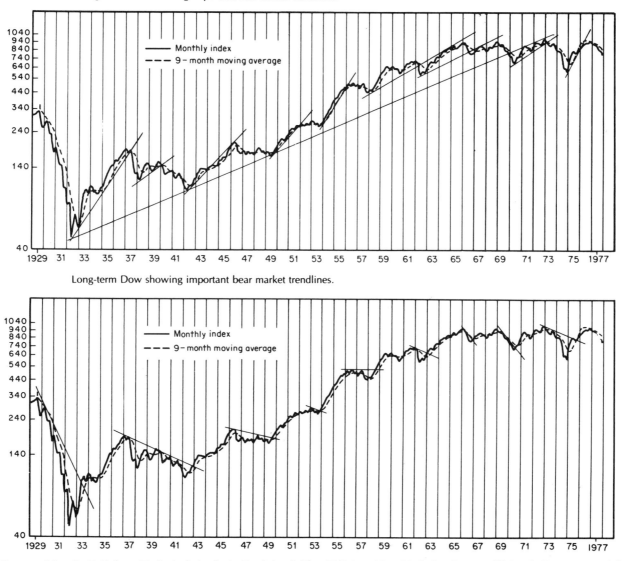

Long-term Dow showing important bull-market trendlines.

Long-term Dow showing important bear market trendlines.

Source: Martin J. Pring, *Technical Analysis Explained*, First Edition, New York: McGraw-Hill Book Company, 1979.

27
Roaring Twenties Revisited?

Want a good scare? How about a big rise in the stock market? Try stacking a 25-year chart of the Dow Jones Industrials on top of a chart for the 25 years leading up to the 1929 crash. They're virtually indistinguishable. These graphs give you the chance to ponder some risks in the current market. One graph commences during 1905 and ends with the infamous 1929 crash. The other one begins in 1965 and ends in 1986.

The similarities are both frightening and exhilarating. Each reveals a prolonged 17-year accumulation base, followed by a subsequent breakout and steep rise. The 1920s market finally broke out above 100 in 1924, on the way to a whopping peak of 380 five years later. The good news is that if these visual similarities represent something deeper, we might see the current stock market—which broke out above 1,000 in 1983—keep going, perhaps as far as 3,500 within five years of then, or early 1988.

The bad news is that the good times would be followed by a sickening bust. Recall the events of October 1929. If we are to believe that the 1987 scenario mirrors those events of 60 years past, we should beware a virtual free-fall.

There is other evidence pointing to similarities with 1929. For example, see Charts 1 and 2, which show that, among other things, the market's 1987 price/earnings ratio was actually higher than it was in 1929. Likewise, as Chart 30 shows, there was a takeover binge in the late 1920s very similar to what we've seen recently. One more point: European stocks headed south in the spring of 1986. As Chart 29 shows, European stocks dropped in 1928, warning of what was to come in 1929.

Also, the first chart was preceded by the late 1800s, including a prolonged bull market, just as the three decades before 1965 saw a tremendous rise in stock prices from depressed levels. By 1965 and by 1905, equities were fully priced. Could it be that in both the 1920s and 1980s, most top bananas, aged 50 to 60, grew up thinking that ever higher prices were the rule? To them, a big, continuous, and pricy market seems like a return to normal, rather than an aberration. They would be unaware of danger.

But the likelihood is that the similarity in these charts is just coincidence and nothing more. The best argument against extreme, 1920s-style vulnerability is the tremendously higher recent inflation. Adjusted for inflation, as shown in Chart 22, the 1980 rise looks nothing like the 1920s. Current prices are high, but I'd bet the similarity between these charts is just a freakish coincidence.

Comparison of Dow Jones Industrials of the 1920s vs. the 1980s

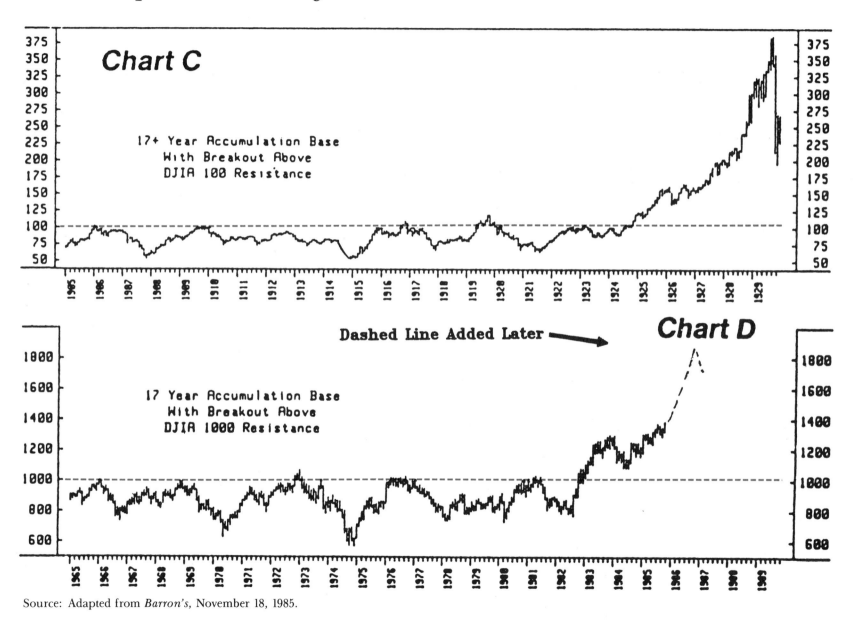

Chart C

17+ Year Accumulation Base
With Breakout Above
DJIA 100 Resistance

Dashed Line Added Later →

Chart D

17 Year Accumulation Base
With Breakout Above
DJIA 1000 Resistance

Source: Adapted from *Barron's*, November 18, 1985.

28
Price/Earnings Ratios Can Be Deceiving

In 1929 prices were sky-high, and any rational simpleton should have seen the bubble that was too big and about to burst. Right? Wrong. You see, earnings, which are what most investors use to value stocks, can be misleading. Lower price/earnings ratios (P/Es) don't always mean stocks are getting cheaper. Even most pros have a tough time believing it, but these were the conditions leading to the Crash of 1929. Despite a doubling since 1926, and a quadrupling from 1913, most folks were suckered into hanging on and buying more overpriced stocks because P/Es seemed OK and were falling lower.

The Dow Jones Industrials' P/E was 20 in early 1927, and the market moved up 30 percent. But earnings increased even more. So why should folks be afraid when by year-end the market's P/E was just 13? Irving Fisher (no relation to me) was by far the most noted economist of his day. From his pulpit at Yale he pontificated that stocks were not too high because earnings were rising still faster. This, Fisher maintained, was evidence of the economy's vigor. His view is shown on the following page. This chart appeared in his 1930 book *The Stock Market Crash and After*—a telling example of how wrong an "expert" can be. In 1930, with the market partway down its three-year suicide run, Fisher argued at length that there was nothing further to fear, because P/Es were reasonable and falling.

The solid dark line on the chart represents the average P/E for each month of 1929, while the dotted line shows the average P/E for each month of 1928 (the individual months apply to both years). By following the dotted line from left to right, you see that the market P/E increased in 1928 (from 13 in January to just over 15 in December). In contrast, the P/E in 1929 actually declined from a high of 16.2 in January to a low of 10.8 at year-end.

In 1929 the Dow Industrials rose 29 percent more, from 300 to a September 3 peak of 386. (Heck, 1985 prices rose that much.) Along the way, earnings rose faster. Actually most of the price gains came in June, July, and August, while most of the earnings boosts came early in the year. But what folks saw was a big earnings gain—seemingly enough to justify the higher prices.

What went wrong? First, earnings reports are announced at least six weeks after a quarter ends. So, you don't find out that earnings are falling until well after it happens. If business turns weak in the quarter's second month, you won't hear about it until months later. Secondly, earnings are misleading. When earnings are temporarily way too fat is just when optimism and stock prices are apt to be highest, but also when the P/E is low due to the fat earnings. That's what happened. Between 1929 and 1932, stocks plummeted, earnings vaporized, and P/Es skyrocketed. The bottom half of the ratio fell faster than the top portion.

How does this relate to today's world? Beware of the experts who forecast rising stock prices based primarily on P/Es or forecasts of future earnings. They can't know what they're talking about. As I've emphasized for years in my *Forbes* columns and before that in my last book, it is better to look at a multitude of other valuation measures. P/Es alone don't hack it.

Price/Earnings Ratio, 1928–1929

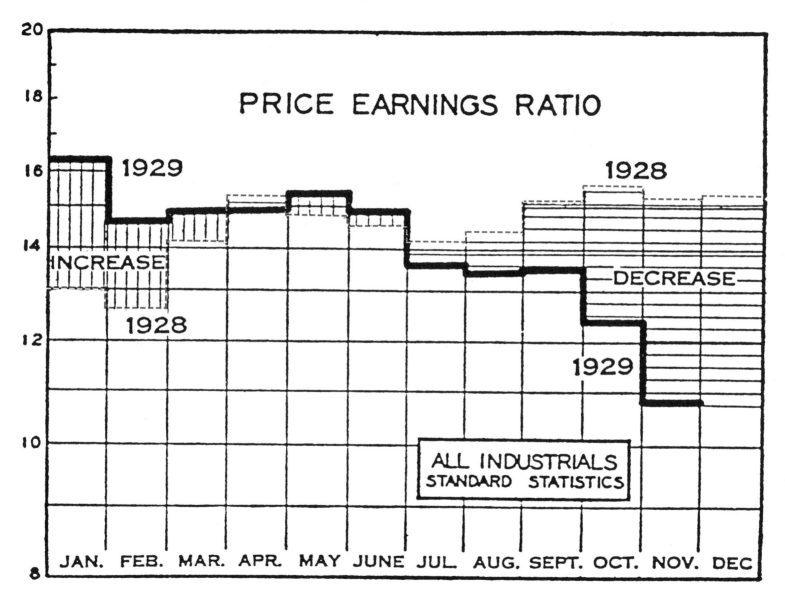

69

Source: Irving Fisher, *The Stock Market Crash and After,* New York: The Macmillan Company, 1930.

29
A Clear Warning

Most folks think the 1929 crash kaplunked with absolutely no advance warning. Not so! The European stock markets sounded a clear warning—one that any contemporary observer could have noted—but few heard it. You can see the warning on this graph, which shows stock price indexes for New York, London, Berlin, and Paris. The events surrounding October 1929 and the precipitous fall of stock prices in New York are well known. But were you aware that:

- The world had other major equity exchanges then?
- London, Paris, and Berlin all suffered major declines too?
- London and Berlin hit their highs in 1928 (point A), a year before the New York crash, and were in an obvious downward trend all the way up until New York's big demise?
- Even Paris had lost its momentum early in 1929 and was moving down through most of the year while New York kept rising?

Another interesting fact is that in 1929 prices in London fell even more than in New York—something few casual observers know. But an American, seeing the early decline in major European markets, had a clear warning that New York was out of whack. As it turned out, and as it usually turns out, no one country was immune from global economic events. It is uncanny how often events happen in parallel around the world—and how it has been that way long before "modern communications

systems." The big October crash took place simultaneously thoughout the Western nations—all within days of each other (point B). But to Europeans the decline was not a new event.

There is another warning here. Point C shows when prices plateaued briefly in New York on their way to a final 1932 bottom. While prices stabilized in New York, they had fallen a much greater percentage in London, were still falling in Berlin, and hadn't yet stabilized in Paris. Here, too, European prices offered further warning that the October crash wasn't merely a correction in a longer bull market as most Americans believed.

This chart's source was Irving Fisher's 1930 classic blooper of a book, *The Stock Market and After* (see Chart 28, too). Fisher believed stock prices would rise. He felt the New York decline came, in part, from pressure from Europeans liquidating stock. With that largely completed, which they weren't, as the chart shows, he reasoned that New York could now regain its ebullience. This widely regarded classical economist seems to have been better at constructing charts than charting his way through the financial waters.

Stock Price Indexes, 1927–1929

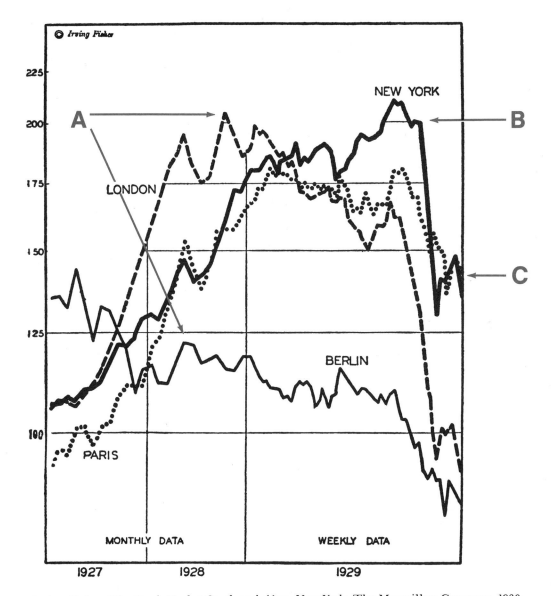

Source: Irving Fisher, *The Stock Market Crash and After,* New York: The Macmillan Company, 1930.

30
The Big Boys Don't Always Buy Cheap

You hear it a lot lately: "Stocks must be cheap. If they weren't, all these raiders wouldn't be taking them over. The leveraged buyout–backed raiders like T. Boone Pickens and Carl Icahn—and the giant corporate acquirers like Philip Morris, which gobbled up General Foods—these guys just don't miss, so stocks must be a good deal, or they wouldn't be on such a buying spree." If you believe that line—that the recent growth in merger-and-acquisition activity means stocks are a bargain—think again! The big boys don't always buy cheap.

While there are some phenomenal coups, the overall results are mixed. In fact, it seems takeover activity can be a reverse barometer of the market's health. Consider a few phenomenal points. First, these guys were nowhere to be seen back in the mid-1970s when stocks were dirt-cheap. The market sold for seven times earnings and has subsequently skyrocketed. Why hadn't they been buying? Interest rates, believe it or not (see Chart 41), were almost exactly where they are now, so their leveraged deals would have cost no more then than now. But the acquirers didn't acquire then, when stocks were cheap.

If these guys were so smart, why is it that the mega-billion-buck oil takeovers like Getty and Gulf happened when oil prices were sky-high, not before? If these highly debt-financed take-overs were a good deal in the 1983–1984 period, they would have been far better ones in 1978–1979, because they would have benefited from subsequent rising oil prices, profits, and the rapid inflation that would have let them repay their debt in much-depreciated dollars.

The answer, it seems, is that like everyone else, takeover artists chase bull markets. On average, these people are no more sophisticated, just more money-laden. Perhaps the best indicator of this phenomenon is the 1920s takeover activity. Here, too, (as with Charts 28 and 29), we turn to the most noted economist of the day, Irving Fisher, who used the then-existing high and rising takeover level as a prime basis for thinking stocks were cheap. He made the same argument then, in detail, that you hear today. On the facing page is a chart from *The Stock Market Crash and After*, where he argued that stocks wouldn't keep plummeting. What you see in the chart is the steady increase in takeovers as the 1920s bull market progressed. Again, if the takeover artists had been real gurus, they would have bought before the rise, when stocks were cheap.

Stocks plummeted in 1920 and 1921. Takeover activity followed right behind. But in 1922, the market started rising and again increased takeovers were right behind. By 1928, just before the crash, annual takeovers had more than tripled. By 1934 many of these "smart" purchases had gone belly-up. This phenomenon has important investor implications. When takeover artists want to buy so many of your stocks away from you, as they have in the last few years, you might consider selling them those, and soon selling some of your other stocks, too.

Mergers Record, 1919–1928

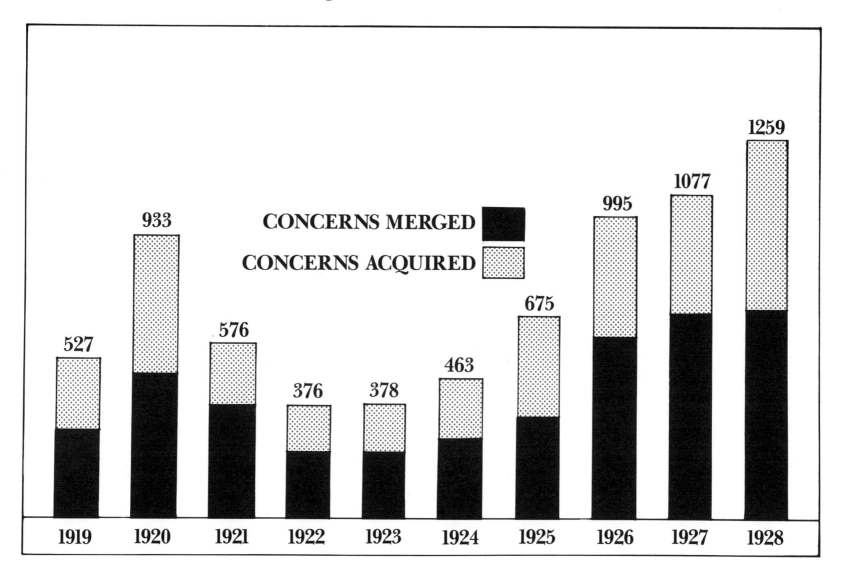

73

Source: Irving Fisher, *The Stock Market Crash and After*, New York: The Macmillan Company, 1930.

31
Preferred Stocks Shouldn't Be

Preferred stocks are great because they're safer than common stocks but have more profit potential than bonds. Right? Baloney! Preferreds provide worse returns than bonds but aren't as safe. Today's preferreds aren't even as safe as common stocks. This old chart compares the returns from common stocks with preferreds from 1908 to 1932. A single glance tells you that if you bought common stocks you would have had many, many years during which you would have been able to sell at a profit far greater than anything you could have gotten with preferreds. From the very beginning, common stocks increased in value relative to preferreds.

By 1915 the common stocks started paying more dividends, too. From World War I through the 1921 recession, common stock dividends declined, but they remained above the preferred dividends continually. Even in the 1932 Great Depression, dividends from common stocks bought 10 years earlier were higher than preferreds that were also bought in 1922.

Common stock prices also increased relative to preferreds, rather regularly from 1908 through 1929. Stocks then fell; you sure wouldn't have wanted to own common stocks in such a decline. But 1929 to 1932 is the only four-year period on record, before or since, where preferreds performed much better than commons. Most of the time, both during this period and since, preferred stocks have been real dogs, having *none* of the upside potential of common stocks but being less safe than bonds in periods of trouble.

Preferred stock promises a fixed dividend and liquidation advantages relative to common stock. But that's it. Preferred holders seldom have voting rights unless dividends aren't paid for a long time; then they have insignificant rights. So, in effect, a preferred is like a bond without the one really fine feature of bonds—forced repayment, which provides a path to liquidity if things really sour.

Preferreds have little protection relative to stocks in today's bankruptcies, because in Chapter 11 proceedings, companies are rarely liquidated. Instead, they're reorganized, largely under management's direction with a bit of nudging from the judge. They take bondholders' losses out of the equityholders' hides. In practice preferred holders do even worse than common holders in court because management, which is running the show with the court's protection, rarely owns any preferred stock and has no basic loyalties to preferred holders. Preferred holders don't have to be repaid and don't have enough votes to throw the rascals out. It's the common holders who elect the board that elects the management. So the preferreds get raped. In reorganization they are diluted through the creation of enough new securities that their old preferred shares become virtually worthless.

So, remember what this chart teaches. Common stocks offer appreciation potential, while preferreds offer almost nothing at all. If you want long-term safety, buy bonds. If you want appreciation potential, buy common stocks. And if you want nothing at all, buy preferreds. Common stock is the preferred stock to own, and preferred stock shouldn't be.

Comparison of Industrial Common and Preferred Stocks, 1908–1932

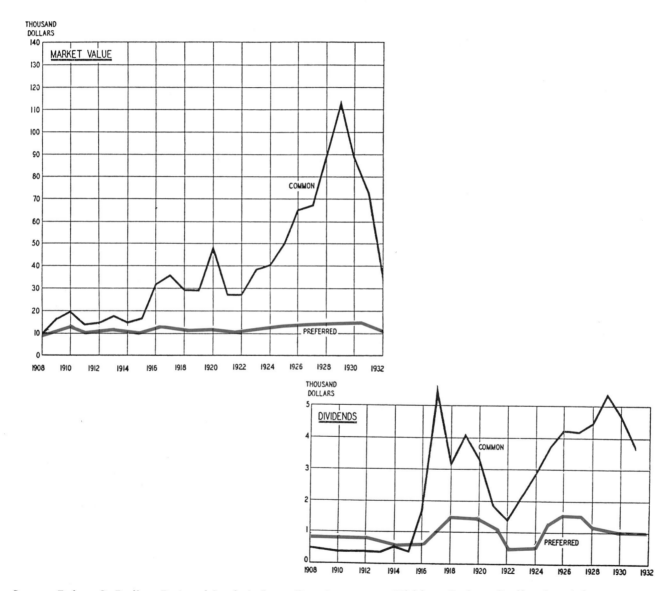

Source: Robert G. Bodkey, *Preferred Stock As Long-Term Investments,* Michigan Business Studies, Ann Arbor: University of Michigan Press, 1932.

32
The 2 Percent Rule

As a kid my goal was to grow up to be a baseball catcher. My hero was Yogi Berra, a phenomenal catcher and a stunning philosopher—take the time he said, "Sometimes you can see a lot just by looking." It was because of Yogi that I started counting the frequency of recurring events—just to see what happened and how often. If it was good enough for Yogi, why not me? One counting led to my 2 percent rule, which says major declines in the stock market occur at an average rate of about 2 percent per month.

This chart explains it. It shows an index of 12 industrial stocks during the legendary panic of 1907. Interestingly, this index mirrors the action of the Dow Jones Industrial Average (DJIA) almost exactly. That is, the DJIA peaked on January 19, 1907, at 103, as in this chart, and it bottomed out on November 22, 1907, at 53, as in this chart. For purposes of this lesson, you can ignore the lower chart with its 20 railroad stocks.

In the term "the Panic of 1907," the year is when the bulk of the drop occurred, including the decline's ending "wash-out" crisis. But the "panic" is always long after the decline begins—very long. The 1907 panic had its seeds in early 1906. Since 1904, stock prices had doubled, but they peaked in mid-January 1906. From there prices declined, but by year-end they recovered—but not quite to their January highs. Throughout 1907, prices resumed their decline, washing out and forming a bottom in November, and then beginning a rally which lasted throughout 1908 and would, in 1909, take stocks back up to their 1906 highs. It was a strong but fairly typical stock market debacle that was caused by a combination of excessive speculative zeal and tight money. In all, stocks lost 49 percent of their value in 22 months.

That's 2.2 percent per month, and that's the lesson. Most big declines happen at a rate of about 2 percent per month—a little more, a little less, but not by much. It may be as little as 1.5 percent per month, or as much as 3.0 percent, but that's about it. Look at recent history for further confirmation. The 1968–1970 decline dropped from 995 to 627 in 18 months—2.1 percent per month—almost exactly the same as in 1907. The 1981–1982 decline dropped 25 percent in 16 months, or 1.6 percent per month. That's about as slow as they get. The 1973–1974 decline was 2.1 percent per month, and the 1976–1977 decline was 1.7 percent per month.

Big bear markets are a tradeoff between magnitude and duration. Bear markets need to turn everyone pessimistic; they end when almost no one remains optimistic. For this to happen, time is more important than the magnitude of the drop. A short, sharp drop always leaves many who remember the recent past when prices were rising. Enough duration is needed for folks to feel like the avalanche will just never stop. Investors need to be emotionally drained.

So remember 1907 and the 2 percent rule. If the DJIA's 1987 high of 2,200 was a major cyclical top in the market, as some suspect, and if you expect the market to drop at least 25 percent in a subsequent decline (which would mean a DJIA of 1,650), then don't look for a bottom fast. The 2 percent rule says it will take between 8 and 16 months, and most likely about 12 months, to create enough pessimism for a real bottom. Be patient.

The Panic of 1907

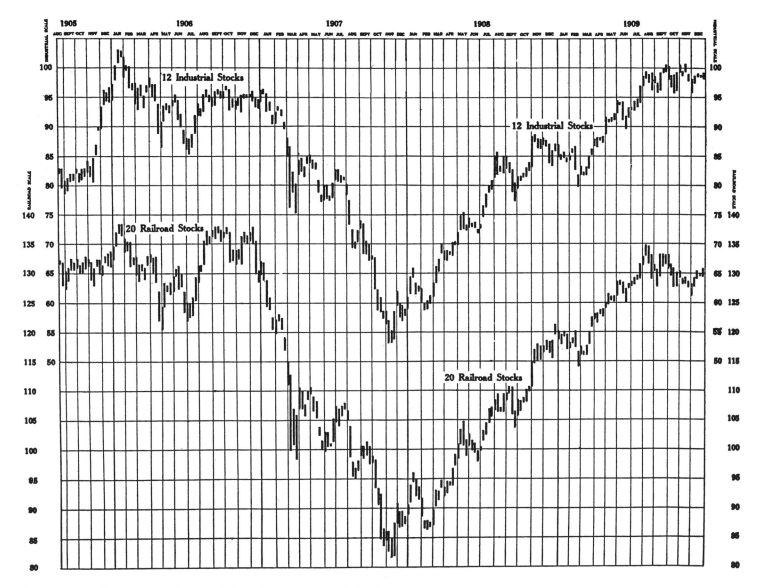

Source: Philip L. Carret, "The Art of Speculation," *Barron's*, 1927.

33
Remember What the Rich Man Forgot

This chart is similar to Chart 32 (the Panic of 1907) but includes three other important features: bond prices, the "Rich Man's Panic" of 1903, and an important lesson—that major stock market tops are usually preceded by at least a few months of falling bond prices. Bonds are represented in this chart by the single line. Look at 1905. Bonds had risen since mid-1903, but then they peaked and started falling in early 1905. Stocks kept rising until early 1906. Then they fell, which finally led into the Panic of 1907. Bond prices fell in line with stocks throughout 1907, and then they both rose together until year-end 1908. But again, falling bond prices in early 1909 foreshadowed the sharp decline to come in stocks.

Bonds fall before stock prices because of the relationship between bonds and interest rates. They move against each other. As interest rates fall, bond prices rise; as rates rise, bonds fall. Why? Bond prices adjust to interest rates, not the other way around. A bond's interest payment is a fixed yearly amount of dollars. As interest rates bounce around over time, an existing bond's price must bounce just the opposite way to keep the yield on that fixed yearly payment competitive with the newer interest rates from newer bonds.

But stocks also compete with interest rates. As seen in Chart 4, the earnings yield from stocks (earnings divided by stock prices) has to compete with interest rates. So, when bond prices fall, it means interest rates are rising. And when interest rates rise, stocks have to have higher earnings to avoid falling. If the higher earnings don't materialize pronto, stocks go floppo.

Is that always true? Not always, but usually. Most big stock declines are preceded by at least a few months of falling bond prices (higher interest rates). This chart shows one of the few exceptions. While the railroad stocks (dark squares) always conformed to the rule, in 1899 and 1901 industrial stocks (light squares) didn't. The industrials dropped in 1899 and again in 1901 without any prior drop in bond prices. There are exceptions to every rule, and while this one may not look like much, it was a full 20 percent decline. Then, without a breath of bullishness, the industrials fell again in 1903—a whopping 37 percent— which was known as the "Rich Man's Panic" because supposedly only the rich weren't already scared away by the 1902 drop in bond prices.

Despite the exception, if you just remembered what the rich men forgot, you could have enjoyed most of the bull market in railroad and industrial stocks, while missing most of the decline. Remember, since stocks rarely fall in a major way without a prior slump in the bond market, don't expect stocks to fall unless bond prices dip first. In 1986, as bonds rose steadily, this rule was one of the few time-tested and truly bullish signs for stock buyers.

I first saw this beautiful old chart in the Jackson Library at the Stanford Graduate School of Business. It was fully three feet by 18 inches and was stashed in the stacks as part of an old bound subscription service that prepared dozens of charts and sent subscribers periodic updates to replace outdated charts.

The Average Market Price of the 20 Leading Railroad and 12 Leading Industrial Stocks and of 5 Standard Bonds, 1896–1912

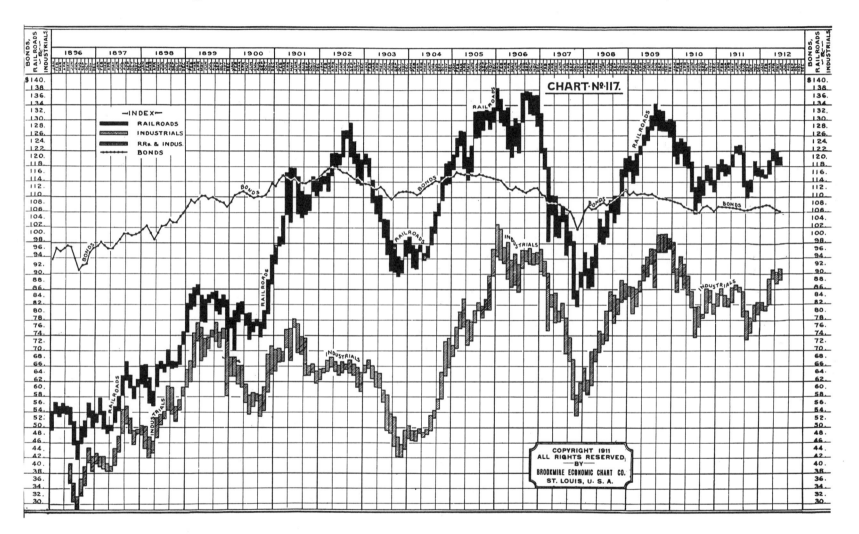

CHART·Nº·117.

—INDEX—
RAILROADS
INDUSTRIALS
RR.s & INDUS.
BONDS

Source: Reprinted by Permission. Copyright © 1911 by Les Euell and John R. Euell Anthony, *Brookmire Investment Reports*, P.O. Box 586, Daytona Beach, FL 32015. All Rights Reserved.

34
Monthly Railroad Prices, 1843–1862

Interested in learning how to avoid a serious problem that may have already cost you big bucks? The big losers in the recent computer stock downturn could have learned two lessons from 19th-century railroad prices—one would have already become a money saver, the other may be key right now. The railroads were the big growth stocks of their day with unquestionable long-term prospects—comparable to today's electronics stocks. But that didn't stop them from plummeting. Speculative booms, like railroads then or electronics of the early 1980s, are usually followed by a severe and, just as important, a *long* decline.

Background: In 1843, the nation was emerging from a seven-year depression. During the 1830s, unsound banking practices, overly ambitious infrastructure investment (railroads, canals, etc.), and rampant real estate speculation paved the way for the Panic of 1837. Economic devastation followed in a crisis of major proportions. Stocks crashed. Urban food riots erupted. Stores and warehouses were looted, and banks ceased to honor their notes. Many railroads were simply abandoned. By all accounts, it was among the worst economic periods ever, rivaling the 1870s and 1930s.

The Boom: But by 1843 recovery was beginning, along with a renewed interest in stocks—and a spectacular 1843–1844 price rise (note the advance from A to B), which resulted from these stocks having been beaten down too low. By 1850 railroad building boomed. With prosperity and new land acquisitions after the Mexican War and the California gold discoveries, U.S. railroad building now rivaled that of all other countries combined. Stocks more than tripled from 1843 to 1853 and seemed the world's one sure shot. Buyers took comfort in these growth-oriented shares, holding them and buying more. But many failed to realize that railroad projects weren't always profitable—or easy or quick.

The Bust: As supply outstripped demand, freight rates fell drastically and the stocks started down, eventually plummeting nearly 70 percent from their 1853 peak. What went up for ten years gave it all back in five. For five long years (from point C to point D), railroad stocks declined without a single bull rally of 20 percent or more. The tough times undermined asset values—which were pledged to back bank borrowing—which led to the Panic of 1857 when banks announced a total suspension of payments. Even the bluest of the "blue chips" couldn't escape the onslaught.

The Lessons: Big booms are followed by big busts. That which sounds like a sure shot is more often a backfire. But just as vital, the longer the boom, the longer the bust. So, for electronics fans who saw a very long boom unfold, remember the rails of the 1850s: The continued bear bust can last an astonishing five to seven years. Beware or be patient.

Indices of Railroad-Stock Prices, Monthly, 1843–1862:
Index I (8 Selected Stocks), 1843–1852;
Index IIc (18 Selected Stocks), 1853–1862; and All-Inclusive Index, 1843–1862

(Base: 1853. Logarithmic vertical scale)

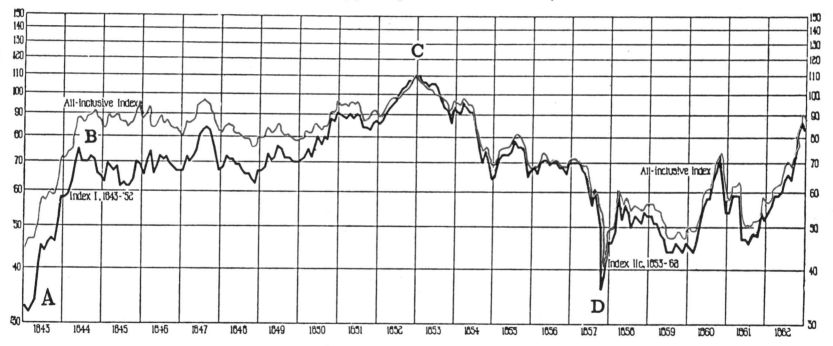

Source: Walter B. Smith and Arthur H. Cole, *Fluctuations in American Business Cycles, 1790–1860*, Cambridge, MA: Harvard University Press, 1935.

35
Financial Fluctuations in the 18th Century?
You Can Bank on It!

Did the pre–New York Stock Exchange era have financial markets that fluctuated violently? Of course, but recorded history gets a bit gray back then. London was the center of the financial world, and there were no indexes like the Dow Jones. What investors did have were individual stocks, which traded six days a week. (Stocks traded on Saturdays in the U.S., too, until the 1950s.) Stocks were speculative and prone to wild gyrations tied to company rumors.

A useful measure of the timing and approximate magnitude of fluctuations can be found in the stock price of the Bank of England, often referred to merely as "Bank stock." The "Bank" was England's central bank and in many ways similar to the U.S. Federal Reserve System. But the Bank also competed directly with other, lesser banks, creating profit opportunities. While we can't buy stock in the Federal Reserve, in those days you could buy the Bank. Folks bought Bank stock for a safe yield with appreciation potential. What could be safer? The mentality was like that of Americans who bought pre-break-up AT&T preferred stock, when stock in a regulated monopoly-utility seemed like the world's safest stock.

But there were violent fluctuations anyway. This chart is based on Joseph Francis's 19th-century book, *History of the Bank of England*. It shows yearly high and low prices for Bank stock from 1732 until 1846. Look at 1769. In less than 2 years, Bank stock plummeted 40 percent from a high of 175 to 105. Then it rose 47 percent the next year. The market drifted lower until 1781, when it bottomed out at 105 again. But in the next 10 years it more than doubled to 219.

Does this seem like some calm and peaceful financial picnic to you? It shouldn't! Take the early 1770s again. While some colonials were busy being proper in Boston, others were engaging in terrorist acts against the realm on board her Majesty's ships, and calling it all a "tea party." The prolonged bear market of the 1770s reflected the beginning of the end of England's ability to hoard natural resources via colonization. When England lost the United States, the Queen lost her crown jewel. It certainly seems worthy of a major bear market.

Ironically, while the market bounced around a lot, prices did not nosedive during the Napoleonic Wars (1804–1815). An old legend says that Nathan Rothschild, using message-laden carrier pigeons, knew before the rest of the crowd of Napoleon's defeat at Waterloo in 1815. Legend has it that as prices crumbled, Rothschild bought, and made a fortune. But these data indicate that the crumbling and fortune might not be as great as Rothschild's PR.

What's the point of all this? While there are always new evolving details, like computers and financial instruments, nothing really important has changed in the financial markets in the last 200 years. Wild fluctuations, bulls, bears, rumors and inside trading have long been with us. Financial manias are nothing more than mass psychology allowed to endure over time (or overtime). In 1986 it became popular to think that new "program trading" had made the financial markets more volatile. But every time I hear drivel like that, I'm reminded by charts like this that there is nothing really new under the financial sun—just new wrinkles on old faces.

The Bank of England—Stock Prices, 1732–1846

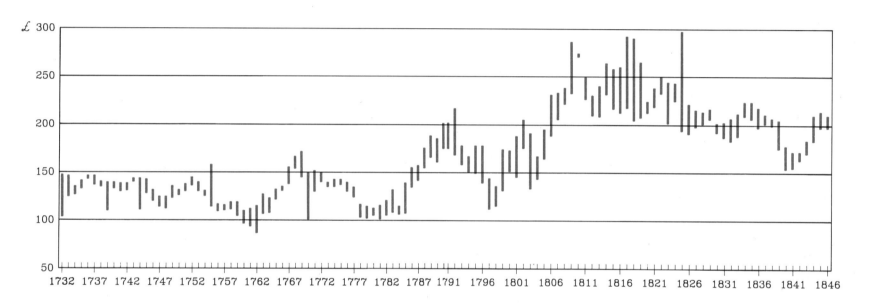

Source: Joseph H. Francis, *History of the Bank of England*, Chicago: Euclid Publishing Company, 1888.

36
Charting the South Seas

There's been little news of any importance for centuries in the financial markets. New twists? Sure! But the keys to making and hanging on to money don't change. For example, avoid manias. Financial manias have been with us almost forever. I first read about them in Charles Mackay's classic book from 1841, *Extraordinary Popular Delusions and the Madness of Crowds*. It covers gyrations like the Dutch Tulipmania of 1636, the French "Mississippi Scheme" of 1720, and the 1720 English South Seas Bubble. Some say 1720 was the first Kondratieff wave peak (see Chart 84). This never-before-published chart chronicles the South Seas mania that started in 1711 when King George chartered the South Seas Company (SSC), made himself its governor, and granted it sole rights to the South Seas trade (basically the Pacific Ocean). No one could really assess the commercial potential. Manias often involve phenomena that can't be detailed precisely—that's how they get speculative.

The SSC was contrived by financial promoters who were less keen on South Seas trade than on doing deals. As stocks soared in 1719, they concocted a scheme to swap the entire English national debt for SSC stock—plus more of the future take from their South Seas pipe dream. Parliament loved the something-for-nothing nature of it. As the scheme unfolded, ever more people, particularly politicians, who were generally rich in those days, bought SSC stock. Other stocks boomed too—like that stodgy old Bank of England stock (see Chart 35). As that chart shows, Bank of England stock rose 33 percent by May. But meanwhile SSC stock rose 225 percent from £123 to £400. Stock offerings were floated to the public.

As politicians bought more SSC stock, SSC's power rose, which led to still more financings. Along the way, SSC got parliamentary backing to let investors buy stock on time—speculating on borrowed money. SSC was just a pyramid based on ever more money from a greedy public in ever larger rounds of offerings at ever higher prices. In this ebullient environment, other pipe dream–like stock companies were formed to cash in on the public's greedy binge—most lacking sound plans and qualified management. But in a binge, who cares?

By summer, dreams of South Seas wealth had workers retiring to invest their life savings in SSC stock, which promptly plateaued at £1,000. To keep the upstart stock companies from siphoning off potential investor funds, SSC got overly greedy and persuaded Parliament to outlaw all companies that weren't royally chartered. Since even the King wasn't sure exactly who was chartered, all but the biggest stocks plunged. SSC, which of course was chartered, didn't fall at first. Then, loss-ridden investors, particularly those who bought stock on debt, soon needed to liquidate funds from big names, too—like SSC and the Bank. But SSC had no real business. By October it fell to £200, and by year-end the "great" company, which aspired to assume the English debt, was broke. Most other stock companies went broke too—except for the Bank, of course, which survives to this day.

The lesson? When you see the public embracing some new panacea, be sure to beware the emerging mania. There are no new financial dances, just variations of the Wall Street Waltz.

The South Seas Bubble, December 1719 to October 1720

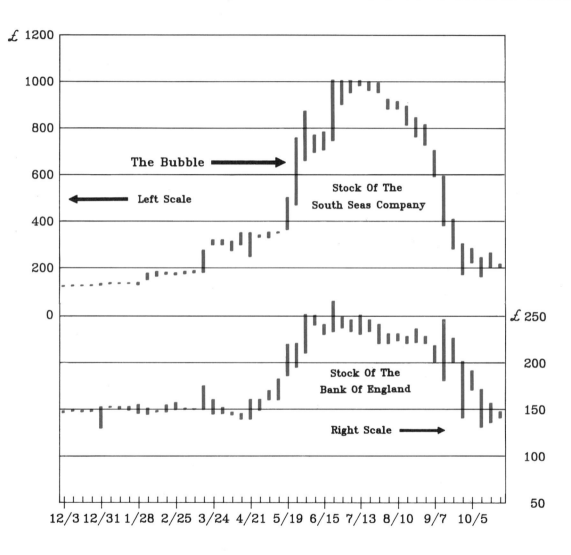

Source: James E. Rogers, *A History of Agriculture and Prices in England, 1703–1793*, New York City: Clarendon Press, 1902.

37
190 Years of Stock Market Movements

By itself, this chart may be of less interest than when combined with other charts in this book or elsewhere, but any student of the market should be familiar with it. It pinpoints the market's major advances and declines from 1790 through 1980. It comes from *Cycles* magazine, published by the Foundation for the Study of Cycles.

What this chart does best is tell you when the market was going up and down, and which were the biggest moves. You can see long periods, like from 1880 through 1910, when stocks moved very little in any direction. If you can believe this chart, stocks rose only 2.3 percent per year during that period. On the other hand, Kondratieff wave freaks (see Chart 84) like to point to the three giant bull markets that occurred during the 1830s, 1870s, 1920s areas. They see them as speculative superbull markets, which come at a particular stage of the ultralong, 55-year economic waves they envision. Many of these observers envision that we are at just such a stage now. But their three superbulls weren't the only big advances. As shown in Chart 34, the 1840–1853 period is perhaps the most unheralded major bull market of all time. And, of course, the post–World War II advance dwarfed all others.

Notice my words, "if you can believe this chart." I don't. Because of numerous other accounts that confirm when stocks were rising and falling, we can be fairly confident of this chart's accuracy as to when stocks were rising and falling. But I distrust the accuracy of the chart's first 100 years with regard to how much the market rose and fell. There just weren't enough good records kept from those early days to construct truly useful stock market indexes.

The Foundation for the Study of Cycles, which is a respectable and professional organization, did the best it could, splicing together five different, and in some ways inadequate, indexes to make this chart. The first index was a bank and insurance index for 1790-1831. Obviously that didn't cover enough other types of stocks. The same was true for the Cleveland Trust Rail Stock Index, which was used for 1831-1854. The Clement Burgess Composite Index took over for 1854-1871, and the Cowles Index of Industrial stocks ran during 1871-1897. All but the last of these are somewhat suspect in terms of their ability to correctly measure the magnitude of major moves. Only after 1897, starting with the Dow Jones Industrials, does the chart become fully comparable to what we're used to seeing.

So, if you believe this chart with respect to magnitude, stocks increased at only 3 percent per year over the entire 190 years. But of course, that doesn't take into account dividends and the inaccuracy of the various indexes. By comparison, the Dow Jones Industrials reflect an increase of only about 3.5 percent per year since the mid-1920s, much less than the 9.5 percent returns chronicled by Ibbotson/Sinquefield and Fisher/Lorie studies (see Chart 12), which include dividends and all stocks on the New York Stock Exchange.

Annual Average Stock Prices, 1790–1980

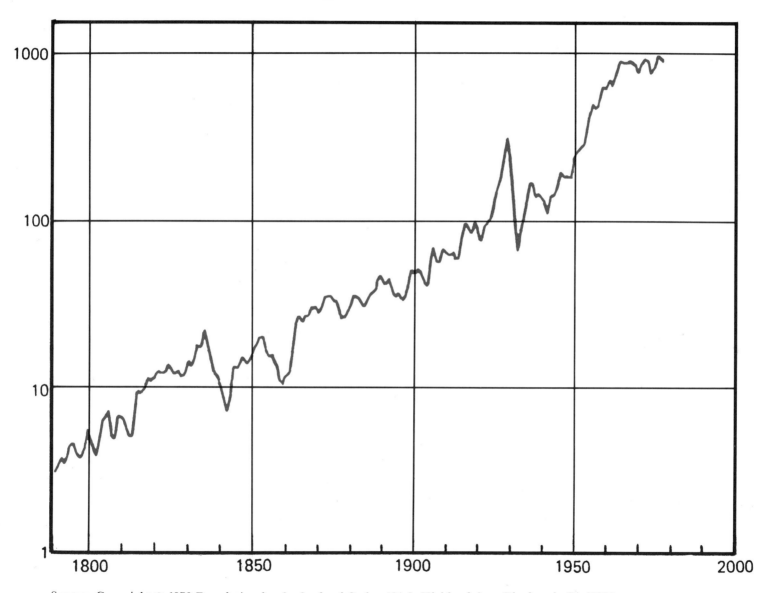

87

Source: Copyright © 1978 Foundation for the Study of Cycles, 124 S. Highland Ave., Pittsburgh, PA 15206.
Note: Current figures are Dow Jones Industrials.

38
Do You Figure They Earned Their Keep?

When Uncle Morris died in December 1949, he left you a cool quarter of a million smackaroonies in a tax-free trust—with your dad as trustee. In 1975 you became 35 years old, and based on the trust's provisions, the money became yours. But during the years Dad had it, he turned it over to a money management firm, and you've always wondered whether the outfit really earned its keep. Specifically, you want to know if your trust funds beat the market over those 26 years. How do you find out?

Figuring the rate of return on your trust funds is the easy part. Just get a financial calculator and put it in the compound-interest mode. Enter the $250,000 starting value as the "present value." Enter the amount you received from the trust as the "future value." Enter "26" as "N" for number of years, and punch "ans" and "i"—out pops the compound annual rate of return. (From calculator to calculator, the keys will have slightly different labels; read the instructions.)

The hard part to figure out is an exact average return for the market against which to compare your trust's results. You've seen lots of statistics bandied about regarding the market's rate of return in recent years, but nothing to let you pinpoint the market's return over a specific, but seemingly long-gone, time period. How do you do it? Use this table, which comes from a book by Lawrence Fisher of the University of Chicago (no relation) and his sidekick, James Lorie. They researched average annual returns for the New York Stock Exchange back to 1926, including dividends and appreciation, and laid out the results in an easy-to-use format.

The chart works like a set of steps, stepping down as the page moves to the right. On the far right-hand edge of the fifth step you'll see "12/49," which represents the December 1949 date when the money-management firm in the example was first employed. Running down the tallest step's left-hand edge are dates too. Close to the bottom is "12/75"—December 1975. If you find the intersection of the 12/75 row with the 12/49 column, you will see the number 11.2, which means that from December 1949 until December 1975 the New York Stock Exchange provided total returns averaging 11.2 percent per year. That's your cut-off. If your father's money-management firm did better than that, after deducting for their fees, then they probably earned their keep.

This table is the one most folks will want to see, but the book by Fisher and Lorie, *A Half Century of Returns on Stocks and Bonds*, is available at major libraries everywhere. It contains other useful series too—like the ones that demonstrate period-specific rates of return for long- and short-term Treasury securities. And the Fisher/Lorie book lets you see the returns of stocks or Treasury securities based on varying tax-rate assumptions, so you can pick the period-specific returns that match your own special tax circumstances. Or if you had to live off the dividends or interest, it lets you see the price-appreciation returns assuming no reinvestment of income. Hopefully, someone will soon provide an update that extends the data up to the present.

Annual Rates of Return on Common Stocks, 1925–1976

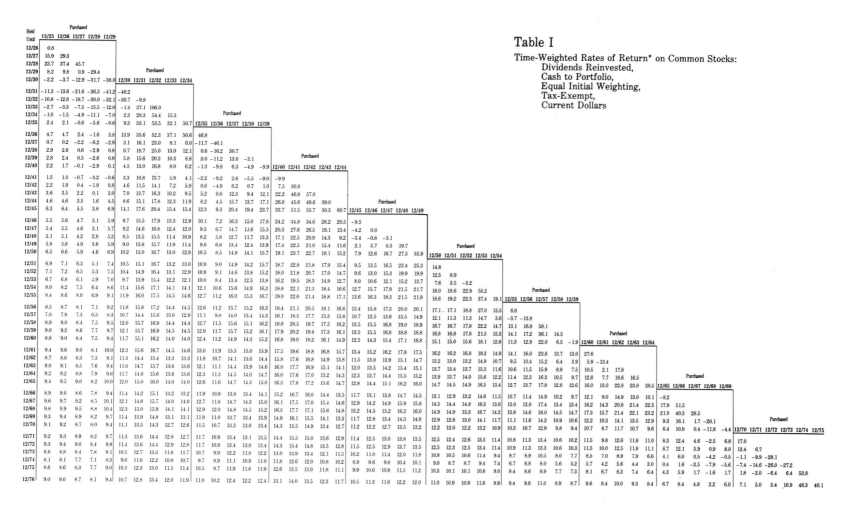

Table I

Time-Weighted Rates of Return* on Common Stocks:
Dividends Reinvested,
Cash to Portfolio,
Equal Initial Weighting,
Tax-Exempt,
Current Dollars

*Percent per annum, compounded annually.

Source: Lawrence Fisher and James H. Lorie, *A Half Century of Return on Stocks and Bonds,* Chicago: University of Chicago Press, 1977.

39
Two Ways to Make a Million

Do you sincerely want to be rich? You're not alone. While the American dream is little more than "lottery delusions" for most folks, it needn't be. There is a way, and it isn't a get-rich-quick scheme. Using the power of compound interest, practically anyone can pile up a million by retirement. All it takes is a modest willingness to save and reasonable investments.

These charts show two ways to amass a million bucks. One is the lump-sum approach, and the other way is to sock it to 'em periodically. The first example presupposes you're 30 years old with $10,000 in a tax-free IRA. If you make your investments grow at a 15 percent average annual rate, which is impressive but not impossible, you will have $1.3 million when you're 65. Amazed? Such is the awesome power of compound interest.

What if you don't have $10,000? The second chart assumes you're 30 years old and sock away $1,000 each year into your IRA. You again make your boodle grow at 15 percent annually. At age 65 you will have just over a million bucks. Is this realistic? I think so, but it involves some "ifs." The 15 percent rate isn't impossible. The S&P 500 has averaged better than that over the last decade. But the example doesn't account for inflation. If inflation averages 4 percent annually, you will need 19 percent annually (15 plus 4) to amass the million dollars of real purchasing power. This is tougher, but not impossible. More than 30 mutual funds have grown faster than that over the last decade.

Even if you consider that to be too much, think again. There is still another obvious way, which these charts imply but don't clearly state. Try combining the two effects and starting a few years earlier. If you start at age 25 and sock away $2,000 a year into your IRA (lots of folks are doing it), you will have built the $10,000 by the time you're 30. If you keep socking away $2,000 a year, and the whole kit and kaboodle grows at 15 percent annually, you will have amassed a whopping $4 million by age 65. To end up with a mere million bucks, you only need to get a 10 percent annual return—hardly a high-falutin' goal. The average stock on the New York Stock Exchange has done that well averaged out over the last 60 years (see Chart 12).

So, almost everybody in America can be a millionaire. We of the younger generation need not be concerned about a bankrupt social security system if we plan individually for our own future. This conclusion assumes that tax laws will continue to allow us to invest money tax-free in IRAs and other tax-deferred retirement/pension plans. Let's hope the politicians don't strip this "tax dodge" away from us, because if they do, the American dream of being a millionaire will return to pipe-dream status for millions of everyday Joe Lunch-buckets.

Two Examples of the Power of Compound Interest

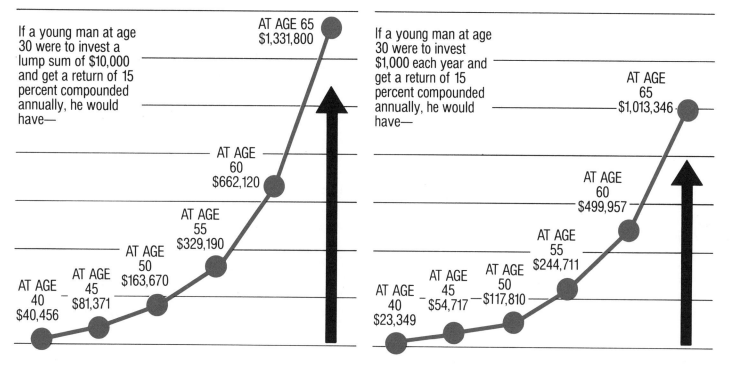

If a young man at age 30 were to invest a lump sum of $10,000 and get a return of 15 percent compounded annually, he would have—

AT AGE 65
$1,331,800

AT AGE 60
$662,120

AT AGE 55
$329,190

AT AGE 50
$163,670

AT AGE 45
$81,371

AT AGE 40
$40,456

If a young man at age 30 were to invest $1,000 each year and get a return of 15 percent compounded annually, he would have—

AT AGE 65
$1,013,346

AT AGE 60
$499,957

AT AGE 55
$244,711

AT AGE 50
$117,810

AT AGE 45
$54,717

AT AGE 40
$23,349

Note: Examples assume reinvestment of all dividends and payment from other income of taxes due on annual dividends.

PART 2
INTEREST RATES, COMMODITY PRICES, REAL ESTATE, AND INFLATION

As an economics undergraduate I had trouble getting a handle on interest rates. They always seemed somehow mysterious. Were they a cause or a result? It seemed that the professors had conspired to make the whole subject complex. But interest rates are nothing more than what you pay to rent money—the price of money, if you will—which isn't much different from the price of anything else. The same kinds of phenomena that boost other prices tend to boost interest rates, too. In this section you will not only learn about interest rates, but about many of those other prices too, like commodity prices, wholesale prices, real estate prices, and inflation in general.

Interest-Rate Movements

One of the beauties of graphic visualizations is that you can see at a glance what took others years to learn. For starters, you will see that long-term and short-term interest rates tend to go up and down at the same time, but not by the same amount. Short-term interest rates, such as rates for 90-day Treasury bills, tend to be more volatile than for 30-year Treasury notes. That makes sense when you understand how emotional the financial markets are. Wall Street has a uniquely hysterical way of thinking that the world will end tomorrow but be fully recovered in the long run, and then a few years later believing that the immediate future is rosy but in the long term the subway still stinks.

Also, you will see that short-term rates are usually lower than long-term rates, because there is more fundamental risk in the long term. Then you will see that the spread between long-term and short-term rates is a kind of barometer of economic vitality. When short-term rates are a lot less than long-term rates, the economy is pretty healthy, and when the two rates are close together, it is a rumbling of risk. The beauty is that you can learn all of this from one chart, a simple story, in a short time.

These charts illustrate much more. You will learn the vital lesson that interest rates move up and down together all around the Western world, as do commodity prices and inflation in general—and they have for close to forever in France, Germany, Switzerland, England, Belgium, the Netherlands, and yes, the United States. You will see interest rates in all these countries bounce up and down together. It's all because, contrary to what they taught me in Econ school, we've been one big intertwined economic world ever since the dawn of capitalism. Ironically, economic theory has largely been dominated by Keynesian and monetarist economists, who all believe that we can jiggle our economy and get considerably better results than what's going on all around the world. You saw in the last section how that isn't true for stocks. In this section you'll see that it isn't true for interest rates or prices in general.

Other Lessons About Interest Rates

You'll also learn how closely interest rates tie into economic growth and corporate profitability, and why. You'll see that they are so tightly tied that you can outguess most economists' earnings forecasts just by watching the trend of interest rates. Critics might contend that you could outguess most economists with a Ouija board, but that doesn't negate the validity of understanding the link between interest rates and profitability. For example, suppose you wanted to forecast oil prices. The pros have been terrible at it; on average, they've missed all the big moves up and down. Oil prices have been so tightly linked to interest-rate movements, as you will see in Chart 44, that you could have stayed on the right side of the major trends just by having an interest in interest rates.

In addition, you will learn that, contrary to what you've always believed, high interest rates are not a new phenomenon. Most folks think that interest rates were always low until after World War II, and then rose steadily as our economy was ever more mismanaged. In a poll I conducted among investors, more than 95 percent of all investors seem to believe that 19th-century American interest rates averaged in the range of 1 to 3 percent per year. Nothing could be further from the truth. As you will see in Chart 45, short-term rates rarely got below 5 percent, and were often as high as 10 percent. Several times (while the country was at peace), they got as high as 20 and 25 percent. Why? The United States was a third-world-like country of that era, and with risks high, it needed sky-high interest rates to suck capital out of Europe.

By comparison, England was to the world then what the United States is now—the fortress of economic stability. So money cost the English less to borrow than anybody else. But in chart 46 you see a fascinating chart that links several of these lessons. It shows how English and American interest rates have moved up and down at the same times since 1860—and that as England's economic ship faltered progressively throughout this century, it cost them ever more to borrow money relative to the rising American ship.

In fact, a rigorous understanding of economics today is impossible without understanding how England dominated the economic world of the 18th and 19th centuries. After seeing the volatility in American interest rates, you will learn from Chart 47 how powerful England was by remembering that England's dominance and steady cost of money prevailed throughout disasters like our revolution, the Napoleonic Wars, mass industrialization, and World War I.

The Role of Inflation

But interest rates don't exist in a vacuum. If interest rates are one tune Wall Street waltzes to, the flip side of the record is inflation and commodity prices. The rise and fall of interest rates tend to coincide with the rise and fall in inflation. Most folks have as little real grasp of the history of inflation as they do of interest rates. They usually assume that inflation is a modern event and that inflationary prices only rise and never fall back into deflation. The truth is, inflation has come and gone many times before. In Chart 51 you will see that wholesale prices (of goods sold to producers) surged and sank in five major phases during the 200 years ending in 1950. Then, in Charts 49 and 54 you will see that it was just part of inflation's continuous worldwide waltz.

But it's been going on longer. Chart 50 will let you see inflation's ebb and flow in England going all the way back to 1300. England is the only place where we have such a long record to examine. For 50 and 100 years at a time, inflation skyrocketed, only to taper off and die back later. These violent gyrations masked the real long-term trend of inflation, which has been as low as you might have imagined, both in this country and around the world, but there have been lots of violent inflationary hiccups along the way.

It is fascinating to explore our own inflationary past (Chart 52). Visually, it looks like there has been oodles of inflation since 1900, but your financial calculator helps put this in perspective. Inflation since 1790 has averaged only 1 percent per year, and since 1900 has averaged only 3 percent. The scary thing is that 3 percent inflation generates more than a tenfold increase over 80 years. If that rate continued for the next 8 years, a $10,000 car today might cost your grandkids $120,000. Everyday houses could cost millions. Egads!

A Hard Look at Real Estate and Commodities

Real estate and inflation are tied together in people's minds, and they probably should be, because, as you will see in these charts, real estate is an inflation hedge at best (maybe a tax dodge too).

At worst, real estate is a good way to fool yourself about investing. Contrary to popular notions, real estate has been a terrible investment over the longer term, barely keeping up with inflation over the longest term and sometimes not keeping up for decades.

If you compare real estate's long-term returns with stocks, you will be amazed at how poorly real estate has done. It gets worse if you buy raw land, where you really get a raw deal. Homes have done better than land, but again no better than inflation. In fact, it has only been in recent decades that homes have been considered "investments." Before that they were considered the longest-term form of consumer spending.

Then why is it that everyone thinks real estate has been so profitable? Because folks forget that most of their real estate profits came from leveraging themselves to the hilt during one of the few extended periods when real estate has risen rapidly in price. When you buy a home, you typically borrow four dollars for every dollar you put up yourself. So, if the house price increases 10 percent, you've made 50 percent on your money. While you can increase your potential profits through borrowing, you also boost your risk. Folks have forgotten the risks in real estate, thanks to the inflation-driven boom that pervaded the post–World War II era. But these charts will teach you to acknowledge and remember those lengthy long-ago periods when real estate prices didn't do so well—and prepare you for realistic expectations of the future.

Then consider commodity prices, because inflation and real

estate prices have rarely increased when commodity prices have been weak. You will learn in Chart 56 just how weak commodity prices have been. So if you want to buy real estate, you might just hold off until you see some strength in commodities—because just the same way that real estate is an inflation hedge, and little more, so are commodity prices.

The ultimate inflation hedge to most folks is gold. You will learn in Chart 57 that gold's inflation-hedging merits have come and gone in flurries that have given most truly long-term gold holders the cold shoulder. With the exception of a few periods of a very few years, gold hasn't kept pace with inflation or anything else. And that is true of most major commodities. Without huge amounts of inflation to fuel them higher, these so-called inflation hedges have been better to avoid.

Over the long term, inflation merely reflects how much the world's governments overprint currency. Commodities, real estate, and currency are essentially the same (via inflation and interest rates). They're all tied roughly together in pricing.

Historically, inflation has come during wars. Some folks think war is good for the economy. Wars may be good for speculators, who can learn from Chart 55 how commodity prices soar before and during the war and drop in the years afterward. But wars certainly aren't good for the economy. There is no real evidence to the contrary, but there is lots of evidence to suggest that wars are injurious. Wars generate short-term scarcity and disruption, which boosts prices and creates economic chaos.

So, if you want to avoid inflation, high interest rates, and volatile commodity prices, the first step is avoid wars. The second step is to take the power of printing money out of the government's hands. By the time you are finished with this section, you won't need any prompting to read between the lines and see the merits of a rigid goldlike standard to avoid inflationary boom-bust cycles—the same way England did so successfully for so long while it dominated the world's economy.

40
The Interest-Rate Shuffle

This chart, covering 25 years of short- and long-term interest rates, crossed my desk in 1974, the year of the worst post-war recession in the United States by far. From the chart come several simple lessons. First, short- and long-term interest rates usually move the same way at about the same time. Look at 1953 or 1957 to see that they peaked virtually simultaneously. In 1970 short-rates peaked before long-rates, but only by a few months. In this case short-rates were a warning to investors of the likely road ahead for long-rates (see Chart 42). But what about 1973? Short-term rates peaked, then fell, rose again, and rates were still climbing when the chart found its way to my hands in late 1974.

Nothing's perfect, but this chart's imperfection demonstrates another imperfect rule. When rates fall steeply for months, the economy tends to be very weak. The shaded areas represent recessionary periods as measured by the National Bureau of Economic Research (NBER), the official recession record keeper for the United States. With the exception of 1966, every time interest rates took a nosedive, the economy was just starting a recession.

In late 1974, facing an economic cliff, Gerald Ford & Co. were arguing for tight money to help "Whip Inflation Now"—remember the W.I.N. buttons? Ford was also arguing us further down an already faltering economic cycle. He could have heeded a clear warning by seeing short-term rates flashing their tell-tale "peak" in 1973, but he didn't. So 1974 could have been far less nasty if Ford had known what he was doing instead of fighting the wrong battle. It turns out that late 1973 was actually the start

of the recession—it's just that on this chart the NBER hadn't cataloged it yet. Starting in late 1974 rates fell, as they normally do throughout an economic decline. In this case, following the rule that peaking short-term rates lead to an economic decline would have steered you well—the path of interest rates, after hiccuping, would have fallen in place.

There are other lessons to be learned on this chart. Short-rates tend to be more volatile than long-rates and to stay lower than long-rates. This is because lenders normally want more per year for taking the risks of lending for longer periods; more things can go wrong and they undertake greater risk. So, another warning sign that has worked well over the years is that when the more volatile short-rates approach or exceed long-rates, watch out.

How do these lessons relate to the late-1986 environment? The rates falling through 1985–1986 are telling you the economy is weaker than current government statistics indicate, but with 6 percent short-rates staying 2 to 3 points below long-rates, these indicators also tell you there is not a lot to worry about.

Long-Term vs. Short-Term Interest Rates, 1950–1975

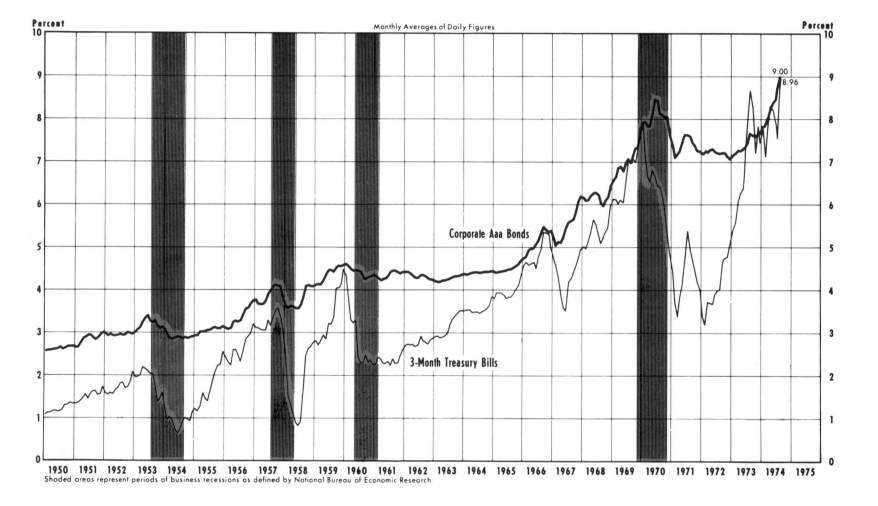

Percent

Monthly Averages of Daily Figures

Corporate Aaa Bonds

3-Month Treasury Bills

9.00
8.96

Shaded areas represent periods of business recessions as defined by National Bureau of Economic Research.

97

Source: Federal Reserve Bank of St. Louis.

41
Long-Term Interest Rates: Four Countries in the World Economy

This chart reveals a secret most economists refuse to acknowledge: We live in a world economy and cannot escape what's going on outside our borders. Here are 20 years of long-term interest rates in four Western nations. Note that none of the countries avoid the major peaks, such as 1970 or 1974. The major troughs happen at about the same time, too. When one country's rates rise, so do rates in the others; when rates fall, they do so in all the countries.

While folks stubbornly cling to the notion that a country can buck the trend, it rarely happens—and then usually by going down the tubes. Economists are heavily misguided by political thinking and thereby prone to argue that we can control our destiny separate from the destinies of other nations. Politicians spout economic isolationism and their own prescriptions. After all, who would vote for a riverboat captain who didn't claim abilities to control his boat—regardless of wherever the currents might meander? But in matters economic, history's force argues that we're all in it together. While President Reagan took credit for taming recent U.S. inflation and high interest rates, he didn't generate these results; he was merely along for the ride. Almost no one looks overseas to see that these developments were unfolding all over as a global phenomenon.

It's been this way forever. Note the charts of commodity and wholesale prices from the 1920s and the 19th century in Charts 51 and 57. We cannot escape foreign activity even though only a small amount of our GNP comes from foreign trade.

The lesson from this is to always look at what is going on overseas to get a cross-check on what you think is going to happen here. In 1986, with interest rates falling in most Western nations, there is likely to be little pressure for rising interest rates in the United States, and a lot of room for falling rates—which speaks to why the stock and bond markets have been booming.

This chart came from the monthly *Bulletin* of the Federal Reserve Bank of St. Louis in October 1981. The St. Louis Fed is one of the best sources of economic data. Chart fans will also love their *International Financial Statistics* and *U.S. Financial Data*—all available via subscription—free of charge, by mere written request.

Long-Term Interest Rates in Selected Countries, 1960–1980

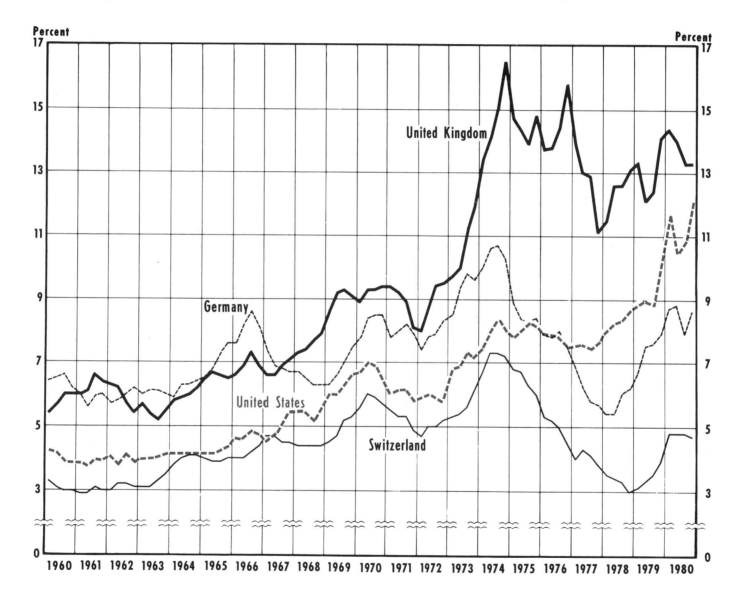

Source: Federal Reserve Bank of St. Louis, October 1981.

42
There Seems to Be a Bond Between These Yields

As with the last chart, here you see the synchronous movements of financial events in different countries. This time you see them for interest rates and dividend yields, and how they are tied together in four European countries. Look at interest rates. These are for long-term government bonds—the highest-quality available in those countries. The rates moved up and down simultaneously in the different countries. There seems to be a bond between them. In 1957, interest rates peaked in all the countries but the United Kingdom. They rose very little thereafter in the U.K. Rates then fell until 1959, when they established a simultaneous bottom in all four of the countries.

There are some variations, however. The 1960–1962 period shows some jiggle. Germany and the United Kingdom acted similarly, but differently than Belgium and the Netherlands. But then starting in 1963 they move almost in lock-step again. And if that doesn't convince you, look at the dividend yields on stocks. Except when Germany's dividend yields peaked out a year before the other three in 1958, and the Netherlands didn't rise in 1960, and Belgium didn't in 1961, the yields in these countries look like mirror images of each other from year to year.

The message here is no different from the others that point out the intertwined nature of most major economies. But you can see some simple lessons in these charts that are case studies on this theme to hone your Wall Street wits. First and most obvious, synchronous movements involve many events. If one country makes a change, it will have to compete with each of the other countries, whether that change involves interest rates, dividend yields, stock prices, currencies, commodities, real estate—on and on, ad nauseum.

Next, this chart is a classic lesson in divergence. Look at the dividend yields in 1957. Germany signaled that it was the key country to watch when its yields turned down while the other three were still rising. Either Germany's yields would turn around and go back up, or the others would soon come down. The longer that Germany marched out of step with the others, the more likely it became that the others would move down too. And so it happened. You see the same phenomenon in 1961's declining Belgian yields while other countries' yields kept rising. Either the other countries would soon see falling yields, or Belgium's yields would likely reverse and go back up. Here, too, Belgium was the warning sign. By breaking a trend and maintaining it, it was warning you of the likely future direction.

Of course, divergence isn't always meaningful. Often a country dashes out of step for a short while, only to come back in line with other countries. And sometimes a country will go off its own way for a long time, particularly if things in the country are going haywire. So, remember, divergence isn't a sure thing, but it is a powerful warning.

You can get European rates in the London *Financial Times*, and to a limited extent in the *Wall Street Journal* and *Barron's*. Watch 'em and watch out.

Bond Interests and Common Stock Yields of Four Countries, 1955–1965

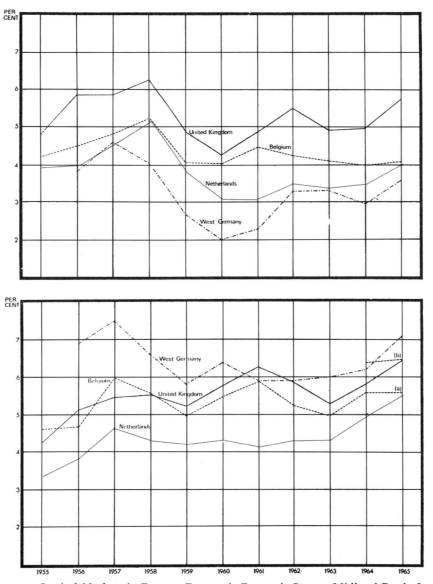

Source: *Capital Markets in Europe*. Economic Research Group, Midland Bank, London.

43
The Snake

The "snake" depicts one of the fundamental trade-offs for stocks and bonds over the next few years. This chart shows the average interest rate of quality corporate bonds versus the growth rate of corporate earnings as represented by the S&P 400. It's a trade-off between business's ability to get money through earnings growth versus its cost of money through borrowing. The interest-rate scale is on the left side; the earnings-growth scale is on the right. As you see, interest rates and earnings-growth rates have correlated neatly with each other. When earnings growth has been fast, usually during the latter part of rapid economic expansions, interest rates have been high. As interest rates have fallen, so has the growth rate of earnings.

This means that if historic relationships continue and interest rates keep falling, then so might the growth rate of earnings. If earnings don't grow quickly, then the stock market has a problem. Why? As of this writing, the Dow Jones Industrial Average was at about 2,100 with about $115 of underlying earnings. That translates into a P/E of 18. The P/E chart (Chart 1) says 18 is a historically high P/E.

How do you justify a high P/E? To simplify this, imagine a P/E of 20. Inverting it gives an E/P, or earnings divided by price, of 1/20th or 5 percent. You can think of that as the earnings yield of owning a business—or stock—directly comparable to the interest yield from a bond (see Chart 4). If the earnings yield is lower than bond yields, it makes little sense to buy the stock unless the earnings will increase enough so that the average earnings yield of the next few years will rise above the bond yield. After all, bonds pay up front, whereas much of a stock's earnings are reinvested in the business—and bonds have less fundamental risk than stocks.

So the Dow's P/E of 18 is an earnings yield of 1/18th or 5.6 percent—versus bonds, which are currently at 8.5 percent. Unless earnings soar, interest rates must fall 3 points or more for stocks to be a good deal. If bond rates fall but only a little, earnings still must rise to justify a 2,100 Dow.

But the snake says that as bond rates drop, so do the prospects for earnings growth. The snake predicts that 8 percent bond yields will result in 5.5 percent earnings growth, which means the Dow's earnings might increase from $115 to $121 in three years. At 2,100, the Dow's P/E would then be 17.3 (2,100 divided by 121). That means an earnings yield of only 5.8 percent (1 divided by 17.3), which is still much too low relative to 8.5 percent bonds.

So, according to the snake, bond rates must fall all the way below 6 percent, which is a big drop, before the trade-off shifts to favor stocks. A bond rate of 5.5 percent would be an enticement relatively equal to the stock market's earnings yield. The snake then predicts annual earnings growth of 4 percent, which boosts the Dow's earnings in 3 years to only $129—at which point its earnings yield would start to rise, but at 6.1 percent it would just barely beat bonds. That's the tradeoff between earnings, interest rates, and the stock market in the coming years: a real snake in the grass.

AA Bond Rates Compared to the S&P 400 Earnings, 1960–1986

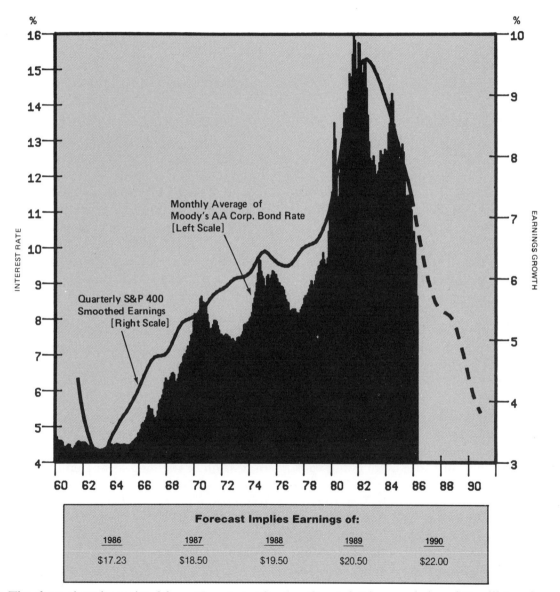

Forecast Implies Earnings of:				
1986	1987	1988	1989	1990
$17.23	$18.50	$19.50	$20.50	$22.00

Source: The above chart is reprinted from "Investment Strategy Quarterly" by permission of Merrill Lynch, Pierce, Fenner & Smith Incorporated. Copyright © 1986 Merrill Lynch, Pierce, Fenner & Smith Incorporated.

44
Why the Interest in Oil?

Will oil prices keep plummeting? Will interest rates fall? To answer those questions, keep an eye on the relationship between interest rates and oil. They've been quite tight-knit up until now. This chart is structurally a lot like the snake (Chart 43). It chronicles the amazing oil price–interest rate relationship since the beginning of the OPEC-induced oil crisis. As shown in other charts (see Charts 40 and 45), what happens with any major interest rate, such as the 20-year Treasuries used here, tends to mirror (and be a good proxy for) trends in other debt securities. In this chart, interest rates are measured on the left-hand vertical axis, while oil prices are shown on the right-hand vertical axis.

From 1973 to 1986, major oil price moves and fluctuations in Treasury notes matched each other in direction within 12 months of each other. The trends diverged only briefly in 1983–1984. Oil prices and interest rates remained rather flat between 1975 and 1978. Then they both started up. Interest rates led the way. But oil peaked out first, in 1980, soon followed by Treasury rates in 1981. From there the path was basically downhill, with only that one interest-rate hiccup of 1983–1984 coming between them. Interestingly, the relationship would have warned you in 1983–1984 that either oil prices were going back up, which they didn't, or else interest rates were going to turn around and head lower, which they did. After that, as interest rates fell steeply in 1984–1985, their decline would have warned you that the late-1985 upspike in oil prices would likely turn into what became the subsequent 12-month oil price free-fall.

Why has the oil price–interest rate relationship held over the years? Oil is perhaps the most basic single commodity for an industrialized economy. You can't do much without power. But another key commodity is money, whose price is measured by interest rates. The economic forces that make the economy expand or contract move aggregate demand for most major parts of the economy—these two included. They are such huge components of the overall pie that they just can't escape each other for long. Additionally, like any other commodity, money and oil are both sensitive to inflationary trends and, in the short term, even the fears of inflationary trends.

What does this relationship forecast for the immediate future? In mid-1986, oil prices started to firm up and rise, while interest rates continued lower. The pattern of the past may wither. But the weight of history says their divergence is not likely to continue, which means that either oil will head lower or interest rates will stop falling, turn around, and go up. Which will happen? I certainly don't know, but there is a good clue to watch for in the months and years ahead. When one of them makes a really big move in any direction, the way Treasury rates made a big move downward in 1982, that is likely to be an indication of the long-term trend for both oil and interest rates. You may get whipsawed this way from time to time, but probably not terribly badly (see Chart 23).

Yield on 20-Year Treasuries and Price of Crude Oil, 1973–1986

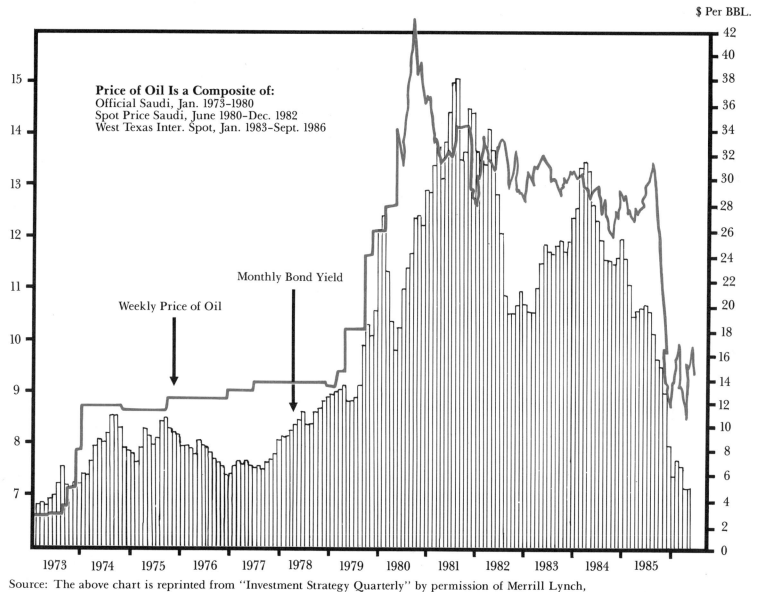

$ Per BBL.

Price of Oil Is a Composite of:
Official Saudi, Jan. 1973–1980
Spot Price Saudi, June 1980–Dec. 1982
West Texas Inter. Spot, Jan. 1983–Sept. 1986

Monthly Bond Yield

Weekly Price of Oil

Source: The above chart is reprinted from "Investment Strategy Quarterly" by permission of Merrill Lynch,
     Pierce, Fenner & Smith Incorporated. Copyright © 1986 Merrill Lynch, Pierce, Fenner & Smith Incorporated.

45
High Interest Rates Have Been a Recurring Nightmare

"Oh, for the good old days." You've often heard it said. Perhaps you thought high American interest rates were a phenomenon unique to the post-Vietnam era. Not so. While many folks believe that interest rates had never risen over 10 percent before World War II, this graph gives you a quick overview of a financial America few can conceive. This chart may convince you that high short-term interest rates were so high so often in the 19th century that high rates may be more normal than not—and perhaps you should prepare for their return.

The chart shows interest rates on short-term commercial paper from 1841 through 1918. Commercial paper is the class of short-term notes from the largest and best-financed corporations and is highly competitive with, and a good proxy for, short-term interest rates in general.

Look at arrow A, which shows that for brief periods, like just before the Civil War and again in the 1870s, short-term annual interest rates got as high as 25 to 35 percent. Even more interesting, from 1845 until 1875 there was rarely a year where short-term interest rates didn't exceed 10 percent at some time. Look at the length of time covered by arrow B.

Why were rates high? Partly rates were high around the world because it was a very risky world—wars, booms and busts, poor communication, plaguelike fatal diseases, and little regulation or insurance. High risk made lenders want to be well paid to part with their money. But perhaps the main reason was a high level of demand for money. The United States was a second-rate nation undergoing an industrial revolution. The nation needed high interest rates relative to other nations to suck European capital into America to finance the new machinery necessary to industrialize.

The chart suggests three conclusions. First, high interest rates are not new. They have recurred throughout American history (see Chart 46 for another example). Second, the high rates between 1979 and 1983 were only extremely high by recent, not long-term, historical standards. Third, with high interest rates having come and gone before, they may well come again. Arrow C lays out the current level of 30-day commercial paper rates as of April Fool's Day 1986. Rates are low now. High rates are apt to return, just like in "the good old days." When you hear folks start yearning for yesteryear, remember, a hamburger was cheap, but money was dear.

This graph is believed to be the first authentic record of money rates before 1870. It appeared in *A Century of Prices* by Theodore Burton and G. C. Seldon (published by *Wall Street* magazine in 1919). The sources were authentic newspaper records of three- to six-month commercial paper listings. The authors had attempted to carry the records back before the Panic of 1837, an economic collapse rivaling the 1930s and 1870s in magnitude, but could not find sufficient records. This graph is a classic.

U.S. Money Rates, Prime Commercial Paper, 1841–1918

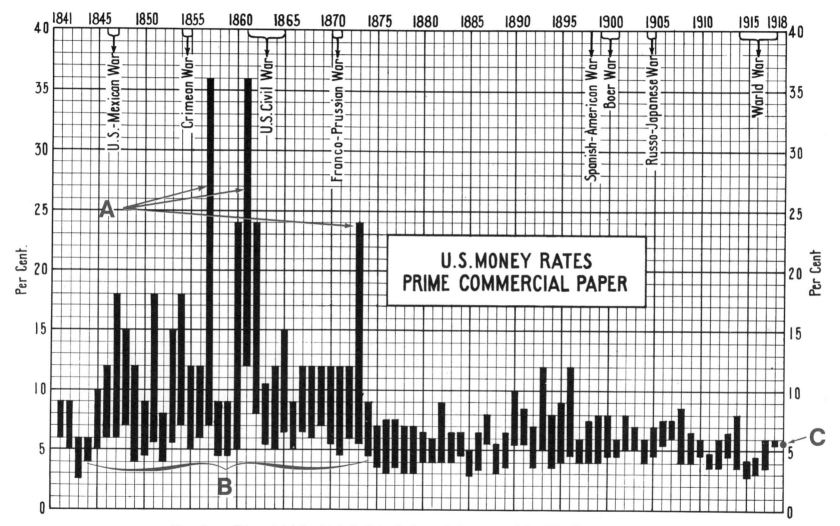

MONEY RATES—This graph is believed to be the first authentic record of money rates before 1870. The rates were compiled from the daily reports given by the newspapers of that time, a research involving a great deal of labor. Prime three to six months commercial paper was selected as a better reflection of actual conditions than call or time money, and it has the additional advantage of permitting earlier quotations. An effort was made to carry the graph back to the panic of 1837, but no adequate records were found before 1841. There were times in the late thirties when money was unobtainable at any rate. The evident scarcity of capital and the high rates obtained previous to 1873 shed an interesting light on our financial history.

Source: Burton, "A Century of Prices," *Magazine of Wall Street*, New York, NY, 1919.

46
125 Years of the Counsel of the Consols

Kondratieff wave freaks (see Chart 84) love this chart because it helps make their case. I like it because, in parallel fashion to others in this book, it shows how interwoven are the financial threads of different major Western economies. The chart shows the yields of U.S. railroad bonds plotted against English consols from 1855 to 1980. Railroads were America's prime blue chips from 1860 until the 1929 Great Depression. They captivated America in the mid-19th century and were to U.S. financial markets what autos became in the first half of the 20th century—the major new technological development affecting the infrastructure (see Chart 34). In contrast, English consols were the English realm's long-term debt—the world's conservative investment of choice throughout the 17th and 18th centuries while England reigned supreme (see Chart 35). Consols were to the pre–World War II world what U.S. Treasury notes are today—the ultimate liquid safety haven.

Notice how over the entire 125-year period, the two interest-rate yields moved up and down in harmony. Early on, railroad yields were much higher, but they should have been higher. The railroad bonds were only as safe as the safety of the businesses themselves—certainly less than the full taxing power of the world's mightiest nation, which backed the consols. Even worse, railroad bonds represented businesses that not only transported folks in the civilized portions of the United States but also on the frontier—Indian battles, bison, and barren wilderness included. So, investors had a bit more to risk with railroads than they did with the Queen.

Interest rates fell in both countries rather steadily until 1900 and then rose until 1920—almost identically. This interest-rate fluctuation is what Kondratieff wavers see as the tell-tale sign of their longest business cycle's major downward phase and upward phase. After 1920, rates dropped, leading up to the 1929 worldwide debacle (see Chart 29). Railroad yields spiked during the crash; consols didn't. The difference? In depression there was real risk that railroads might be unable to repay their debt, but there was no solvency risk with tax-backed consols.

Note how yields lock-stepped their way lower until the late 1940s and then up together through 1980. Interestingly, rates fell during World War II, just the reverse of during World War I. This led Kondratieff wavers to see their cycle's power as greater even than world wars. During the postwar upswing, the yield on consols rose above railroad yields. Why? Actually, starting in 1900, consols started losing their competitive advantage as England slowly lost its preeminent world position. After World War II, the risks of railroad defaults seemed less dangerous than socialization and inflation risks in England.

The lesson from all this? U.S. interest rates, like the nation's economy and stock markets, are part of a world economy and seldom move far out of sync from the rest of the world—for long. So, don't blame the country's economic problems on the politicians. It is only their fault on the rare occasion when the nation is far out of sync. We have as much to learn about what is going on in America by looking overseas as by looking for the dirt under our own rug.

A Comparison of Yields on Consols and U.S. Railroad Bonds, 1860–1980

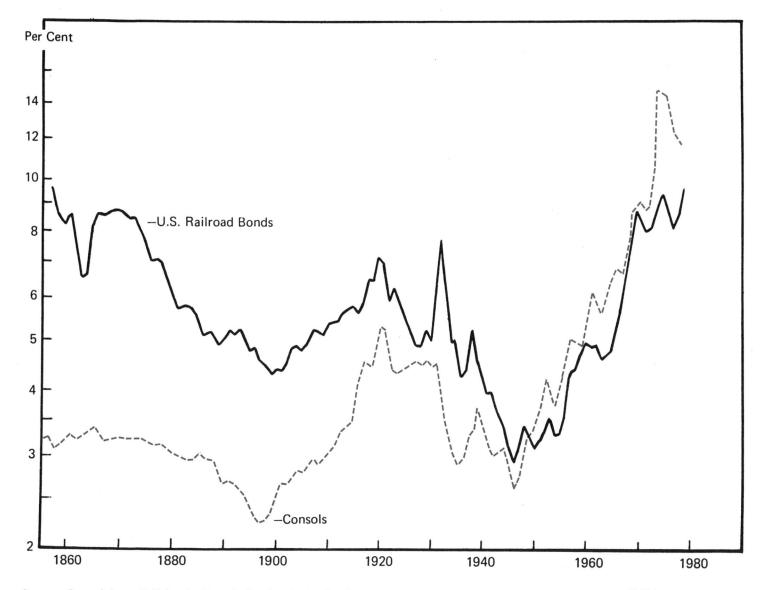

Per Cent

—U.S. Railroad Bonds

—Consols

Source: Copyright © 1980 by the Foundation for the Study of Cycles, 124 South Highland Avenue, Pittsburgh, PA 15206.

47
The Source of England's Stiff Upper Lip

Whenever anyone suggests that interest rates are volatile, always will be, and have to be, I suggest they consider the English experience. It may also motivate you to favor a gold standard. The briefest glance at this chart of 240 years of English interest rates shows why gold bugs are bug-eyed. For more than 200 years, England maintained stable long-term interest rates through a rigid gold standard. Long-term rates never got above 6 percent and never fell below 3 percent, and in most years wiggled hardly a jiggle. And England suffered little of the inflation that periodically racked other countries. And they did all this throughout the course of famines, pestilences, numerous major wars (Napoleonic Wars, World Wars I and II, etc.) and the greatest upheaval of modern times, the Industrial Revolution.

Compare this with the volatile 19th-century American experience (see Chart 45). Now you know why gold fans hope that replacing the current U.S. monetary system with a gold-based system would generate similar results. In England, gold was rock-steady.

It is quite clear from this chart that an economy can operate without wild interest-rate gyrations. What is needed? The prime requisite is a supreme confidence in the value of money. Before World War II, England played much the same role for 200 years that the United States does today. They were the center of the world's economy, and other countries tended to peg their economic fortunes to England's. When other countries traded among each other, they specified payment in English pounds, because they believed in their value. It was only because everyone had such supreme confidence in the stability of England's currency that their system survived intact for so long. This system survived because England maintained the continual right of conversion from paper money to gold to insure the value of the currency.

The United States has effectively had a paper-backed system since the 1930s, and along the way has proved that central bank–controlled paper systems are not good ways to avoid inflation or violently fluctuating interest rates. Note also that England's interest-rate stability vanished a decade after Bretton Woods—when they tied their economic wagon to the paper-backed U.S. dollar.

A constitutional limit on the growth of government spending is unavoidable (see Chart 80). Couple that with a goldlike standard, and the kinds of chaos we've seen in recent decades would quickly become ancient history. (Note the word *goldlike*— a pure gold standard won't work these days—see Chart 69.) So, if you feel, as lots of folks do, that the recent volatile interest-rate swings are unavoidable, remember that they are not caused by a severe economic problem. They are caused by a political problem of controlling government.

It is well to remember that the English overcame their economic problems for hundreds of years with a stiff upper lip— and they did it through much more difficult times than anything the United States has faced in decades. They did it through discipline—not a politician's discipline, but the discipline imposed by a rigid gold standard.

Long-Term Interest Rates, U.K., 1731 to 1970

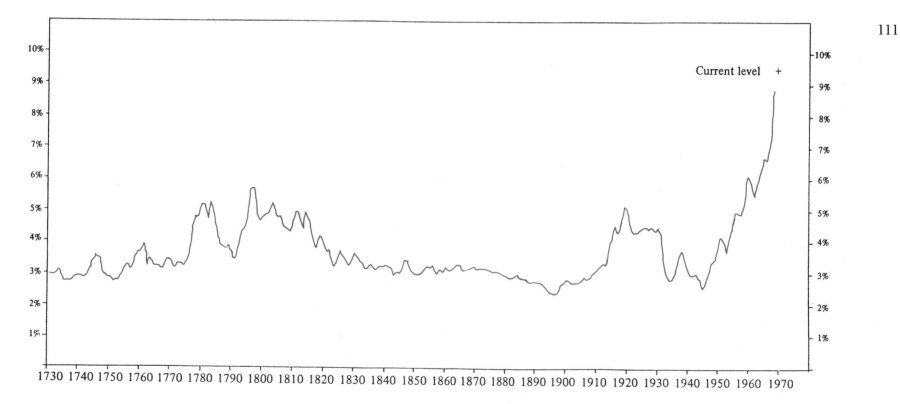

Current level +

Source: Fifth International Investment Symposium, *Investment in the Seventies*, Bellagio, Lake Como, Italy.
Published by P.N. Kemp-Gee & Co., The Stock Exchange, 1970. Courtesy of Scrimgeour Vickers & Co., London.

48
When High Is Low—and Vice Versa

The early 1980s were a time of historically high interest rates and tight money—true or false? Try recalling the period. The prime rate was in the high teens, business activity was sluggish, and unemployment was up. Most folks thought high interest rates were stifling economic activity.

But when you adjust for inflation, interest rates weren't historically high. This chart shows 190 years of interest rates, but it adjusts them to reflect inflation or deflation during each time period. This adjustment results in the interest rates being labeled *real*. When rates aren't adjusted for inflation, they are often called *nominal*. This adjusting process allows interest rates to be considered positive or negative numbers.

How can a real interest rate be negative? Suppose the average long-term rate of return on 30-year Treasury notes is 5 percent. If inflation averages 8 percent during the same time period, then in real terms the interest rate is −3 percent. Inflation adjusting reveals a different story than you might imagine. Historically, the real interest rates of the the early 1980s (point A) aren't very different from historical averages.

During the 1950–1970 period, real rates weren't volatile. But the chart's brief flatness in that period was short and unique, given a longer perspective. Before the 1950s, real rates tended to move up or down violently—often over 5, 10, or even 20 years (note area around point B).

The real interest rates of the mid-1970s also hint that the early 1980s were not a period of tight money. In the mid-1970s, real interest rates were actually negative. That is to say, inflation was galloping along at a higher level than interest rates. The system was paying you to borrow money, which is rare. This chart shows that negative long-term real interest rates have existed only a few times before—and all during war-induced inflations—1812, the Civil War (early 1860s), and during and after World Wars I and II.

Ironically, recent nominal rates have fallen drastically from those high levels of the early 1980s—to about 7 percent. But inflation has fallen even faster, so that real, inflation-adjusted rates have *risen*. With inflation somewhere between 2 and 4 percent, real long-term rates are now up to between 3 and 5 percent.

So, while some folks have been happy about the declining interest rates, those focusing on real rates are concerned. If the recent disinflation slips into deflation, as some fear and as suggested by some charts herein, real rates could actually sky-rocket as they did in the 1930s. This could be the worst environment for investors. From here inflation may be bad, but full-blown deflation is worse.

Historical Record of Real Interest Rates, 1790–1980

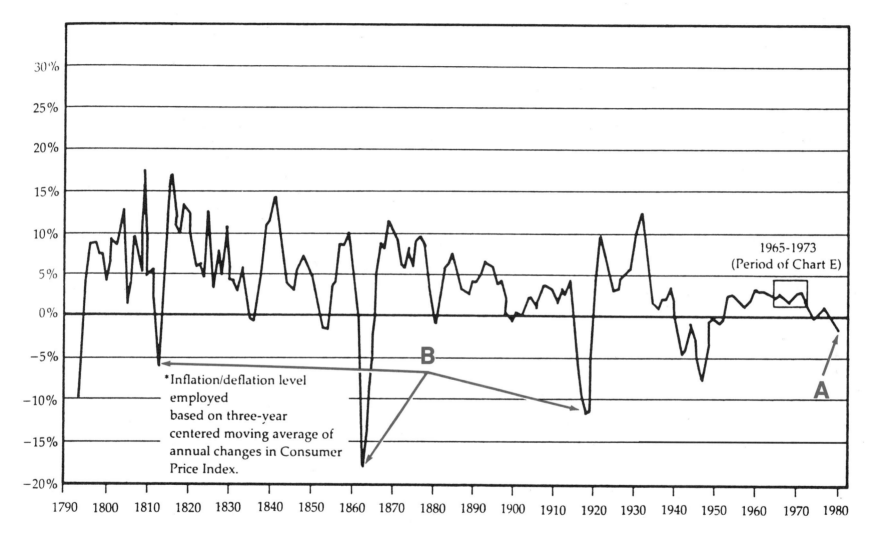

113

*Inflation/deflation level employed based on three-year centered moving average of annual changes in Consumer Price Index.

1965-1973 (Period of Chart E)

Source: Steven C. Leuthold, *The Myths of Inflation and Investing*, The Leuthold Group, Crain Communications, Inc., © 1980, data from U.S. Department of Labor. U.S. Department of Commerce.

49
Comparing Domestic and English Wholesale Prices

Not only has inflation come and gone in U.S. history, it has in every other nation's history too. These charts show wholesale prices in America and England from 1793 through 1932, including the broad, sweeping increases and decreases in overall price levels that came and went many times, affecting all capitalistic economies. England's price history was the most stable in the world, and it is in remembering that fact that the similarities between American and English inflation seem so astounding.

The top chart posts 140 years of wholesale prices in the United States, in similar fashion to Chart 51. You can clearly see the broad recurring inflation-deflation cycle stretching out every 50-odd years. That cycle has been the rule in U.S. history. Note how prices have inflated during and immediately following major wars. Prices soared around the War of 1812, the U.S. Civil War, and World War I (see more detail of this in Chart 55). This phenomenon helps explain the post–Vietnam War inflation.

In fact, these swings generally occurred at the same times throughout most Western countries. Russian economist Nikolai Kondratieff was banned to Siberia when he noticed this trend in the early 1920s and speculated that capitalism may not self-destruct as Marx predicted, but instead purge itself of inefficiencies through long and self-cleansing cycles (see the Kondratieff wave in Chart 84).

To see how similar the price swings were, compare the United States to England in the lower chart. Prices generally rose in England when U.S. prices rose. English inflation is interestingly evident during the Civil War, but at a much reduced level.

While England fared better than the United States did during the mid-19th century, comparison shows that events in different countries tend to go in the same direction in roughly the same time frame since at least 100 years before modern communications.

Even during England's mild inflation of 1850–1870, the similarities are strong. Note that both inflations clearly started before the U.S. Civil War, suggesting, as discussed with Chart 55, that wars may result from worldwide inflation and not, as usually assumed, the other way around.

These charts come from the book *Prices*, by George F. Warren and Frank A. Pearson. These two eminent Cornell professors continually sought to relate general business conditions to agricultural, commodity, and wholesale prices. Their many works provide the most comprehensive information available on early pricing throughout the world. See Chart 53 for another chart by, and a further description of, these two key statisticians.

Wholesale Prices in England vs. the United States, 1782–1930

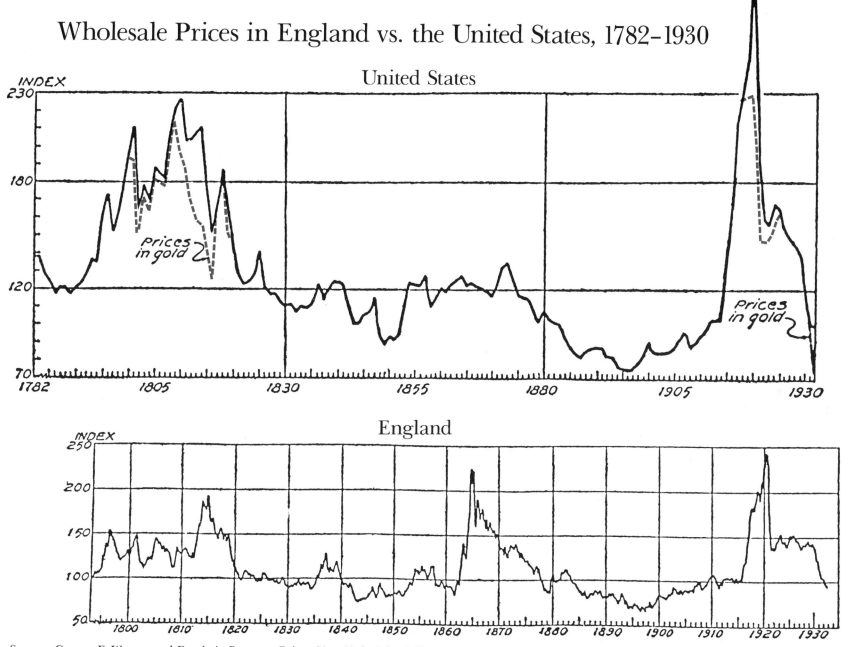

United States

England

Source: George F. Warren and Frank A. Pearson, *Prices*, New York: John Wiley & Sons, 1933.

50
Prices in Southern England

Could the world go on for hundreds of years with virtually no inflation? In fact it has. The long-term inflation rate since the year 1290 has been less than 1 percent per year. The price index pictured on this chart is the oldest existing continuous price chart and the only true long-term inflation measure we have. The chart has lots of little jiggles, so you can see why chasing short-term, and even intermediate-term, trends can be confusing. But the unique perspective of a 660-year time span provides useful insights for the future.

Inflation appears less random over the long haul than in shorter periods. Notice the trendlines A and B. For 210 years, 1290–1500, prices remained relatively static, bouncing around a growth rate of about 0.5 percent per year (see trendline A). Then, eight years after Columbus discovered the Western Hemisphere, prices started rising more steeply (trendline B). This was due to the increased gold supply brought back to Europe by the explorers, which in turn brought down the value of gold, the money of the day. Still, explorers and all, for the next 450 years (1500–1950), inflation bounced around an annual average of 0.50 percent.

To be sure, inflation has often risen much faster than the averages indicate (for example, note the big spike around 1800, which was a 25-year spurt averaging 5 percent annually). But the important point is that, despite these short, sharp rises, after a while inflation always came back down to this low average level. Inflationary peaks can be seen rising high above line B. But they've always come back down to the trendline. Three of these cyclical bounces have been completed since 1290 and have always come back down much as a ball returns to earth after each bounce. But with inflation, the bounce gets higher each time. A fourth bounce began in 1910 (see arrows 1–4).

The lesson to learn from this chart?

- Sharp, short-term swings in the inflation rate tend to cancel each other. Each big rise, even if lasting for decades, is followed by a big fall. So, while your lifetime experience leads you to think big inflation will resume and probably go on forever, it probably won't.
- Your grandkids will probably see much higher inflation levels than your kids, but not as much higher as you currently expect for them.

This chart, which came from *Cycles* magazine (a great source for unique charts), argues well that we may return to low inflation—or even deflation—for many years until we have clawed our way back to that lower trendline that seems to govern us in the longest term.

Price Index of Southern England, 1290–1950

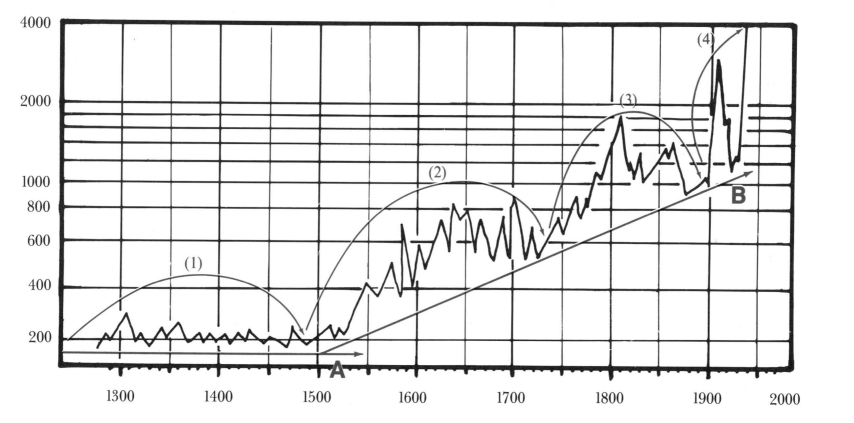

51
Wholesale Inflation

Do you believe that persistent high inflation is an unavoidable fact of economic life? If so, think again. Along the way, study the chart of wholesale prices for 1749-1980. The word *wholesale* refers to goods sold before their incorporation into a finished product. The index is based on commodities (like sugar) and manufactured products (like wire or shoe soles).

There are several ways to view this chart—all good ones. First, compare the number of years when prices rose against the number of years when prices fell. Interestingly, they are about equal. Starting with the cyclical upspike of 1779, there have been 103 years of rising prices out of 201 total years. This may not be surprising, since what goes up often comes down. But in looking at America's five prominent inflationary spikes, you are immediately struck by three interesting facts: First, inflationary spirals have tended to occur during or immediately following major wars. Second, they do not appear very often. Third, inflationary peaks have occurred about every 50 years.

Allow the vertical scale at 80 to represent the average for prices for the chart's first 200 years. This is another way to show the same thing, namely, that prices have been low for far longer than we've suspected.

What does all this mean? Recently most folks have expected that prices will continue rising forever. But there is nothing from history to say that inflation runs in only one direction. Although inflation has been uncharacteristically persistent in recent years, history indicates that it is most likely to stop. Some of the events that helped fuel the recent inflation—like the Vietnam and Korean wars and the Arab oil embargo—are no longer factors. Barring a new outbreak of war or some other major calamity, history argues that we may well enter a long period of moderate prices, or perhaps even deflation, which is scary.

Of course, others would argue that the recent inflation is different from prior ones because this 50-year price spike was fueled by deficits, printing-press money, spiraling federal debt, and general social decay. They may be right—but they may be wrong. Those things are all internal symptoms, which we may be able to control. It is always smart to consider how society's consensus might be wrong. Right now, with most folks on Wall Street and off still expecting inflation to be with us forever, it is good to remember that the inflationary era through which we've all lived is unusual only by a factor of two in magnitude, and by not much at all in terms of duration.

Cycles magazine built this chart primarily from U.S. Bureau of Labor Statistics data. It is one of the oldest data series the government maintains, starting with an 1893 Senate investigating committee. A lack of hard data on the severe post–Civil War deflation prompted Congress to gather old journals and ledgers of merchants and manufacturers on more than 250 equally weighted items, from which this index was constructed.

Wholesale Prices: All Commodities—Yearly Averages, 1749–1980

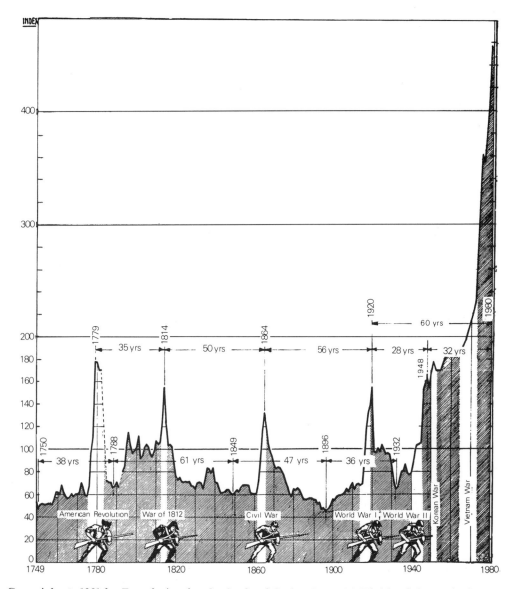

Source: Copyright © 1981 by Foundation for the Study of Cycles, Inc., 124 Highland Ave., Pittsburgh, PA 15206
Note: Date for 1950–1980 provided by David Williams.

52
Inflation—The American Experience

You've heard stories of how cheap things were in your grandparents' day, but do you really know how much inflation has developed in our history? This clean, simple chart provides a visual perspective that few have ever seen or known. The original version showed 190 years of the Consumer Price Index (CPI), from 1790 until 1980. The index stopped at 252. By the beginning of 1986, the CPI had risen another 30.5 percent, raising the total to 329, so I've tacked on the last 5 years in pencil.

Interestingly, low rates of inflation have generated big absolute gains over history. It's another expression of the power of compound interest—the same phenomenon that lets small contributions to a pension plan become big bucks within a lifetime (see Chart 39).

In recent years, the highest rate of inflation was 13.5 percent in 1980. But looking back over a longer time frame, the results look more mellow. My financial calculator computed compound annualized rates of inflation from this chart, for various time periods. They are:

Dates	Change in Index	Annual Inflation Rate
1970–1985	100 to 329	8.26%
1937–1985	41 to 329	4.43%
1900–1985	26 to 329	3.03%
1790–1985	34 to 329	1.17%

So, all told, the CPI rose 8.26 percent annually since 1970, and has risen 10-fold since 1790.

But that 10-fold increase was at an amazingly low annual rate of 1.17%. Does that conflict with your remembrance of steeply rising prices since grandpa's day? If so, in part it is because humans don't naturally think in terms of compound interest (or compound inflation). Also, over long time frames, some product prices rise much more than others. The CPI represents an average, which is distorted when quality changes for better or for worse, when items are no longer produced (buggy whips), and when new products are introduced that can't be compared with the past (TVs since 1945).

Also note that, just as in wholesale prices (see Chart 51), there have been several previous inflationary spikes, which were followed in each case by falling prices. Just recently we seem to have returned to an era of slower inflation. Will we soon encounter falling prices as during the 1820s, the 1870s, and the 1920s and 1930s? Probably not. Mild deflation is even more painful than significant inflation; it causes bankruptcies and depression. Uncle Sam, who is more efficient than he used to be at printing money, will do everything possible to avoid deflation's political repercussions, so it's hard to envision true deflation.

But even the 3 percent average inflation rate since 1984 is too high. At 3 percent it will take only 63 more years to boost the CPI up to 2,000—a 10-fold increase within the lifespan of today's children. Ugh! What would Andy Jackson think?

United States Consumer Price Index, 1790–1985

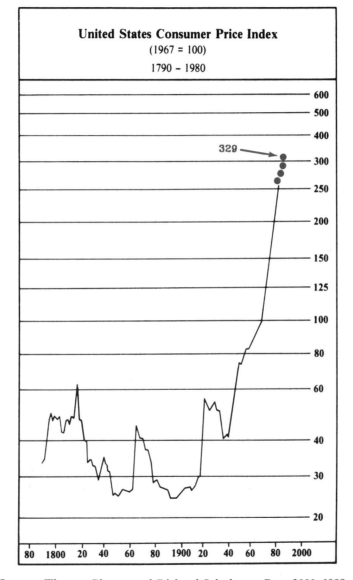

United States Consumer Price Index
(1967 = 100)
1790 – 1980

329

Source: Thomas Blamer and Richard Schulman, *Dow 3000*, 1982.

53
Gold: The Litmus Test for Commodity Prices

How tightly are U.S. commodity prices tied to those of the other Western economies? More so than most folks imagine—much more. And they always have been. This chart shows how similarly inflation ran through the U.S. and its trading partners in and around the huge inflationary spiral of World War I.

Prices is the key word here, and this chart looks at the prices of forty basic commodities in nine countries—all from 1913 through 1937, but expressed in gold, not dollars or local currency. This minimizes the effect of differences in the amount of short-term monetary inflation in each country. Note how the prices all tend to go up and down almost precisely in unison throughout this 24-year period. The nine lines look almost like one. While war-generated inflation raged throughout the Western world to varying degrees, the real, inflation-adjusted, prices of commodities varied almost not at all from country to country. The key to the cohesion of prices among the nine countries was that gold is the price-measuring tool in this instance.

Perhaps the most interesting point is that not one of the nine countries avoided the post–World War I inflationary spiral. But why so much conformity 60 years ago? As with stocks and interest rates, even in earlier decades prices tended to move together. Despite the modern fads that lead folks to believe they can diversify by investing overseas, that view really isn't realistic. Prices rise and fall together around the world. Kondratieff wave fans, who believe in a 54-year cycle, will take heart that it looks awfully like the worldwide inflation spiral that began 55 years later following the Vietnam War.

The lesson to learn from this chart, as seen in other charts throughout this book, is that, more or less, prices tend to move together in most major countries. Investors are well served by keeping an eye overseas to see if a consensus trend is developing there that hasn't yet surfaced in the United States. If so, it probably pays to keep an eye out for that trend's emergence in the United States too. When a fundamental force is emerging across the globe, a single country can rarely escape its influence.

These charts came from Dr. George F. Warren and Dr. Frank A. Pearson, both from Cornell and the leading agricultural economists and statisticians of their day. They provided the early data for most of what has become the current Wholesale Price Index series. Their legendary work, along with that of a very few other folks, provides most of what we know about the prewar economies.

Prices, in Currency and Gold, of 40 Basic Commodities in Different Countries, 1913–1936

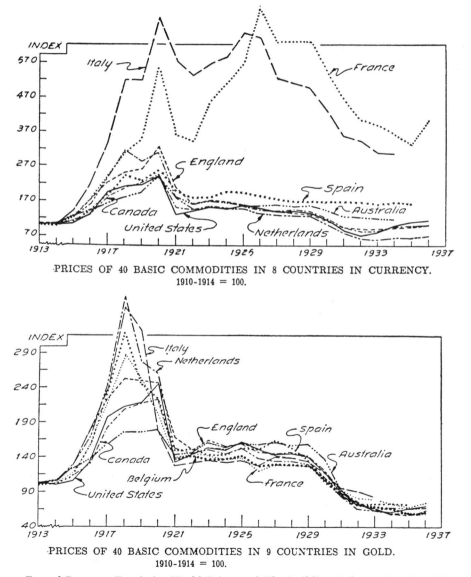

PRICES OF 40 BASIC COMMODITIES IN 8 COUNTRIES IN CURRENCY.
1910-1914 = 100.

PRICES OF 40 BASIC COMMODITIES IN 9 COUNTRIES IN GOLD.
1910-1914 = 100.

Source: Warren, George F., and Pearson, Frank A., *World Prices and The Building Industry*, London: John Wiley & Sons, 1937.

54
Prices in Three Countries

This authoritative old chart provides another way to see that the major economies are linked and long have been. It is from A. C. Pigou's *Industrial Fluctuations* (see Chart 67 for another). It shows prices in England, Germany, and the United States from 1860 to 1910, and is in many ways similar to Chart 49.

Note how tightly the three countries' prices move together. For example, the steep price declines that started in 1873 began in England, but prices were plummeting just as steeply in both other countries within months. In fact, the only time in the whole 50 years when one country was moving significantly out of phase with the others was 1862, when English prices increased while American and German prices fell.

This chart demonstrates another visual perspective of the fact that the world's economies were tightly linked long before there were modern communication systems. If prices in 3 major countries moved so tightly together in the 19th century, shouldn't we expect them to be at least as tightly tied together now that communications are faster and trade is heavier?

The implications are heavily political. Every time things go well in our economy, the President claims credit. When things go badly, everyone blames him. The same thing happens in every other country. This is so self-centered; no country avoids the major trends happening around the world. At best, a country can avoid making a bad situation worse. Why should the President and other politicians take the credit or the blame? They can affect what goes on here, but, as we see in so many charts throughout this book, they can't buck the global trend for the better.

Recently, President Reagan has claimed the credit for all the good economic news that has come down the pike: falling unemployment, falling interest rates, booming stock markets, four years of economic expansion. Almost everyone gives him credit for that good news. But few stop to notice that parallel developments have been going on around the world—some a little slower, some a little faster. But it's happening.

Of course, economies can do better than the global trend to an extent; the Japanese have proved that in recent years. But doing so has little or nothing to do with federal economic masturbation. Instead it has to do with the culture and ethics by which the country operates. A country that saves, works, reinvests, and builds will generate an above-average trend of long-term growth. A country that doesn't, won't. It isn't a lot more complicated than that.

Every time I hear folks blame a president or praise one for unemployment or the stock market or interest rates or whatever, I am reminded that those individuals are demonstrating how little they understand of the global economy. Yes, the government can be managed for better or for worse, but if folks knew what Pigou knew, they wouldn't expect the government to bail us out of the world's booms and busts.

Retail Prices in Germany, England, and the United States, 1860–1910

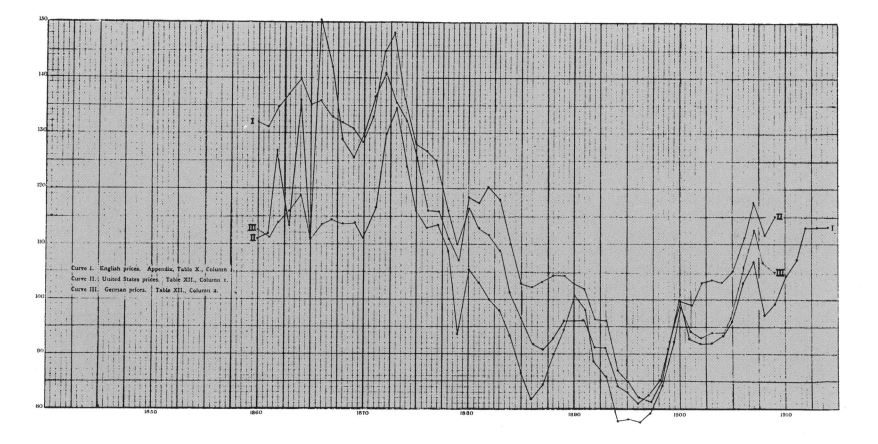

Source: A.C. Pigou, *Industrial Fluctuations*, 2nd Edition, London: Macmillan & Co., Ltd., 1929.

55
A Lesson in Avoiding Wars

Have you ever wondered if they were right? Back in the 1960s it was fashionable to lambaste the Johnson and Nixon administrations as warmongers. The liberal mindset of the day argued that wars were good for the economy and that politicians and corporate leaders were quite willing to shed a little blood in the name of profit. Well, Johnson and Nixon had plenty of shortcomings. But if you really believe they thought wars were good for the economy, then you also have to believe their principal shortcoming was not warmongering, but ignorance.

There isn't much to see in this chart, except that wars cause tremendous inflation in commodity prices. This chart shows five wars and plots how commodity price indexes behaved during them. The scales at the bottom show the number of years before and after the wars' peaks. A first glance reveals that commodity prices rise about 100 percent from the beginning of a war to its peak. Later, after the war, the commodity prices subsequently fall back to previous levels. This decline is a similar percentage but occurs more gradually, at roughly half the pace of the increase. The decline seems to continue unabated for roughly 15 years. In a singular exception, prices reinflated after World War II, but maybe that's because the Korean conflict came so quickly on its heels.

The early years of the Vietnam War were similar to these other war periods, only more moderate. But then again, the Vietnam War, while smaller, was much longer than the others. If folks had seen this chart, they shouldn't have been surprised to see commodity prices falling recently. They should have been surprised for it to take so long after the Vietnamese conflict ended for prices to fall. If you believe there is more to these charts than coincidence, you will lean toward the notion that inflation will not soon resume—we are still in the 15-year post–Vietnam War period—and commodity prices could fall further (see Chart 56).

So wars cause higher prices—that's clear—but usually only temporarily. Wars also cause tremendous dislocations to the economy, and they put commodity prices, which are one of the key economic barometers (again see Chart 56) through wild gyrations. Usually overall business conditions are no better off after the war than before. In fact, each of these wars, plus Vietnam, was followed by recessions that make up what I perceive to be six of the nine worst all-time U.S. economic declines in history. So, it's most unlikely that Johnson and Nixon would put that kind of blemish on their records intentionally.

Is this the only lesson here? Maybe not. The chart also raises a question. Note that commodity prices often begin escalating *before* the wars begin. Some theorists speculate this may mean that increases in commodity prices aren't a symptom of war, but a cause. They argue that, to avoid wars, we need to avoid the social conditions leading to inflation, which cause social disease and the desire to look overseas for scapegoats. Being a basic contrarian, I sort of like that maverick idea myself.

Effect of Wars on U.S. Wholesale Prices

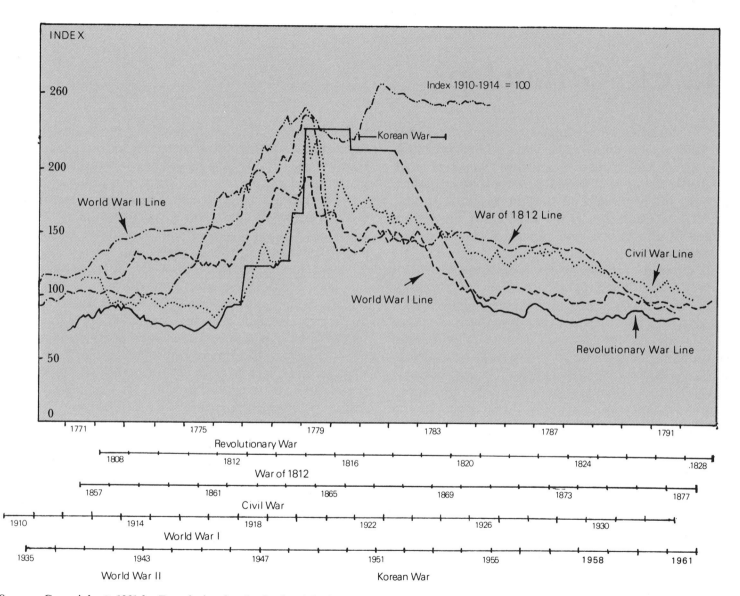

INDEX

Index 1910-1914 = 100

Korean War

World War II Line

War of 1812 Line

Civil War Line

World War I Line

Revolutionary War Line

Revolutionary War

War of 1812

Civil War

World War I

World War II

Korean War

56
No Place to Go but Up?

What are we to do now? Money market accounts no longer provide those juicy double-digit yields. The stock market is sky-high, and real estate has a negative cash flow. So where *aren't* prices sky-high? For an answer, as well as several other lessons, look at this chart. Just as movements straight up generally don't keep on forever (see Chart 18), most broad-based free-falling markets eventually stop falling and provide a chance to buy bargains almost for free.

The chart shows spot market prices of 23 commodities for the 5 years to mid-1986. These prices lost about 26 percent of their 1984 peak value. While that isn't the world's biggest decline, averaged out over the 23 different prices it's enough to raise eyebrows. Why? First, it argues strongly against the folks who, based on their lifetime's experience of ever-increasing inflation, expect still more inflation immediately ahead. As seen in Chart 51, inflation isn't a one-way street. Commodity prices are a key to measuring inflation potential. There has rarely if ever been a significant inflation that was not preceded by spiraling commodity prices. Why?

Commodity prices reflect the demand for the basic materials that fuel an economy. As goods are produced, inflation is built in via stages—starting with commodities, adding labor to create intermediate materials, and finally adding labor to create finished goods. It's a long way from the iron ore to a finished auto or tape measure. This chart reflects lackluster demand for goods in the marketplace. As long as commodity prices keep acting poorly, it is a sure sign the economy isn't strong, which means

there are none of the tight-economy conditions necessary for rapid inflation. So you can expect to see no major inflationary spiral in the coming months unless commodity prices first firm up and then go up.

Similarly, lots of folks claim that double-digit interest rates are also right around the corner. Hogwash! Here, too, weakness in commodity prices argues that interest rates won't show much strength in the immediate future. Will interest rates go down? That is less clear, but don't bet on steeply rising rates unless you first see a warning rise from commodities.

So, what's the answer to the initial question? Well, you might consider gold as an investment, since it's way down from its peak. But gold, too, as an inflation hedge will require a prior boost in commodity prices before it will really shine. Perhaps the answer is right in front of our faces. Basic commodities are the cheapest in years and are perhaps the contrarian's perfect dream. After two years of steadily falling prices, it is unlikely that commodity prices will keep falling much longer. Of course, it is next to impossible to buy something that seems to be in free-fall. The way many traders would handle this is to wait for "relative strength." They might measure this by daily figuring out the average price of the last 40 days. When the price finally pops above its 40-day moving average, they would get bullish.

Commodity Prices, 1982–1986

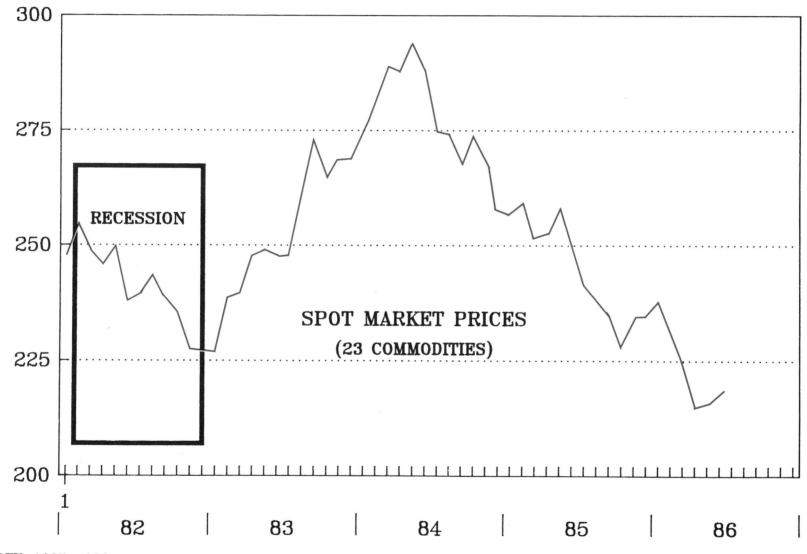

129

RECESSION

SPOT MARKET PRICES
(23 COMMODITIES)

INDEX: 1967 = 100

Source: Data from Commodity Research Bureau, a Knight–Ridder business information service.

57
Long-Term Gold Holders Get the Cold Shoulder

If you want to hedge against inflation, your best bet is gold, right? Hardly! Eyeball the next chart and match it to some others in this book. You'll see it differently—quickly.

At first glance, gold looks like a winner. We've just come through one of the worst inflationary cycles in history. In the decade of 1970–1980 alone, consumer prices more than doubled. Yet gold skyrocketed 2,400 percent (from $35 to $850 per ounce). That's an average compounded rate of 37 percent annually. It's no wonder scared money sees a lot of glitter in gold.

But the broader history of gold prices shows less sparkle. Dramatic surges in gold prices are few and far between; only three major peaks appear in 200 years—one during the Civil War, another after the Arab oil embargo, and the third during the double-digit inflation of 1980. Making matters worse, each of these three big bull markets lasted a brief 3.7 years on average, which means that over the 200 years, someone seeking an inflation hedge suffered 190 years of patient and profitless waiting.

What's the upshot? The long-term evidence suggests that gold does not provide great returns. Looking at the entire 200-year span from 1781 to 1981, gold appreciated at a paltry 1.58 percent per year. The appreciation to gold's peak in 1980 was only marginally better at 1.9 percent. How would you like to bank your retirement on that? Consider a more recent period, say, the 55 years from 1926 to 1981. This was gold's heyday, and it increased 5.77 percent annually, nicely beating the average 3 percent inflation rate and 3 percent rate of return from short-term Treasury bills (see Chart 12). Yet all the action came in ten years. In four out of every five years, you would have waited empty-handed. Meanwhile gold yielded 4 percent per year less than the average stock on the New York Stock Exchange—despite the Great Crash of 1929.

So it seems that all that glitters is not gold, and gold doesn't glitter brightest. Over 200 years, gold did well recently—but only briefly. Experiences of the last few decades should be discounted by gold's poorer longer-term record. If you want an inflation hedge, it seems that a buy-and-hold strategy with a diversified list of average stocks would have served you better and probably will again now. Since gold has had its few good and glittering years and they've mostly been recent, they are unlikely to come again soon. I'd look elsewhere.

This chart came from *Cycles* magazine, a great source for charts of all types. Note that the recent past is shown in greater detail. The right half of the chart covers 1955 to 1983, while the left half goes back to 1781.

200 Years of American Gold Prices, 1781–1981

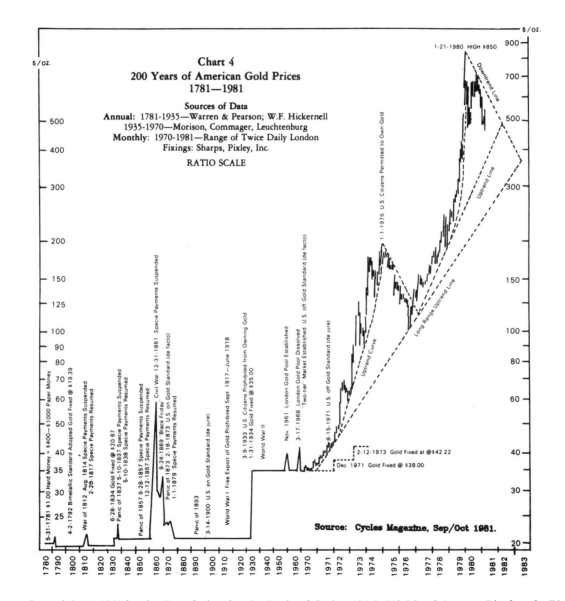

Chart 4
200 Years of American Gold Prices
1781—1981

Sources of Data
Annual: 1781-1935—Warren & Pearson; W.F. Hickernell
1935-1970—Morison, Commager, Leuchtenburg
Monthly: 1970-1981—Range of Twice Daily London
Fixings: Sharps, Pixley, Inc.

RATIO SCALE

Source: Cycles Magazine, Sep/Oct 1981.

58
The Long Cycle in Real Estate Activity

Does real estate have cycles? Yes, very definite ones; they're just longer than most folks' memories can grasp—and harder to see. The daily availability of stock prices and interest rates make financial markets emotionally volatile and short-term swings highly visible. The stock market is like a silent partner who is always offering to buy or sell your part of the business—an offer dangled in front of you like bait, luring you into stupid transactions. Not so with real estate—there is no daily bait.

Instead there is an 18-year sweeping Long cycle, named after Princeton's Clarence Long, who first wrote about them in 1940. This chart traces the Long cycles back to 1870. (Disregard the top part, which covers turf similar to Chart 62.) In your business lifetime, you might see two or three Long cycles at most, but you don't think of them as cycles. The wipe-outs seem like unique disasters that happened several times in your life.

Without stocklike daily prices and volume to help you envision these cycles, it helps to see them as cycles stacked on top of other cycles. First comes the Kondratieff wave (see Chart 84), which is the most powerful underlying force. Then stacked on top of and swinging around that fluctuating base is the Long cycle shown in this chart. These Long cycles are caused by the interplay of Kondratieff-generated interest-rate fluctuations and the satisfaction of generational demands for shelter. Finally, stacked on top of both these cycles and swinging around the Long cycle are the three- to four-year business cycles that we're used to seeing (often called Kitchen cycles, after Joe Kitchen).

We tend to notice only the Kitchen cycles. But they're at their most mild when the Kondratieff and Long cycles are both in the upswing, like in the late 1950s and early 1960s. They're at their most deadly when the Kondratieff and Long cycles are both in their down phases, like during 1928–1935 or 1873–1878.

You don't believe it? Most folks don't. But look at the predictive powers. This chart stops at 1960. The last cyclical peak it shows was 1945. The next peaks? Adding on 18-year increments gives us 1963 and 1981. Old-time real estate buffs know that the market stumbled badly starting in 1963. Since 1981, farm real estate has collapsed (see Chart 59), nonresidential real estate is in extreme overcapacity, and residential prices have stopped galloping ahead the way they were in the late 1970s. Why had prices soared so much since the early 1970s? Could it be the Long cycle? After the 1954 trough, adding 18 years would have put the next trough at 1972, after which this chart says that the Long cycle upswing should have started, which in fact seems to have happened.

What does this cycle predict for the future? The next Long cycle trough isn't until 1990, which means real estate has some bad years still coming—perhaps until 1992. Seeing that trend doesn't take much, particularly factoring in the current terrible changes in the tax law. But after that, the Long cycle predicts 10 boom years. So buy later, not now, and hold on for the golden 1990s.

Idealized 18⅓-Year Real Estate Cycle, 1870–1955

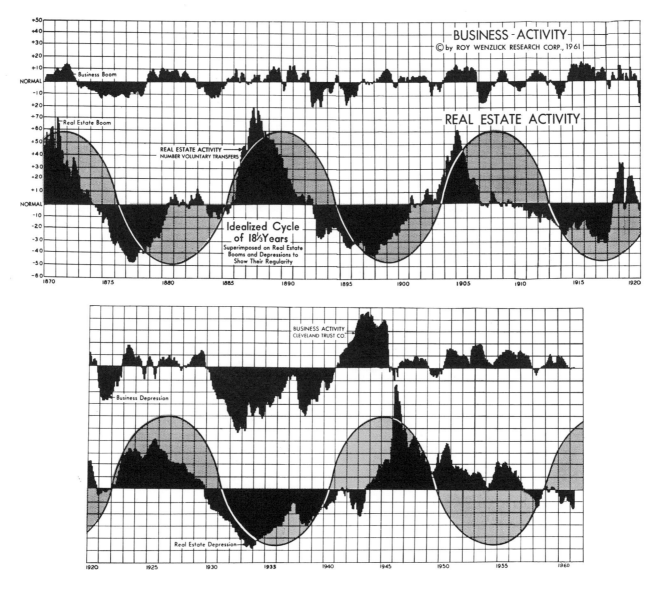

Source: Roy Wenzlick, Research Corp., St. Louis, MO.

59
Rural Real Estate: The True Story

I remember her telling me, "Real estate could only go one way." It was back in 1980, and everyone "knew" real estate was the one sure-shot investment. She was a financially ignorant older widow who was making a boodle buying real estate. The point, she assured me was that "you can't lose." My next-door neighbor accumulated millions, seemingly overnight, buying highly leveraged land.

A 19-year-old employee/laborer offered insights on where I could buy particularly choice, but undiscovered, pieces. Then he told me that Will Rogers once said, "Buy land; they ain't making any more of it." But he offered me a still better insight. His blathering reminded me that Bernard Baruch once said, "When beggars and shoeshine boys, barbers and beauticians can tell you how to get rich, it is time to remind yourself that there is no more dangerous illusion than the belief that one can get something for nothing."

While Will Rogers's quip may be amusing, buyers of raw land in recent years should have listened to Baruch. Before 1980 rural real estate had risen 15 percent annually for years—spurred on by strong farm-product pricing and spiraling inflation during the Nixon-Ford-Carter years. But just when the party got going good, somebody took away the punch.

This map shows the percentage change in agricultural land values for each state (and collectively for New England) for 1981–1985. As you can see, farm land values plummeted. This is a reasonable proxy for rural land in general. The Midwest Grain Belt, which is also referred to nowadays as the Rust Belt, has some of America's finest dirt, but values dropped more than 40 percent on average—49 percent in Iowa. Only four states posted gains. Only Texas showed a big gain, and even its 45 percent rise works out to less than 10 percent per year on a compounded basis. Whew!

As of this writing, with continued weak farm-product prices and government efforts to reduce crop price supports and loan programs, experts predict that farm real estate prices may not reach their 1981 blowoff peaks for decades. But why listen to them? They didn't warn us about 1981, so what makes them think they're right now? But one thing's for sure: I'd much rather buy rural real estate now, after a steep drop, than before it.

The bottom-line lesson to learn from this map is no more complicated than Baruch's wise words. Whenever everybody believes something will make them big bucks, it won't. Why? Quite simply, if everyone believes it, it means they've already spent their money on it (that happens awfully quickly), and there won't be enough additional buying to push prices still higher. For prices to go higher, there still have to be gobs of skeptics who will be converted to your way of thinking.

Change in Average Value of Farm Real Estate per Acre, 1981–1985

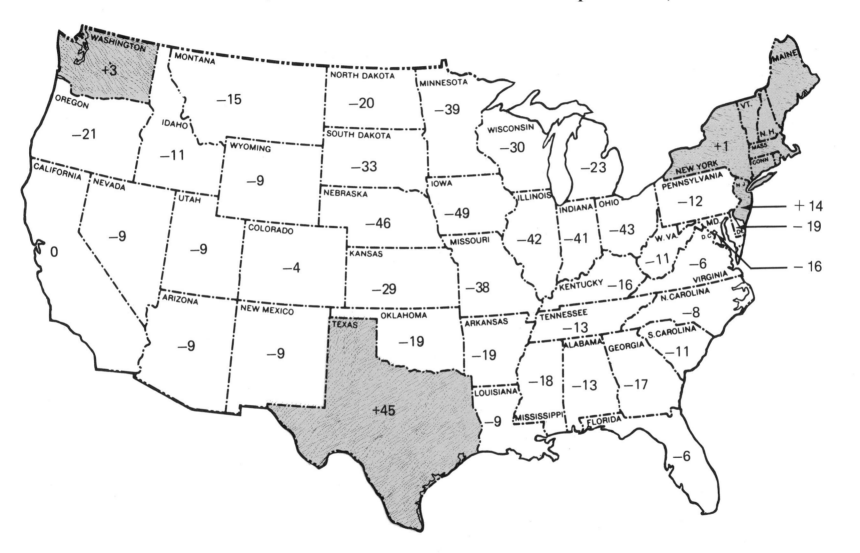

Source: U.S. Department of Agriculture, Economic Research Services, Agricultural Land Values, June 7, 1985.

60
And It Never Was, Either

So you accept that farm real estate was a disaster in recent years, but what about over the long term? Farm land hasn't been an above-average investment in any long-term time frame except the 1965–1980 superinflationary era. If you don't believe it, take a look at this chart. It shows the history of farm real estate prices from 1912 through 1975, both in nominal dollar terms and adjusted for inflation.

The index increased from about 82 in 1965 to about 220 in 1975. A quick pass with your trusty financial calculator indicates that to be an average annual increase of about 10.4 percent, which doesn't seem too bad. Of course, you actually wouldn't have done quite so well. First, when you sold your farm, you would have suffered a real estate commission—which is about 10 percent on raw land. So the 220 would have dropped to about 198 net to you, reducing your annual return to 9.2 percent. Then, throughout that time period, property taxes would have averaged about 1 percent per year of the property's asset value—which would drop your average annual return to about 8 percent. So the best period in history for farm real estate was worse as an investment than the average return on stocks over the last 60 years (see Chart 12).

The bigger picture looks worse. If you bought in 1912 at 25 and sold in 1975 at 220, and netted 198, your 63-year average annual return would have been only 3.3 percent—before property taxes. That's about equal to inflation or the rate of U.S. Treasury bills over the same time period (see Chart 10). Another way to see this is to look at the line that shows the trend in farm real estate prices in constant, 1967 dollars (meaning that prices have been adjusted for inflation). That shows almost no real, after-inflation appreciation at all, spanning a whole lifetime—and that's before property taxes.

But isn't that OK? Lots of folks want little more than an inflation hedge. The chart disproves that myth too. As a long-term inflation hedge, farm real estate was poor. If you had bought in 1912 and needed to sell in 1942, fully 30 years later, you would have lost a little more than 40 percent of your original purchasing power, before the effect of commissions and taxes. How long does somebody have to wait for a little inflation hedging? In this case it seems about 56 years, or until 1968.

Of course, if you factored in commissions and property taxes, you never would have been quite able to get back all your bait. And as a final kicker, to get that mediocre return, you would have had to suffer continual illiquidity. The nice thing about fixed-income securities (Treasury bills and bonds), which yielded very similar average annual returns over the decades, or stocks, which did much better, is that you could have cashed in your chips any old time you wanted to.

So, my conclusion is: If you want to make an above-average return on your money, take a lesson from history and don't try to do it with raw land. You're apt to end up with a raw deal. Farm real estate isn't your best bet over the long-term, and it never was either.

Trend in U.S. Farm Real Estate Prices, 1912–1976

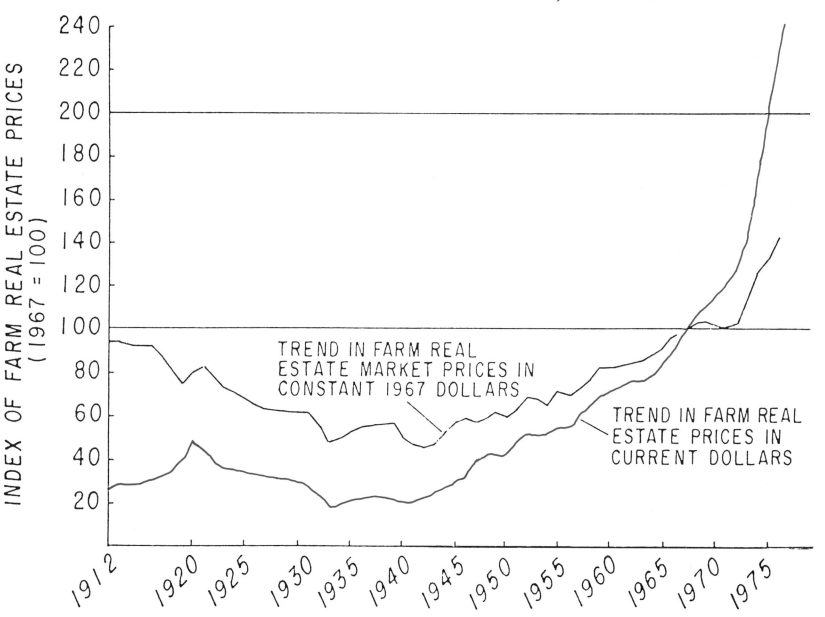

Source: Raleigh Barlowe, *Land Resource Economics: The Economics of Real Estate,* Englewood Cliffs, New Jersey: Prentice-Hall, Inc., 1978.

61
U.S. Housing Prices

At least I know my house has been a good deal—right? Maybe. Few folks understand that most of their gain came from borrowing money, not price appreciation. This chart (which uses numbers from the U.S. Department of Commerce) shows the average price of an American home from 1885 through 1980. On first glance, it looks great. The index rose from 60 in 1935 to 1,000 in 1980. But looks are deceiving, so here's what you should learn always to do. Get your financial calculator and compute the compound annual increase involved in that rise since 1935. Believe it or not, that seemingly huge move from 60 to 1,000 is a compound return of less than 6.5 percent per year—hardly the greatest imaginable. You could have done much better on the New York Stock Exchange (Chart 12).

Perhaps you recall making much more than that with your home? Maybe you forgot that you only put up about 20 percent to buy your home and borrowed the rest via your mortgage? So, in your mind you didn't pay 60 in 1935, you paid 12. The important point to remember, which a generation learned in the 1930s and has been largely forgotten ever since, is that mortgages must be paid off. They provide potential for greater returns, but only by providing comparably greater risks. If for any reason the value of your home falls, as home prices did between 1925 and 1935, you can get stuck with interest payments and a big fat loss.

Imagine buying a house in 1925, which our index says cost about 100. You put up 20 and borrow 80. You pay interest each year. But in the early years, very little of an amortized loan contributes to principal repayment. So, by the mid-1930s, you still owe just about 80. By then your home's value had dropped to 60. Remember, you still owe 80. So your homeowner's equity is −20. It would have taken you until the late 1940s just to break even—not counting all the interest payments you would have made over the years.

And who would have believed that those falling home prices could have occurred over two decades when interest rates were generally dropping? Just a great investment! In fact, if your grandma had bought in 1885, priced at 60, your folks held on for 95 years, and you sold in 1980, priced at 1,000, without any adjustment for commissions or property taxes, your 95-year average annual return would have been only 3.0 percent.

How is all this relevant today? Home prices are high. Rents are minuscule if you think of them as a yield relative to the home's market value—far less on average than you could get in the bank. And contrary to the fantasies of some real estate jocks (those that don't understand how long-term bonds get priced—see text for Chart 33), rents don't rise to match real estate prices. The prices fall to match rents. Just like bonds, real estate prices must swing to make rental yields compete with other alternatives in the long-term. With real estate values far from bargain-basement levels and few people seeming to understand that mortgages can wipe you out the way they wiped out legions of folks in the 1930s, it is a particularly good time to remember that real estate prices offered no appreciation from 1890 until 1935 and that it could happen again—or worse.

Single Family House Price Index, 1890–1980

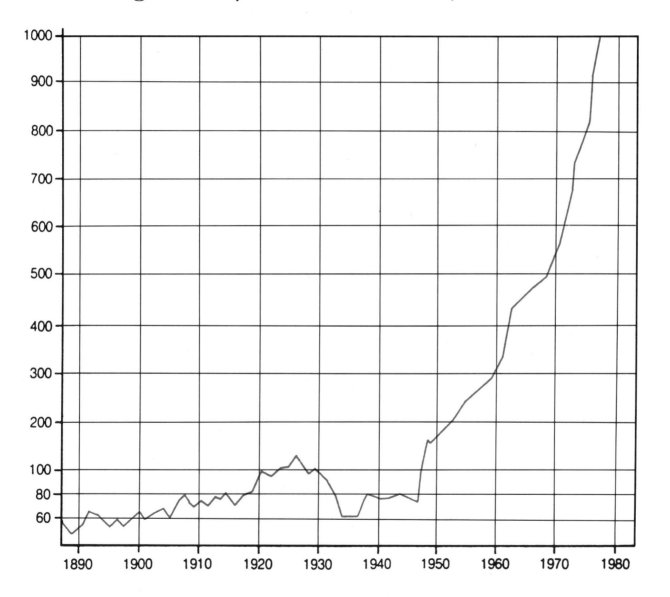

Source: Douglas Casey, *Strategic Investing*, New York: Simon & Schuster, 1982.

PART 3
ANALYZING BUSINESS CYCLES, GOVERNMENT FINANCE, AND QUACKERY

It always amazes me how much unfounded financial mythology pervades human minds, both in social interaction and through the media. Folks flap their jaws without first checking to see if the "facts" they're repeating are even close to being true. Charts can provide a quick visual check on whether the herd's blatherings have any basis in fact, or are merely restatements of accepted mythology. The charts in this part illustrate business phenomena, government finances, and some of the perceived quackery that divides what we accept as fact from what we don't. The charts help provide a clear visual perspective of facts that allow you a better grasp on reality.

There may be no subject that generates more myth and mindless hysteria than government finance. Politicians have a vested interest in pushing mistruths to seek election. The media focuses on sensationalism to sell copy. And we mindlessly pass on what we hear to liven our cocktail parties. It's no wonder that the guy on the street believes the myths he is exposed to. He hears it from all quarters. After all, if everyone says it's so, isn't it likely to be? Bah humbug. This part's nine visual perspectives on government finance cover issues ranging from debt to taxes, deficits, government spending, growth of government, the states versus Uncle Sam, and more.

The Debt and the Deficit

For instance, you will see at a glance that the federal debt "crisis" is a problem, but a minor one—certainly not a real crisis, not even close. The best way to think about the issue is how much debt Uncle Sam has versus his income and net worth. By these measures, Uncle Sam's debt is within comfortable historical averages. For example, you will learn that although federal debt as a percentage of GNP is higher than 10 years ago, that only brings the ratio back to where it was in the mid-1960s and leaves it far lower than in the mid-1950s, and about a third of what it was in the mid-1940s. If we could afford those kinds of debt burdens then, things aren't as bleak they seem now.

In fact, you will even come to suspect that repaying the federal debt may not be the world's best idea. It's already been done once and resulted in one of our three worst depressions ever. As shown in Chart 76, stalwart Andy Jackson repaid the federal debt, which led to a major financial panic and seven steady years of economic decline. Yet you will learn from Chart 82 that if we really want to pay off Uncle Sam's debt, we can do it without raising taxes—the same way Andy Jackson did. How's that? Turn to Chart 82 and read about how Uncle Sam built the world's most valuable real estate portfolio, all financed by 150 years of debt and inflation.

You will also come to see clearly that the much-discussed deficit isn't as crucial as most folks imagine. It may not even exist. If you take out the $100 billion transfer payments Uncle Sam makes to the states and municipalities (funding their $100 billion surplus) and let Uncle Sam depreciate the assets he buys the way a corporation does, you would have vaporized most of the federal deficit without changing a thing. Is that just creative accounting? No, actually it's rather realistic accounting. As you will see in Chart 82, the asset purchases Uncle Sam made over the last two centuries contributed to deficits and the federal debt but are today worth trillions of dollars.

Ironically, while few speak of it, the real fear, instead of deficits and debt, should be the growth rate in federal spending. If Uncle Sam's yearly spending keeps growing as much faster than GNP in the future as it did over the last 20 years, it will take less than 100 years of that relatively higher compound growth rate for Uncle Sam to have taken over the whole economy.

Antibusiness Myths

The world of everyday business has long generated myths, too. As great fortunes are amassed, folks portray the amassers as superhumanly skilled, or devilishly corrupt, or of some other sensational but unrealistic character. Usually they are just people, with all the human strengths and weaknesses of normal folks—hard-working, determined, and intelligent but also lucky—in the right place at the right time. Their businesses are portrayed unrealistically, too—too good or too bad.

But it has always been that way. As you saw in Chart 36, excesses have come and gone for hundreds of years. In my firm's library sits a first printing of Teddy Roosevelt's original *Square Deal*. Close by is a copy of Robert Welch's original "bluebook" of the John Birch Society. Ironically, Welch's zealous conservative rhetoric sounds more moderate than Roosevelt's turn-of-the-century anti-business "yellow journalism," but much of Roosevelt's attitude can be found in antibusiness myths today.

For example, in recent years a widely accepted myth says that business hasn't expanded brick and mortar, but instead has gone on a binge of acquisition and merger. Well, the merger-and-acquisition binge is real enough (as you saw in Chart 21), but business is also spending record amounts on bricks and mortar—not only in absolute terms, but also as a percent of privately produced GNP. You can see the historic figures since 1900 in Chart 68. Then if you don't accept my updates of them, you can look them up for yourself at the library in Value Line, the Conference Board (part of the Department of Commerce), or the original source of Chart 68, the Machinery and Allied Products Institute, which publishes a newsletter called *Capital Goods Review*, which includes this kind of data (1200 18th St. N.W., Washington, D.C. 20036).

Likewise, the last decade's media have portrayed those in the oil business as bad guys and electronics leaders as the bright new breath of fresh air in a bad-smelling environment of dying American industry. There is some truth but more myth to all of that. Charts 71–73 should demonstrate another aspect of the saying that there has been nothing new of importance in the last few hundred years. Take the supposedly "new" learning curve that propelled electronics pioneers to greatness; you'll learn it's hardly new. Likewise, the oil industry was more a victim of politics and foreign powers than a perpetrator of evil. But it's hard to get most folks to consider such things.

For example, another myth that floats around is that labor is overpaid. That's silly (see Chart 70). On a long-term historical basis, adjusted for inflation, labor isn't overpaid. When folks complain that labor is overpaid, they are just demonstrating their own inability to figure out how to use labor productively. In a sense, they are demonstrating their own ignorance and incompetence. The problem isn't the cost of labor, but the brains of management.

Then, there is the recent outcry over foreign investments in South Africa. Some folks raise apartheid as an issue, while others are concerned over the value of South Africa's production of precious metals. This book doesn't deal with moral issues, but Chart 69 lets you see clearly that the real value of South Africa's gold mining isn't a pimple off the S&P 500's back. If South Africa as a whole went down the tubes tomorrow, the rest of us would belch, yawn, and go on.

Quackery Charts

Unfortunately the human race is often more sure of knowing things it really doesn't know than it is willing to admit that there are an awful lot of unexplainable phenomena. This part's last nine charts are what I call "quackery" charts. Most folks would view these subjects as quackery. I hope by the time you've read them that you perceive some quackery, but also some substance. For instance, the Kondratieff wave is much disdained by main-stream economists, most of whom won't even discuss it seriously. But, as you intuitively and correctly know, most economists aren't good at economic forecasting either. Yet most forecasters would have done much better in recent years if they had incorporated the theories of this long wave into their thinking. As you've seen throughout this book, there have been tremendous coincidences among these supposedly quackish long waves. Perhaps economic forecasting is about where explorers were when they thought the world was flat. Forecasters know a lot, but not nearly enough to do their job well.

Perhaps an even stronger example of this phenomenon can be found with sunspots. The evidence of sunspots profoundly affecting agriculture, aerospace, communications, and much more is beyond doubt (see Chart 85). Yet no one even knows why sunspots exist or how they're caused. It is known that sunspot cycles correspond perfectly with variations in the quantities of differing forms of atmospheric radiation bombarding us all. So, is it impossible that sunspots, or whatever causes them, might also affect our emotional mentality and thereby our financial decisions—either directly or indirectly through radiation levels?

Unfortunately, Christopher Columbus may be as able to answer that as anyone alive. Someday scientists may discover the cause of sunspots and further learn of links between the sun and Wall Street. Meanwhile notions like sunspots are unthinkingly accepted by some, and closed-mindedly rejected by most. Sunspots are one of the best reminders around of how little humans actually know. If you're operating to a significant degree out of ignorance, which is always the case on Wall Street, at least you're more likely to do well if you understand your ignorance.

Still, there are useful phenomena for business-cycle analysis, and a few can be charted. Unfortunately, the best predictor of the economy is the direction of stock prices (see Chart 16). It is unfortunate because many folks want to predict the economy so they can then predict stock prices, but it doesn't work that way. What works in terms of tying the economy and stock market together is the 1 percent rule (see Chart 64), which states that the market will soar shortly after unemployment has stopped falling, and in turn will rise by one full percentage point. Folks will also do well to pay attention to auto sales, because as Chart 65 shows, drops in auto sales have preceded most downtrends in both the economy and the stock market.

Putting It in Perspective

To put everything in perspective, this section starts off with two charts showing an overview of the long-term history of business—not only in the United States, but also around the world. The first one is a classic, naming American booms and busts and giving a visual perspective of their magnitudes. Probably you've seen it before. The second, rare chart (Chart 63) is one you won't have seen. It details the tremendous tendency of the Western nations to be tied together economically. Booms and busts have been worldwide since the days before computers, telephones, airplanes, and Dow Jones Industrials.

If you merely learn the lesson of Chart 63, this whole book will have been worth your while. We continue to believe that economic tinkering through the political process can enable us to avoid economic snags. But if the world's countries are economically tied together, it can't make sense for a country's politicians to take credit for prosperity or blame for recessions. We can't avoid worldwide recessions; we've never been able to and won't be able to. Scratch one more myth. Hopefully you can use what you learn from these charts to unravel a few more myths of your own.

62
The One Minute Economic Cheat Sheet

Do you feel insecure? Are you unable to blurt out that key phrase that makes you the hit of the cocktail circuit? If so, this chart is perfect for you. It's a one-minute cheat sheet of American economic history. With it you can stun your friends and dazzle acquaintances.

Your brother-in-law is on the phone badgering your wife into splurging from Dear Old Dad's trust. He wants her to take a flyer on raw Florida real estate that "can only go one way." She's beside herself. She's afraid of blowing the bucks but also never was able to turn down her big brother. Decisively, you step into the cauldron by pulling out your cheat sheet and picking up the phone. "Ed, I've thought long and hard about this. The similarities are just too great. Unless you can convince me that I'm wrong about how much this economy parallels what went on during the Bank Credit Boom of the 1830s, I'm gonna have to lean on Suzy real hard to avoid raw land right now. I'll send you one of my old economic history texts on it—then get back to us." Ed will never call you again, and to Suzy, you're her hero.

You're at a cocktail party, and some bozo is prattling on about how well his firm has done and the oodles of money he is raking in. Someone turns to you and belches through his gin fizz, "Poindexter, how're things for you lately?" You think back to your chart, then chime in, "Well, John, we've been doing swimmingly well ourselves, but I've been consciously trying to avoid a swelled head. You know, this whole time period reminds me of those easy-profit days of the Industrial Overexpansion Prosperity back in the early 1870s. And you know what hap-

pened after that." Of course, he doesn't—which gives you the perfect final shot: "Just about the longest depression ever—almost as bad as the 1930s—so I've been coining money, but I'm also devising strategies to avoid losing it, too." Two points for you.

I first saw an earlier version of this chart as a kid and was awed by its panorama covering 190 years. It reveals two characteristics. First, the index noted by the red line shows wholesale prices. The shaded areas show a subjective economic perception of good times versus bad. The shaded areas above the "long-term trend" line show periods of economic prosperity. The areas below the line show depressions and recessions.

The graph isn't quite realistic for recent periods. The 1973–1975 and 1982–1983 recessions, which don't show up below the trend line, were at least as significant as many of the others that do show up below the line (like the Rich Man's Panic of 1903–1904). But, for covering what most people think of as ancient history, this legendary chart is fabulous. Not one person in ten knows anything about what happened before 1928. And virtually no one is ready to expose his or her ignorance; society just doesn't tolerate it. Couple this chart with a few minor trivia tidbits picked up elsewhere throughout this book (see Chart 45 for an example), and you ought to be able to snow almost anybody, anywhere. Have fun. You might even find it's fun learning about some of these events along the way. I certainly did.

American Business Activity, 1790–1986

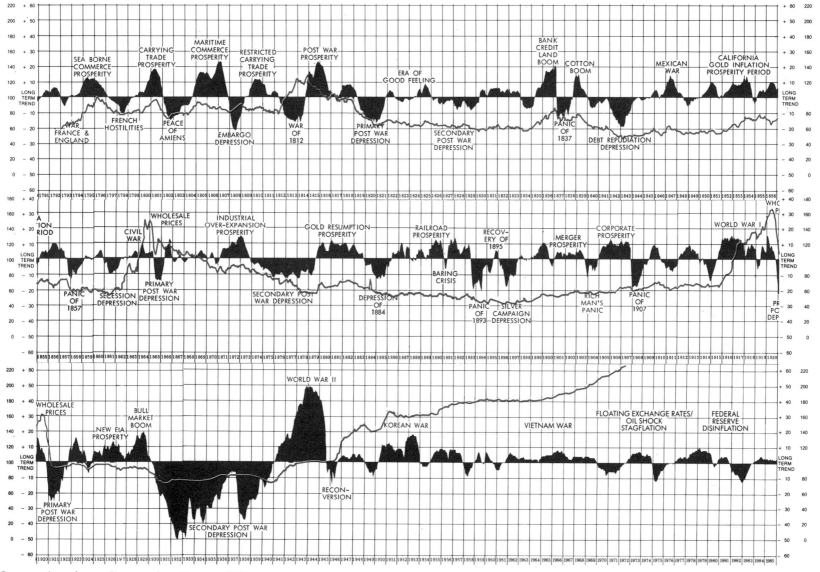

Source: Ameritrust Corporation, January 1986.

63
What Do You See in This Pattern?

No, this chart isn't an ink blot test, but the folks who see lots in ink blots may be the first to learn its lesson. It sure popped my eyeballs when I stumbled on it. It's important for three reasons. First, it's a one-of-a-kind, at-a-glance, thumb-nail, long-term overview of the Western world's business cycles. Second, it is from the earliest authoritative source on world economics, Wesley C. Mitchell's 1927 classic, *Business Cycles*, the 10th-ever book by the National Bureau of Economic Research (NBER). The NBER is the official U.S. scorekeeper for recessions, expansions, and the like. Mitchell was its founder, and for 25 years its director of research, also former president of the American Statistical Association and generally credited for first standardizing economic statistics. Almost without doubt, had Mitchell survived until 1970, he would have been the first Nobel Laureate in Economics instead of Simon Kuznets. GNP accounting work couldn't have existed without Mitchell's prior groundwork. Finally, the chart is important because of its visual lesson.

Looking at the chart, you can learn the lesson without paying much attention to detail. All you really need to see is that it describes the major Western countries, and each different shade represents some different economic event. Notice how most shades line up, neatly stacked on top of each other—the blacks mostly on top of the blacks, the whites mostly on the whites, etc. Whatever happened in one country tended to also be happening in most other countries.

That's the lesson. You hear that a little more in the media these days, but this source shows you it always was that way. So it probably always will be.

Economic declines (the black and gray areas) are usually worldwide. Sure, someone has to get the bug first, and some resist its effects a bit longer. Some suffer worse, while others suffer less badly. But almost everyone, worldwide, catches the economic flu once it starts going around.

Folks have trouble believing this. They want to believe we can do it our own way here and buck the trend. Few ever have. Even most economic theory argues that one country shouldn't be too affected by the rest of the world. Of course, economists haven't been good economic forecasters, and obviously history argues more authoritatively than theory.

As is preached elsewhere in this book, no country is an economic island. There are two tremendous ironies. One is that when one country has tried drastic measures to buck the trend, it usually has suffered even worse. The other is that politicians usually claim credit for economic expansions that were almost always worldwide in the making, yet blame declines on foreign events. Politicians can do almost nothing to avoid a recession once it starts rolling around the world. I wish they wouldn't even try. But the lesson for investors is "keep an ear to the ground" for any divergence between what is happening around the globe and at home (see Chart 42). Expect the home front, financial markets and all, to follow the foreigner's lead.

Conspectus of Business Cycles in Various Countries, 1790–1925

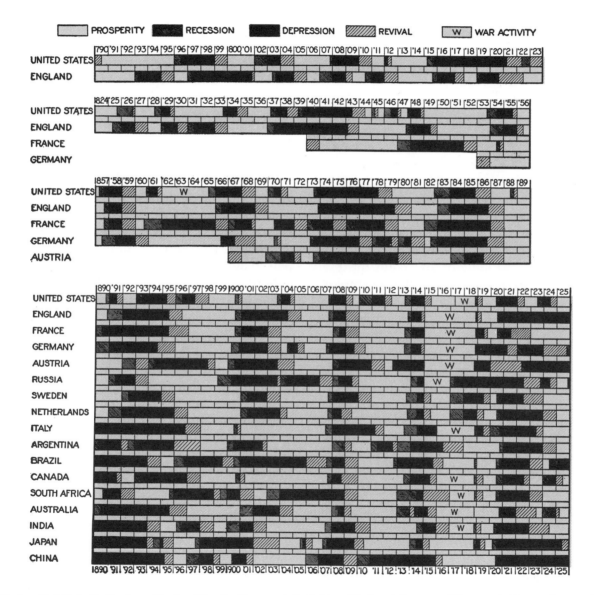

Source: Wesley C. Mitchell, *Business Cycles, The Problem and its Setting*, National Bureau of Economic Research, New York, 1927.

64
Unemployment and the 1 Percent Rule

There has been a historically tight relationship between the stock market and economic recessions (see Chart 25). But there has also been a tight relationship between unemployment and recessions. So, with a twist, you can use unemployment as a nifty warning signal of major buy signs. Here's how.

This chart shows the unemployment rate against a backdrop where periods of economic recession are shaded red. The white sections represent economic expansions. The unemployment rate is defined to be those seeking jobs divided by the total of all employed workers and job seekers. Notice that unemployment falls during expansions and rises during recessions. That may not surprise you. But notice how evenly unemployment rises and falls throughout recessions. For instance, there is not a single case of unemployment rising a full percentage point during an expansion (see left-hand scale). But it regularly rises at least one full percentage point during the first two-thirds of a recession. In contrast, as you see in Chart 25, the market drops before a recession begins; by the time the recession is halfway over, the stock market is already anticipating a better future and soaring upward.

This leads to my "1 percent" rule, which states: If you want to benefit from a major stock market bottom, you had better be fully invested whenever the unemployment rate has just risen one full percentage point. While neither this indicator, nor any other, will perfectly predict market bottoms, the 1 percent rule gets you in the ball park and tells you almost perfectly what inning of the game it is. It places you within a couple of months of the absolute bottom. You will need other tools to fine tune the location of a bottom, but this indicator is a good start.

Another way to say this is that cyclical stock market lows haven't happened without first having a one-point rise in the unemployment rate. A good example is 1970. The market had been falling since December 1968. Unemployment had been falling since 1961, but started rising sharply as 1970 began, which was the warning sign to take note. It rose the full one percentage point by spring. The Dow Jones Industrials hit bottom at 627 on May 26. If you bought using the 1 percent rule, you would be smiling. On your own, you can compare this with the other bottoms of the stock market cycle.

The unemployment rate won't tell you when a market top has occurred. It's less precise for market peaks than it is in relation to troughs. This is because the stock market leads the economy and starts falling long before economic weakness develops—weakness that generates increased unemployment. But you can also see in this chart not to expect a major stock market peak until after unemployment has fallen for at least two years. Where can you find the unemployment rate? Among other places, it's on the back page of *Barron's* every week.

Unemployment Rate for Civilian Workers 1948–1983 (seasonally adjusted)

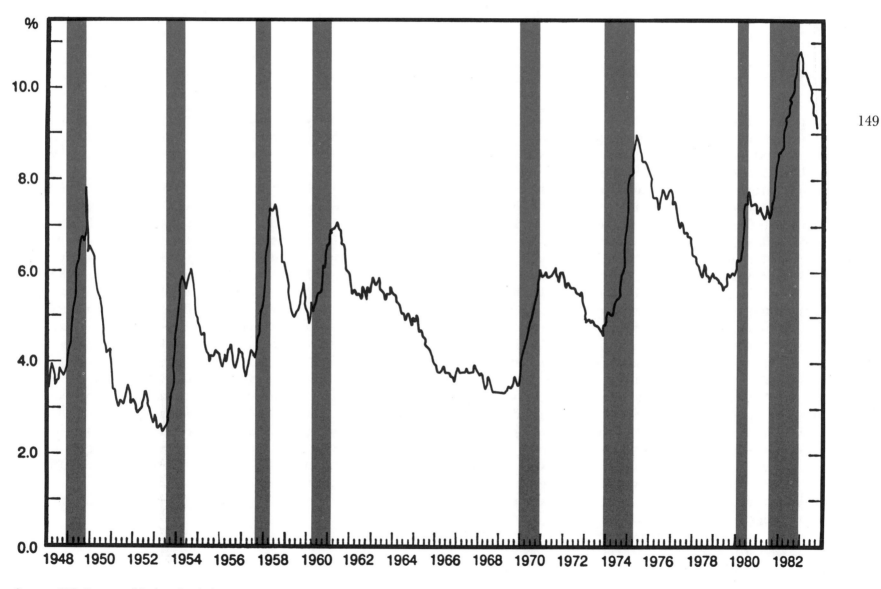

149

Source: U.S. Bureau of Labor Statistics.

65
Cars Crash, Too!

"Watch out! It's going to crash!" That could refer to the market or to a car ride. But when car sales crash, stocks are probably right behind them, and after that the whole economy. As shown in Chart 25, stocks do a good job of forecasting the economy. But as this chart illustrates, so do auto sales, and they tie pretty well to the stock market, too. Again, as with Chart 25, and several other charts throughout this book, the shaded areas represent the periods when the economy was in recession.

Note that auto sales always seem to drop before the economy does—usually by quite a while. Only in 1960 did auto sales fail to fall long in advance of a recession. The 1981–1982 lead time was short too, but how could it not be? It came right on the heels of 1980's recession. Why do declines in auto sales precede a recession? Autos cost a lot and last for years. Most folks can't pay cash for them but borrow instead. In a recession, people are economically scared, and few stick their necks out far enough to buy cars. As their cars age, and they see ads about how a hot new car would make them a hit, pent-up auto demand rises. As the economy heats up, folks feel less afraid, and let loose that pent-up demand—usually all at about the same time.

In a while, two things happen. First, most of the folks who have long dreamed about a new car will have done their thing and blown their wad. Second, since auto buyers are among the worst credit risks (relative to IBM or mortgage borrowers), as the expansion matures and interest rates rise, many potential car buyers who still want to buy get cut off from credit. These two forces cause auto sales to plummet. But the economy won't go into a tailspin yet, because folks just shift from cars to buying relatively cheap nondurables, like clothes, and luxury items. (Note that economic recoveries are not foreshadowed by rising auto sales.)

But the best part is how the direction of auto sales has matched the market's movements. Auto sales peaked in 1950; the market peaked in 1952. Auto sales peaked in 1955; the market peaked in 1956. Autos peaked in 1959, and so did the market. It happened again in 1965 (both without a recession), and 1968, and 1972. In 1976 it didn't work. The market peaked 18 months before auto sales. But, as you see repeatedly, nothing works perfectly in the market. Again in 1981 they peaked together.

What's the lesson? When auto sales are rising, don't expect to see stocks fall much. And when stocks do fall, check to see whether auto sales are dropping to verify that the plunge is long-lasting and deep. You can get figures on auto sales weekly in *Barron's*. As these words are written, many value-oriented stock market indicators in this book are bearish, but auto sales are still booming, buoyed by falling interest rates and financing from auto makers at below-market interest rates. Along with falling interest rates, auto sales provide a ray of hope on which stock market optimists can base their faith.

New Auto Sales, Domestic Type (excluding imports), 1945–1983

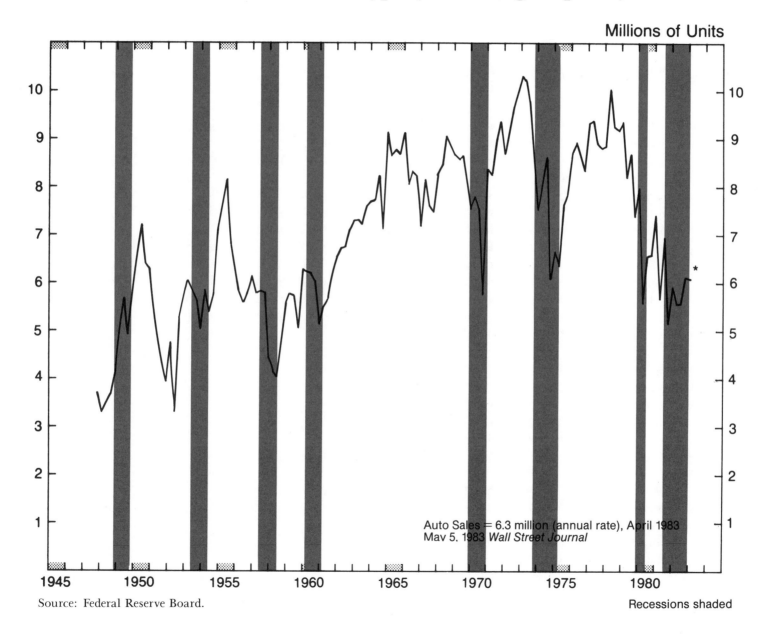

Millions of Units

Auto Sales = 6.3 million (annual rate), April 1983
May 5, 1983 *Wall Street Journal*

Source: Federal Reserve Board.

Recessions shaded

66
Housing Starts: An Inverted Look

How do you forecast the economy? One way is to get perverse and look at housing starts upside down. When they've been up for a while, look for the economy to get worse for a while. When housing starts have been down for a while, look for a rosier world. What are housing starts, and why should you consider them? Housing starts are the number of new houses and house-equivalent apartment units being erected at any time. Housing starts swing in cycles and are an important part of the overall economy. It's hard for business to be strong if housing is falling apart, and it's hard for housing to be strong for more than a few years in a row. The market just gets overbuilt. The economy regularly burns out, and when housing starts have been rising two or three years in a row, the whole economy is usually tired and ready for some time off. Watch out.

This is particularly true when housing starts reach 2 million per year. This chart shows housing starts from 1950 through 1979. It also shows real residential fixed investment (RRFI), which tells the same story in a more complicated and confusing way. So, forget RRFI. Housing starts show a clear enough picture. Look at the big peak in housing starts in 1972 and 1973—more than 2 million starts per year. Then remember 1974, which had the worst of all postwar recessions and followed right on the heels of these high numbers of housing starts. The 1977–1978 period of robust housing starts led into the period that created the term *stagflation*, meaning a stagnant economy drenched in rampant inflation. Just seeing housing starts rise for several years, and particularly reaching the level of 2 million starts would have been enough to tip off astute observers to trouble ahead.

What's been happening more recently? You can look in the back of *Barron's* each week and get the current annualized level of housing starts. They've been rising since 1983 and by early 1986 were back up to the 2 million level. This is ominous for the 1987 and 1988 economies.

This graph came from the *New England Economic Review*, published by the Federal Reserve Bank of Boston. The graph is derived from data published by the U.S. Department of Commerce in its Survey of Current Business. You can also get housing-start numbers directly from this source at your library.

Housing Starts and Real Residential Fixed Investment, 1950–1979

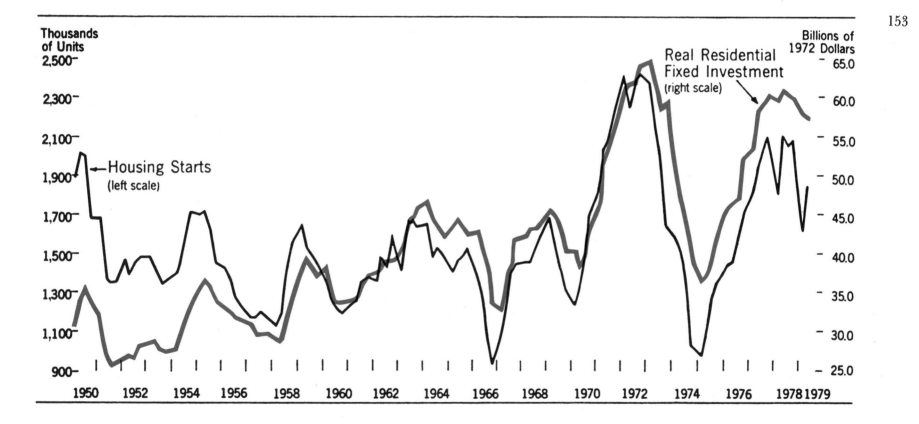

Source: *New England Economic Review*. Federal Reserve Bank, Boston, 1979.

67
Breadlines in Britain

Most people think that until just recently unemployment was minimal—except during the 1930s. That may be correct if you only look back through the 1920s. But it isn't if you think back further. During the later 19th century, when England dominated the world economically and militarily, unemployment came and went like a yo-yo. As shown here, English unemployment hit 7 percent regularly and several times was at 10 and 11 percent—high even compared to the United States' recent past.

This 1929 chart came from A. C. Pigou's book, *Industrial Fluctuations*. Pigou was at Cambridge and was perhaps the preeminent English economist of his period, just before the so-called Keynesian revolution. His book charts a world little regarded and mostly forgotten today. But English economic history is significant to the present because England's late-19th-century position shared elements in common with today's world.

As the recent U.S. unemployment rate reached records for any period since the 1930s, it helps to remember commonalities with England and its cyclic unemployment. First, remember that England was the driving force in the Western world, as the United States is today. U.S. trade makes up half the free world's trade, as did England's then. Other countries base their central banks' monetary reserves on U.S. Treasury bills, as they did then with English consols.

Most important, note the huge swing in unemployment in Pigou's chart. As shown in Charts 47 and 49, English commodity prices and interest rates weren't particularly volatile relative to other countries, so why the yo-yo-like unemployment swings?

Other countries exported their unemployment to England. As England maintained its gold standard, its currency value was relatively fixed—like a sitting duck. Whenever the world economy declined, other countries aimed for a piece of England's international trade by devaluing their currencies via inflation to make their products more price-competitive internationally. Of course, that only works for a while. In time, the inflating country's inflation winds back into higher costs—but in the short term, printing money is a good way to boost international demand for your products and thereby boost your employment at the expense of the sitting duck.

Today the United States is the sitting duck. It isn't all inflation now. It's partially federally subsidized loans for Japanese companies. It's nationalized companies that don't have to make a profit and can sell ultracheap. And it is inflation, too. Everyone outside the United States knows that the only way to keep their unemployment low is to export it to the United States as fast as possible. So, in a recession like 1982, the U.S. dollar rises in value relative to other countries' currencies. Then, in a recovery, like the recent one, the dollar and unemployment eventually drop back.

The upshot? Although the dollar is down recently and unemployment is back down to 6 percent, expect them both to skyrocket again when the next economic downturn arrives—and other countries try to "duck out" on their own jobless rates. The only alternative is for the United States to outgun them with inflation, which, based on past experiences, is just as bad.

English Unemployment, 1850–1914

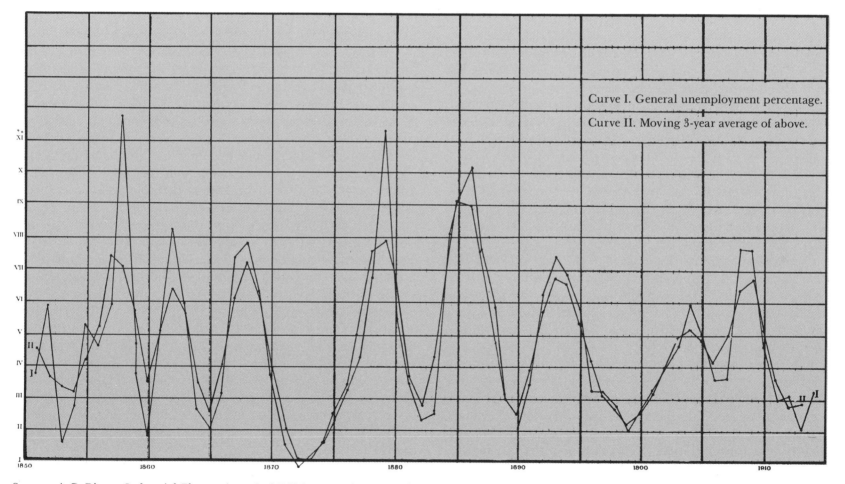

Curve I. General unemployment percentage.

Curve II. Moving 3-year average of above.

Source: A.C. Pigou, *Industrial Fluctuations*, 2nd Edition, London: Macmillan & Co., Ltd., 1929.

68
A Capital Spending Myth

Everyone knows big business is more interested in continuing its merger-and-acquisition binge than building basic plants; it's spending much less than it used to—right? This is another of the many myths the media perpetrate on us. Actually, business has been pushing harder than ever before to build plants.

This chart of 1900 through 1960 shows spending for business plant and equipment as a percentage of privately produced GNP (the part of GNP other than the government's portion). At a glance you'll see that for 60 years, except during the Great Depression and World War II, business never spent more than 10 percent nor less than 7 percent of nongovernmental GNP on increasing its productive base through capital spending. So this chart gives a long-term benchmark against which we can compare present activity.

Capital spending in 1985 was $476 billion—up from $163 billion 10 years ago. Adjusted for 7.5% annual inflation during the decade, that $163 billion would turn it into about $337 billion in 1980 dollars. So the $476 billion really is an inflation-adjusted increase of about 3.5 percent per year, which is more than the economy's real growth.

But the real test is to compare capital spending against this 60-year chart. If business spends more now in relation to GNP than during the average of those heyday years, then we know business is now spending plenty. According to the U.S. budget, nongovernmental GNP is about $2.9 trillion, of which $476 billion is a whopping 16 percent, much higher than in any year before 1960. Actually business is now spending more than 12 percent of total GNP, including the government's part.

Why is spending so high? The inflation that started ramping up in the 1960s made it ever easier for producers to justify building plants. Inflation generated high prices for finished goods, and projections of ever-further inflation allowed managers to start building plants based on economic assumptions of current capital costs—coupled with future high prices for products. The result was big potential profits from building plants.

Despite recent price weakness, most of the managers running America's big companies are in their 50s and 60s and were raised in an environment of ever more inflation. These are the people who bet on more inflation all their lives, always won, and were promoted in their companies based on their successes. They're still betting on more inflation, and they're doing it the same way they did when they climbed the corporate ladder—by voting to add more capacity.

Ironically, in 1987 we are in the fifth year of the economic expansion that began in 1982, yet the economy is operating well under 80 percent of capacity—exactly because these managers keep building too much capacity. Excess capacity leads to nothing but falling prices (see Charts 56 and 84), which could lead to more serious problems of deflation. It is surely ironic that business is spending too much money adding plant and capacity just when most of the media are reporting that business is lax on capital spending.

Expenditures for Business Plant and Equipment as a Percentage of the Privately Produced Gross National Product, 1900–1960

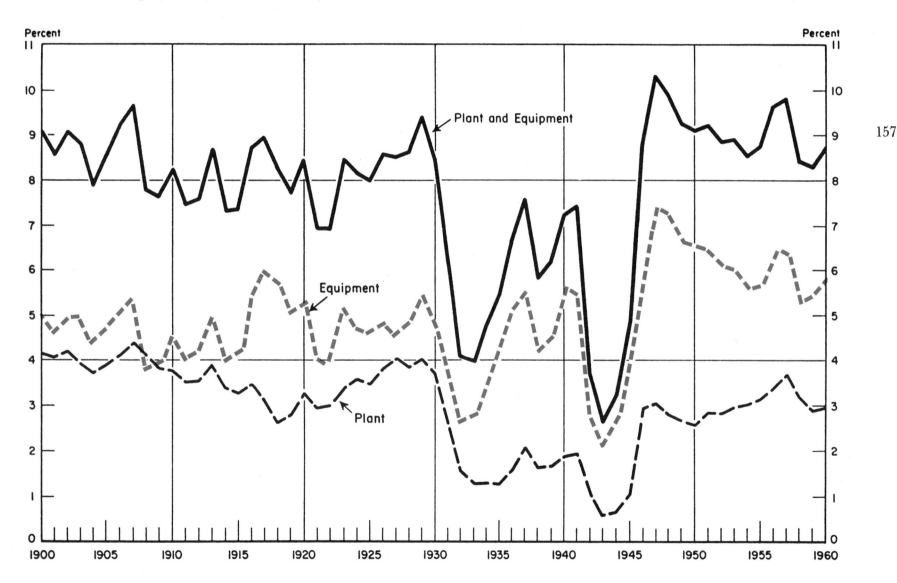

157

Source: George Terborgh, *60 Years of Business Capital Formation*. Reproduced by permission of the publisher, Machinery and Allied Products Institute, 1200 18th Street, N.W., Washington, D.C. copyright 1960.

69
South Africa Gold: How Important?

Is South Africa's gold-mining production so terribly important to the world's economy? Lots of folks think so, but you won't if you study this chart carefully. The whole world's gold production isn't very important when you get right down to it. Why? First consider why South Africa is considered important. It produces most of the world's gold and platinum. This chart shows world gold mining production by source from 1950 through to 1983. South Africa's annual production is clearly marked—the light portion on the bottom. The middle section depicts the annual production of all the other Western, free-market/capitalistic economies. The darkest section, on top, represents the production of the communist bloc.

At first glance, it may seem that South African production has become a bigger percentage of the world's total over the last 35 years. But looks are deceiving, because the vertical scale starts at 10, not 0. South Africa's share of the gold market did rise between 1960 and 1972, but then fell back to 48 percent—about where it was in 1950. On the other hand, the communists have made big inroads into gold. In 1950 they produced about 10 percent of the world's gold, and by 1983 were producing about 29 percent (13 divided by 45). Meanwhile, back at the ranch, the free-market economies, including the United States, have dropped from producing 46 percent of the world's gold to only 22 percent. So South Africa has kept its share while the communists have gained and the other countries have fallen back.

There are those who think this bodes poorly for our future. After all, aren't we losing out in an area that some think should be a critical underpinning to our society? Maybe it should be, but it isn't. The chart has a less obvious but important way to tell us that. Note that the world's total gold production of 45 million ounces, at a gold price of $400 per ounce, is worth only about $18 billion. That may sound like a lot, but it's peanuts. By comparison it's less than half of Texaco's or IBM's annual revenues and less than 0.5 percent of the U.S. gross national product—hardly enough to rattle our cage. So, what happens in South Africa, good or bad in terms of your moral or political persuasions, won't have much impact on the world economy. Even the entire South African stock market is worth only about $55 billion—just two-thirds the value of IBM alone.

What about gold then? And what about a gold-backed monetary system? The world's GNP is so huge today that there isn't enough gold in the world for a gold-backed monetary base to work at even astronomically higher gold prices—not even close. You couldn't do it with bubble gum either (although bubble gum would stand for inflation). The Industrial Revolution unleashed too much real growth. The world's GNP is about 20 times larger than it was then, and it's industrial and service-oriented rather than agricultural.

A goldlike monetary system could work (see Chart 47), but it would need to be based on assets collectively worth a lot more than gold, even if gold were much higher in price. Some folks have discussed a monetary system based on combining a number of assets into a mixed basket. Gold could be one of these.

Total World Gold Production, 1950–1983

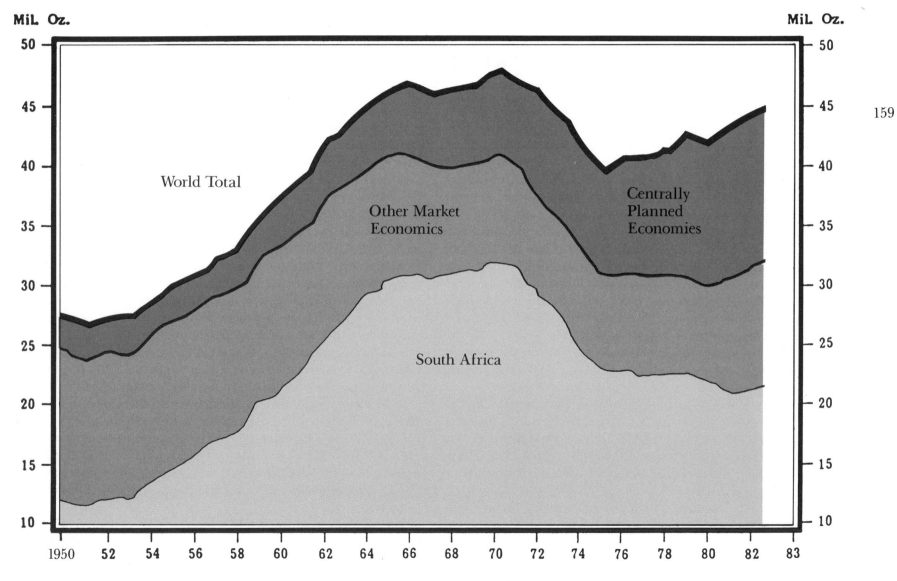

MiL Oz.

MiL Oz.

World Total

Other Market
Economics

Centrally
Planned
Economies

South Africa

159

Source: Goldman Sachs, New York.

70
Is Labor Really Overpaid?

Business can't make money today because workers get paid too much, right? After all, isn't cheap foreign labor the reason that U.S. firms are losing out to overseas price cutters? Wrong! The foreigners have more modern, efficient plants. While labor isn't cheap, the real shortage is in business leaders with the innovative smarts to use labor effectively. Ineffective labor always did cost too much.

Sure, the dollar cost of labor rises with inflation, but so do the prices of the things labor builds. The real cost of labor can only be measured by what a laborer can buy with his or her pay. A laborer gets more "real" pay only if he or she is more productive. As labor becomes more skilled, whether through worker's efforts or management's, wages will rise. But who cares if the worker's output rises at least as much?

This chart puts a longer-term perspective on the issue. It shows 690 years of an English building craftsman's buying power, as measured by consumables like food or clothes.

The chart shows that the real cost of labor approximately doubled in the 186 years from 1264 to 1450. Then it lost all that gain in the next 180 years. A builder in 1800 could buy relatively little more than his predecessor 200 or 500 years earlier. Then, starting in 1800, the real cost of labor roughly quadrupled by 1954.

What does that mean? To find out, rely again on your financial calculator. That steep 1800–1954 rise is a compound real pay boost of 1 percent per year. Seem like a lot? Think again. During that same period, real GNP grew by more than 2 percent per year, which says that labor was getting more but producing more still. Everybody got a good deal.

Most of that gain in real pay accrued during the world's Industrial Revolution, when workers grasped tools such as never before imagined. With their new tools, their real productivity rose, and so did their pay. The average craftsman in 1900 had new mass-production skills that were tremendously faster than were used 100 years earlier. He could drill holes with a brace and bit, use a surveyor's scope to level a foundation, or grasp round nails with needle-nosed pliers. By 1950 workers had power tools, jackhammers, staple guns, and concrete saws. Since 1950 have come products such as laser levels, guns to shoot nails into concrete, plastic piping, and much more. Today's "lazy" worker needn't work as hard to get more done, because he or she is better equipped and knows how to use these tools.

In my personal library sits Halbert Gillette's *Handbook of Cost Data for Contractors and Engineers*, from 1907. It cites the cost of skilled foremen at $5–$8 per day, averaging maybe $6.50. U.S. inflation since 1900, as measured by the Consumer Price Index, is up about 1,000 percent, so that same foreman might get $65 per day now. Instead, he or she gets about $25 per hour, or $200 per day. That's a real pay boost, but it has averaged only 1.3 percent per year—less than half the economy's real gain over the last 85 years. So, while labor got more money, they left lots on the table too.

Frustrated business leaders have griped about labor being too expensive for centuries. But trust this 690-year visual perspective. Labor isn't too expensive now, and if the past 700 years are any guide, it won't be in your lifetime.

Changes in the Equivalent of the Wage Rate of a Building Craftsman Expressed in a Composite Physical Unit of Consumables in Southern England, 1264–1954

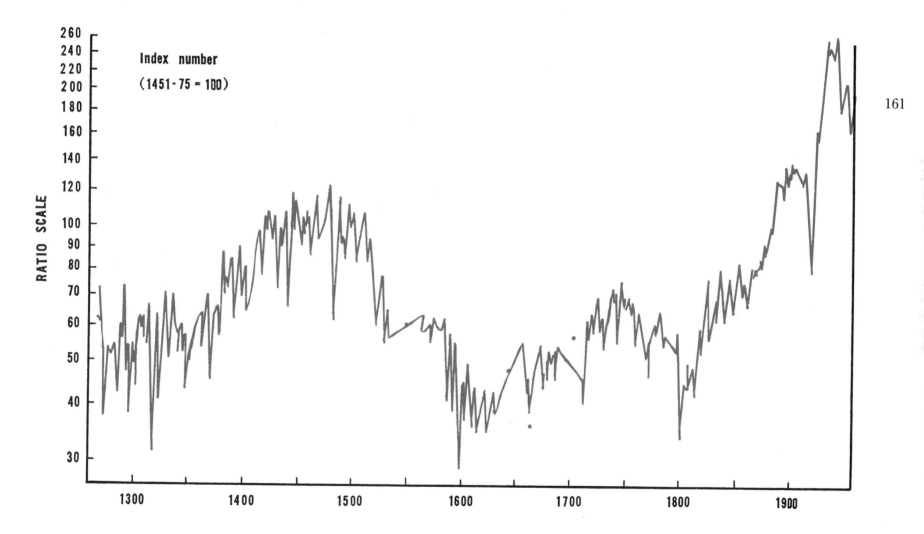

Source: E. H. Phelps-Brown and Sheila V. Hopkins, "Seven Centuries of the Prices of Consumables, Compared with Builders' Wage-rates," *Economica*, New Series, Vol. 23 (November 1956), p. 302.

71
Electricity Use and Economic Growth

This chart is probably the hardest to understand in this book, but it tells a fascinating story, and is well worth the effort. Between its lines, it tells how we got in over our heads with the 1970s OPEC oil crisis.

The chart plots kilowatt-hours of electricity sold versus GNP as expressed in inflation-adjusted dollars (using 1947 as a base). Each dot represents the relationship of kilowatt-hours with GNP for a single year. A number by each dot is meant to mean that the dot depicts the year (52 means 1952). Two lines are drawn: Line A represents the average trend from 1929 to 1945, and it is flatter than line B, which represents the trend from 1946 through 1956. The 1960 and 1965 dots represent projections, because this chart was published in 1958. Actually, the projections came out right on target.

The degree to which line B is steeper than line A depicts a major change in power usage after World War II. Before then, as shown in Chart 72, the United States was able to produce almost all of its own energy via the domestic oil giants that were created around the turn of the century, such as Standard Oil. If you carefully pick points on the chart, you'll see that during that period (along line A), a doubling of GNP resulted in about a 150 percent increase in electricity usage.

But after World War II, things changed. Consumers became gadget buffs. The next doubling in GNP generated a fivefold increase in electricity consumption. Use of "juice" skyrocketed as U.S. industry produced everything from TVs to dishwashers to electric blankets to primitive electronics of all types—to billions of light bulbs. And that's not to mention electric train sets and Christmas tree lights—you name it. The same thing happened with gas consumption. Planes and cars appeared everywhere. So did lawn mowers and golf carts. Power was everywhere.

The same thing was happening all over the Western world. Naturally, the domestic oil industry, which was used to meet power requirements based on the prewar relationship of power to GNP growth, was unprepared for the unprecedented leap in power consumption. Oil isn't discovered easily. Suddenly, starting in the 1950s, the United States was consuming imported fossil fuels at a steadily increasing rate (see Chart 72). The total amount wasn't large, but the trend was up steeply.

As U.S. consumers continued on the gadget binge, foreign oil sources found ever more dependence on them. By 1973 the U.S.'s skyrocketing usage of fossil fuel meant that to double GNP in the next 25 years, as in the last quarter-century, oil usage would be 30 times higher than before World War II—and most of that would be foreign oil. So, in 1973, when OPEC flexed its worldwide monopoly muscle, it was saying, "Either stop using all your gadgets, or give us a few of our own to play with."

Kilowatt-Hour Sales of the Electric Industry
vs. Gross National Product or Expenditure

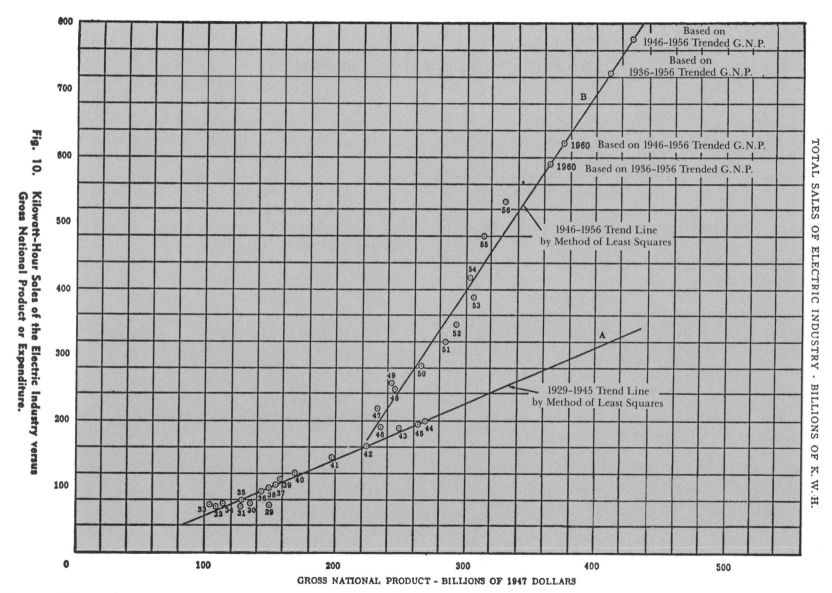

Source: Lillian Doris, *Corporate Treasurer's and Controller's Encyclopedia*, Volume I, Englewood Cliffs, N.J.; Prentice-Hall, Inc., 1958.

72
Crude Oil Supply: A Tale of Government Involvement

164 This is the companion piece that continues where the last chart left off. It shows the trade-offs among domestic oil production, imported oil, and total oil consumption. Between 1950 and 1975, oil consumption tripled. As the last chart showed, an ever larger part of U.S. energy usage was being supplied by electric power, which isn't very efficient and which was built into the economic system via devices that are hard to replace, such as the 1950s craze for electric ranges.

But this chart's real story is threefold. First, foreign oil took a continually increasing share of the growing oil picture, growing from a virtually nonexistent market share in 1950 to fully half of 1976 usage. Second, while domestic production grew, it grew very little. In 25 years, domestic oil production increased by just 54 percent, which works out to a 1.8 percent average annual increase—hardly robust.

Finally, there is the amazing fact that domestic production actually *decreased* once OPEC boosted oil prices. Remember late 1973? OPEC boosts prices. Gas lines take over America. Industrial producers hoard oil-based raw materials. Logic would say, and lots of leading observers of the day believed, that OPEC would quickly fizzle, but it didn't. Voters and the media howled for Congress to do something. As you may recall, President Ford created a cabinet-level Department of Energy and named William Simon "Energy Czar." Then, in classic government form, they imposed taxes so that those "bad" oil companies couldn't "take advantage" of the higher prices created by OPEC to reap "windfall" profits. But that hostility and political vulnerability took away their incentive to produce, too. The effect of the windfall profits tax was to keep the domestic companies from naturally responding to the crisis environment with massive resources to add capacity and oil production.

How does this affect the present? These days you hear lots of arguments for trade barriers to protect American companies from foreign imports. Instead of raising prices like the Arabs did, these foreigners are cutting prices, and many U.S. producers are howling for protection. But whenever government gets involved with quotas, pricing, and the planning of any industry, it is the kiss of death for American sources.

Once the Washington bureaucracy is controlling the levers, U.S. producers will never maximize production, because there will always be too much red tape and too much uncertainty. Producer's won't expand and modernize because of the risk that a different set of politicians may change the rules again in a few years, jeopardizing their investment. And if they don't expand and modernize, they will keep falling backward relative to competition. So this chart's final lesson is that just when it looks like the government should do something, it shouldn't—ever.

Domestic and Imported Crude Oil Supply, 1950–1979

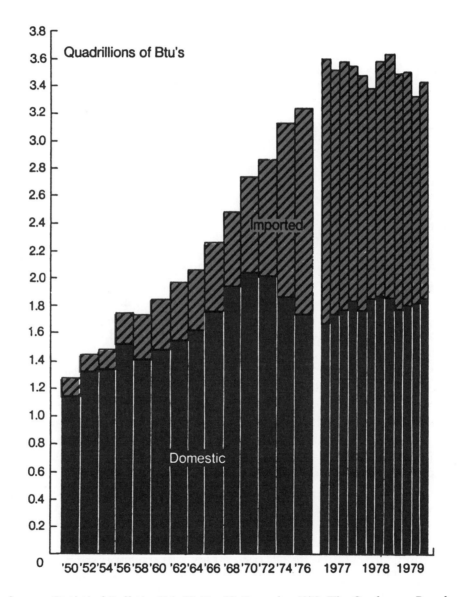

Source: *Statistical Bulletin*, Vol. 12, No. 12, December 1979, The Conference Board.

165

73
Texans Weren't the First to Ride— The Learning Curve

What can you learn from a "learning curve?" Lots, if you study its cyclical nature. When the famous term "learning curve" was coined in the 1960s, it described the way semiconductor pioneers like Texas Instruments learned more as they made ever more electronic devices. The brand-new product technology had little real world experience. Producers learned to count on on-the-job learning to teach them how to slash their per-unit production costs. As they produced more, their knowledge increased, and their costs per unit plummeted in a steady bit-by-bit path.

Since lower costs per unit would make demand grow, the transistor pioneers priced as if they already had those low costs. They took orders, made oodles of chips, and "rode down the learning curve" to lower costs and big bucks. No one had ever seen such a thing. Imagine, having your unit costs drop just by making more of something. To this day, most folks think the learning curve was first discovered by these transistor Texans.

Not so! It's clear from this Investment Bankers Association chart from 1913 that the electric utility industry had its own learning curve in the early 1900s. Notice the dramatic decline in the cost of energy per kilowatt-hour: from 12 cents in 1896 to about 2 cents in 1912, as industry output exploded. So the transistor tycoons merely reinvented learning curves—which are rediscovered about every 50 years—in amazing coincidence with the upward phase of the much scoffed at 50-year Kondratieff wave cycle (see for yourself in Chart 84). Learning curves propelled the railroad boom of the mid-19th century, the electric power and auto industries in the early 1900's, and, of course, the recent electronics boom.

Why do learning curves reemerge and disappear within the 50-year cycle's sweeping curves? It's psychology versus technology versus demand. During the long wave's down-cycle, a generation of business leaders learn to cut back, hunker down, and avoid overextending themselves with unattainable growth plans. With demand low, no one believes in volume, growth, and expansion; it seems too risky, so no one tries. That's why learning curves don't appear and are forgotten in periods like the 1930s and 1940s. Meanwhile, technology accumulates steadily on the sidelines but isn't implemented.

But, as Chart 84 shows, when the 50-year cycle heats up, a new growth mentality emerges. The accumulated process technology that piled up now gets applied all at once. As manufacturers build volume, they adopt and adapt to their own uses process technology developed by others. More volume builds more adoption and adaptation, and what the Texans called the learning curve.

This historical perspective on learning curves teaches important lessons. If we are now early on in the downward phase of a Kondratieff wave, as some suspect, you shouldn't expect large-scale implementation of revolutionary technological breakthroughs anytime soon. The tremendous electronics revolution of the last 20 years won't be replicated over the next 20. Its revolution is done. Kondratieff will allow only evolution from here. But don't expect revolutionary progress to halt forever. Our kids will see another revolution—and another revolution of the mysterious reappearing learning-curve cycle.

Accumulated Knowledge vs. Costs, Electric Utility Industry, 1896–1912

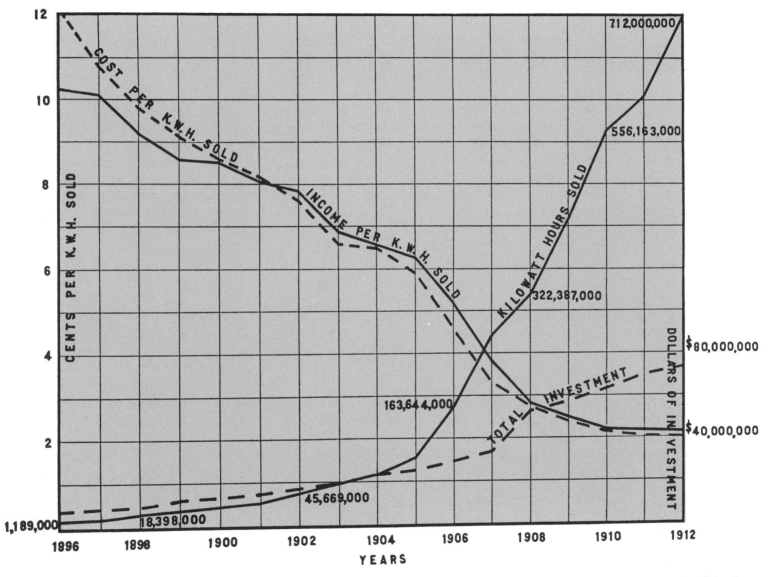

Source: Proceedings of the Second Annual Convention
of the Investment Bankers Association of America, Chicago, 1913.

Note: Sorry this chart is slightly off level,
but what do you want from a 73-year-old chart?

74
In the Know, Or Heavily Snowed?

Despite all the political railing about deficit spending and the media-made hysteria over the burgeoning national debt, the truth is that there is no severe debt problem. While confused alarmists fondly point to our increasing debt level to support fears of impending doom, the more relevant relationship between the national debt and the ability to handle that debt (national income or GNP) reveals that the United States is no worse off now than 20 years ago—and far better off than 30 or 40 years ago.

As this chart shows, federal debt as a percentage of GNP has declined, with a few interruptions since the end of World War II. In 1945 the national debt of $252 billion exceeded GNP of $212 billion by almost 20 percent. By 1982 the national debt was about $1 trillion, which seems like a lot—but GNP had risen much more during the 37 years, to about $3 trillion. So in the 35 years, the ratio had fallen from 120 percent to only about 33 percent. Contrary to all the doomsday babble, the debt burden has become lighter, not heavier.

It is true that this ratio has risen in the last few years after having reached an absolute bottom at about 25 percent in 1974. In fact, it has risen enough in the last decade to return the national debt-to-GNP ratio back up to where it was in the mid-1960s. So, if it keeps rising at recent rates, it may soon get back to its 1950s level. Would that be so bad? By most standards the 1950s were pretty good. The trend is clearly headed the wrong way, but if the country could handle this debt level back in the 1950s and 1960s, are we really to believe that it cannot shoulder the load now?

This debt hysteria is just part of our times—a little like the unrealistic raving and ranting about the federal deficit (see the Appendix). This isn't to say that there aren't real problems associated with government. There are. As shown in Chart 80, it is clear that the growth in total federal spending is a real problem. Perhaps the key lesson to learn from this chart is not to believe everything you hear or read. A lot of what you hear from politicians or read in the media is just self-serving and ignorant poppycock.

How do you know what is real and what is poppycock, either from your local paper, your vote-hog, or me? For issues related to government finance, you can look them up yourself in the library. Believe it or not, just ask for the Budget of the U.S. Government. It is only about two inches thick and amazingly readable. The most interesting parts are in tables and charts, all of which are nicely indexed. That is the source of this chart, although the current edition has data back to only the mid-1960s. To construct the chart, we had to gather the older data from older editions of the budget, which you can look up too. It's all there at the library for those who would rather be in the know than heavily snowed.

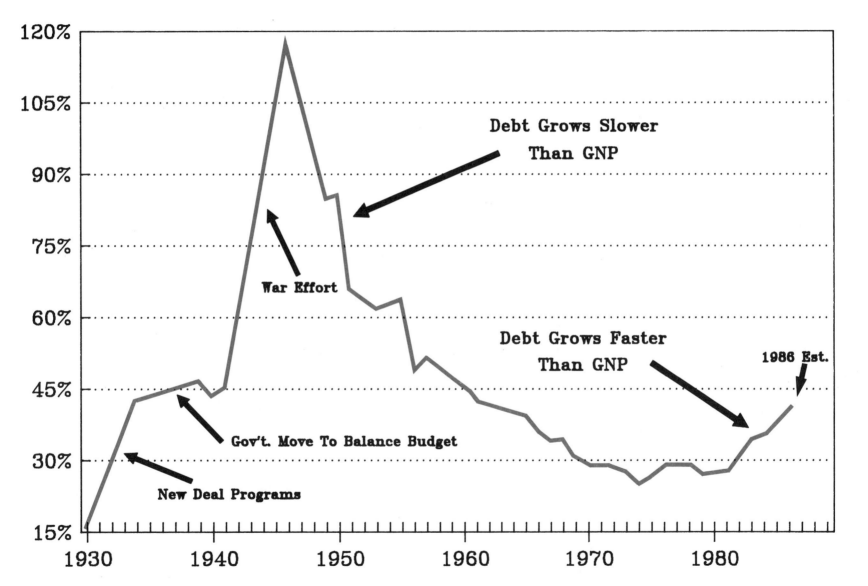

Net Public Debt as a Percentage of GNP, 1930–1986

Debt Grows Slower
Than GNP

War Effort

Debt Grows Faster
Than GNP

1986 Est.

Gov't. Move To Balance Budget

New Deal Programs

Source: Budget of the U.S. Government.

75
Taxes: The Customs of Our Evolution

I'll bet you think the U.S. government grew slowly until recent years. You would be wrong. And I'll bet you don't know when its growth picked up, why, and how the republic financed its early days? Those facts have interesting implications for the future.

This chart says that Uncle Sam financed his early days through taxes based on trade barriers and protectionism, as well as liquor and tobacco excises—a real savage-the-sinners story. But the real growth started blossoming when the government learned how to tax incomes. The left-hand chart shows sources of federal revenues for 1873–1916, and the right-hand chart continues the story through 1940. Note that the scales change. The left-hand chart is in millions of dollars, while the right-hand chart is in billions.

Customs taxes were sufficient to constitute the bulk of the government's sustenance for a long time. Add on excise taxes for liquor and tobacco, and you have virtually the entire shebang. The government's basic policy was to tax foreign trade and "users." On this basis, government growth proceeded only as fast as its funding source. So, as the economy progressed and people bought more from overseas and consumed more booze and stogies (cigarettes weren't common yet), the government grew.

But it only grew that fast, which wasn't fast enough for progressive do-gooders like Teddy Roosevelt and Woodrow Wilson. Your financial calculator will let you see quickly that the growth rate of government spending averaged 2 percent up until 1909. That year introduced the corporate income tax, followed by the personal income tax in 1913. Estate taxes followed in 1916.

After that, corporate and personal income tax revenues soared, rising to $4 billion by 1940. The brief 1918–1921 spike was tied to World War I tax hikes. But after that, the rest of the bulging revenue trend came in peacetime. From 1916 to 1940 total federal revenues grew at a whopping 8.6 percent average annual rate. The point is, once the government had learned how to tax income, it had learned how to fund rapid growth. It is obvious, for example, why prohibition wasn't a socially palatable phenomenon when Uncle Sam depended on taxes generated by booze buyers but became socially palatable once income taxes were in place.

The implications are interesting. Back during the Industrial Revolution, the United States had user taxes, and the government's growth was minimal. But once corporate and personal income taxes were ushered in, government growth promptly exploded. Recently the country has suffered government growth rates high enough to cripple productive capability within our lifetime (see Chart 80). Perhaps, as some folks suggest, we should institute constitutional amendments to limit the growth rate of government spending. But another, parallel approach might be to constitutionally eliminate income taxes and replace them with the good old user-based methodology of yesteryear.

Sources of Federal Revenue, 1873–1940

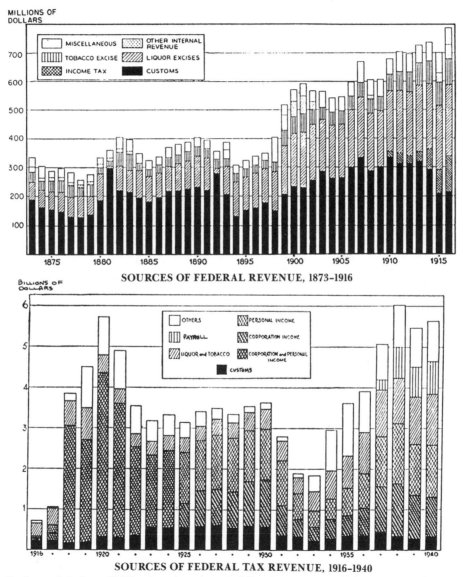

SOURCES OF FEDERAL REVENUE, 1873–1916

SOURCES OF FEDERAL TAX REVENUE, 1916–1940

Source: William J. Shultz and C. Lowell Harriss, *American Public Finance*, 5th Edition, New York: Prentice-Hall, Inc., 1949.

76
Government Growth: The Big Picture

This chart gives the best overview I've seen of government growth. It spans from George Washington's administration up to the 1950s. At the top are the Presidents' terms of office. The chart shows national income (adjusted GNP), federal debt, expenditures, and revenues (taxes). Over the entire 163-year time span, both spending and taxes seemingly grew from about $7 million to about $100 billion—an average annual growth rate of about 6 percent. Federal debt grew from about $98 million to about $300 billion—a growth rate of about 5 percent per year. And national income grew from $950 million to about $300 billion—an average annual growth of 3.6 percent. Since then, the post-1950s double-digit growth rates (see Chart 80) raised the federal budget to about $1 trillion. Tacking that on provides us the longest-term growth rate measurable for the U.S. government (196 years), yet it still averages 6 percent. Cameoed in the upper left are debt and expenditures per capita, which grew about 2.8 percent per year—conveniently, just slightly less than GNP.

An interesting period is the 1830s. For the only time in U.S. history, federal debt disappeared completely. Following the lead of Andrew Jackson's populist philosophy, the government repaid the federal debt completely from the proceeds of selling Western lands to a speculation-hungry populace. Investors believed they were buying America's future. They were, but a few decades too early. Before Jackson's election, Uncle Sam sold precious little land, but in 1836 alone sold $25 million worth to investors, and finished repaying the debt.

Today's governmental leaders might learn a lesson from Jackson and consider selling assets to pay down the federal debt. Not only is Uncle Sam the world's largest asset holder, but its capital acquisitions have been a big contributor to its cumulative debt (see Chart 82). Inflation has raised the value of these assets drastically relative to their costs.

But beware—ironically, whereas most folks believe repaying the national debt would instantly cause the nation to enter into economic nirvana, this mid-1830s period of total debt repayment led also to one of the four largest financial disasters and economic collapses of all time. It started with the Panic of 1837, during which the land speculators and lots of other folks were wiped out, and then on to the subsequent depression that lasted until 1843. So maybe repaying the debt isn't the great idea everyone imagines it would be.

Then there were two periods when debt, expenditures, and revenues went straight up—starting with the Civil War in 1861 and just before World War I, starting in 1911. It's not surprising that federal activity increased during these wars, but it is surprising it didn't fall back further afterward. However, the presidents during these periods were progressives and not hostile to spending. For example, as shown in Chart 75, the arrival of income taxes between 1909 and 1913 fueled governmental growth pangs. The income tax was an offshoot of the progressive policy under Teddy Roosevelt and then Taft and Wilson. President Harding was of a more skinflint persuasion and stopped the trend. Where is Harding now that we really need him?

Public Finance, 1790–1953

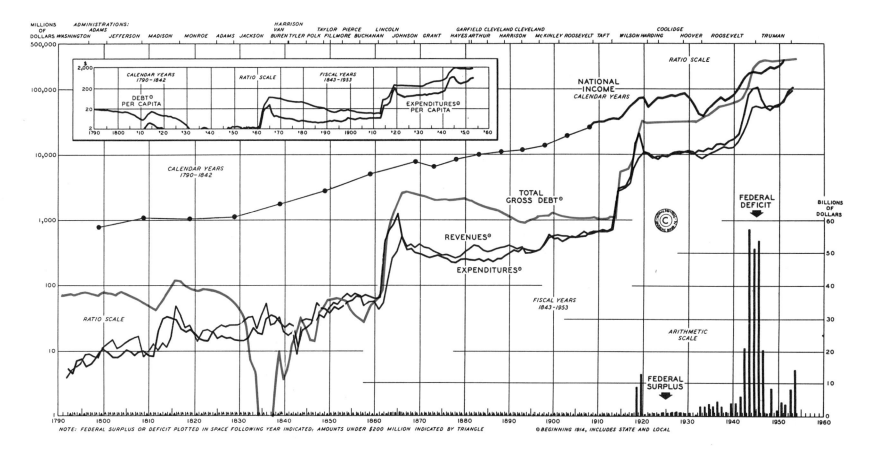

Source: How Much Government, a graphic analysis prepared for the 36th annual meeting of the Conference Board.

77
State and Local Taxes on a Steady Course

Some things just never work the way you expect them to. Take taxes for example. Not only does Congress shake up the tax code every two years, but the effluent runs down from Capitol Hill, first to the states, which often adjust their codes to the feds' jiggling, and then to the municipalities, which often look to the states as their big daddy. But whether they hike taxes or not, as we'll see in Chart 80, the changes don't turn into actual tax cuts. The clamor for tax cuts really changes very little in the overall tax picture. This chart shows why.

When you add together the various components of state and local taxes, as shown in the top line, the result is a growth rate depicted by a line as straight as a laser beam. And that line keeps growing at 11 percent per year—a doubling every 6.5 years. Income tax, sales tax, property tax, and federal government handouts are the foundation of the state and municipal tax system.

While property taxes fell when voters took the issue into their own hands at the polls, nothing else has. Individual income taxes rose 13 percent annually as the slowly rising economy and inflation forced ever more taxpayers into higher tax brackets. The same thing has happened with state corporate income taxes. In many states the rates have been increased and the booming economy keeps pushing the corporate tax take higher, at 12 percent per year with barely a jiggle along the way. Then comes federal government handouts, which have also grown at 13 percent per year.

As it turns out, tax cuts don't cut taxes, and reforms turn out to be nothing more than plans to redistribute income—a way to take a little less from one overtaxed and weary group of constituents and shuffle it off to another whose shoulders will soon grow just as weary. The bulging tax coffers actually have been filling so fast that the states haven't been able to spend all the money. They've been accumulating the surplus and paying down their debts—to the tune of about $100 billion a year.

Ironically, folks complain quite a lot these days about the federal deficit. I'm not even sure it exists (see my October 6, 1986, *Forbes* column in the Appendix). But if it does, it sure isn't as large as folks babble about. Right now the states and municipalities are running this $100 billion surplus, but only because they are receiving $100 billion from Uncle Sam. If the federal government backed off its transfer payments, the states would still run small surpluses, and the federal deficit would shrink more than 40 percent.

Would anything really have changed? Of course not! But while society would be no worse off, we might have to put up with 40 percent less mindless yelping from the dogs who keep whining about the evil deficit—and in the process keep focusing most of us off the real problem—the growth in government spending (see Chart 80).

State and Local Tax Sources, 1960–1979

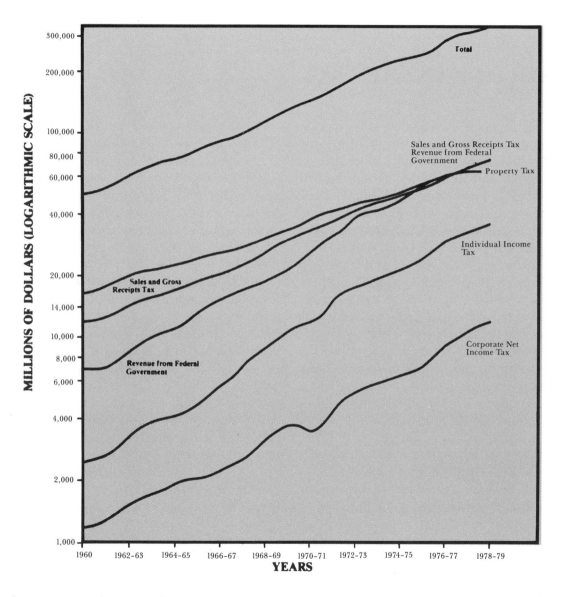

Source: Economic Report of the President, 1981.

78
The States Are Revolting

176 It took the tax revolution of the late 1970s to bring profligate state and local government spending under control, right? Not really. It seems the hometown boys were more anticipatory of voters' mood swings than we imagined and already well on their way to controlling spending before California taxpayers started their revolt in 1978 with the infamous Jarvis-Gann initiative. It also seems Uncle Sam has yet to learn the lesson—largely because he never got quite as far out of line as the states had.

These charts come from the Advisory Commission on Intergovernmental Relations in Washington, D.C. They show the per capita growth of expenditures, adjusted for inflation, for both the federal and combined state and municipal governments. The federal numbers on the left show that after adjusting for inflation, Uncle Sam spent about $700 per year per American in 1954, but by 1982 was spending about twice that amount. The growth rate seems to have picked up about 1959 and galloped steadily ever since. Pulling out your financial calculator allows you to ascertain that Uncle Sam's "real," postinflation spending grew about 2.7 percent per year per American.

The right-hand chart shows that state and local expenditures grew far faster from 1954 through 1974, but slowed to virtually no growth after that. State and local spending grew from a combined $300 million in 1954 to about $700 million in 1974, which works out to a 4.3 percent 20-year average postinflation growth rate. It seems the local pols had been outspending Uncle Sam by a lot for a long while, and finally figured out that enough was enough.

Starting in 1974, four full years before California's Jarvis-Gann-based tax revolt, the states were already pulling in their horns and bringing their growth to a halt. Holding their real per capita spending steady for the next 8 years dropped the total 28-year growth to a 3.3 percent average annual rate, still much more than the federal government's. So while it seems today that Uncle Sam can't learn to control his spending the way the hometown gang has, remember, the hometown crowd learned only recently and after decades of excessive growth.

This chart spells H-O-P-E for the economy. As Chart 80 shows, the most severe problem undermining the economy's long-term vitality is the growth rate in federal spending. Can it be slowed down? Well, 10 years back it seemed unlikely that state spending could be slowed either. For example, when Ronald Reagan ended his 2 terms as California's governor in 1974, he had grown the Golden State's budget by a whopping 17 percent average annual rate (not inflation-adjusted). Reagan talked fiscal restraint, but he spent like a drunken sailor. Ironically, his Democratic successor, crazy Jerry Brown, talked like a spender but pinched the pennies a bit and slowed the growth rate.

My hope is that as ever-popular Ronald Reagan leaves the White House, he and his cronies will be succeeded this time too by politicians who are perhaps less popular but who are more prone to hold spending in line. The voters' challenge is to make politicians of both parties understand the command.

Federal and State-Local Expenditures, 1954–1983

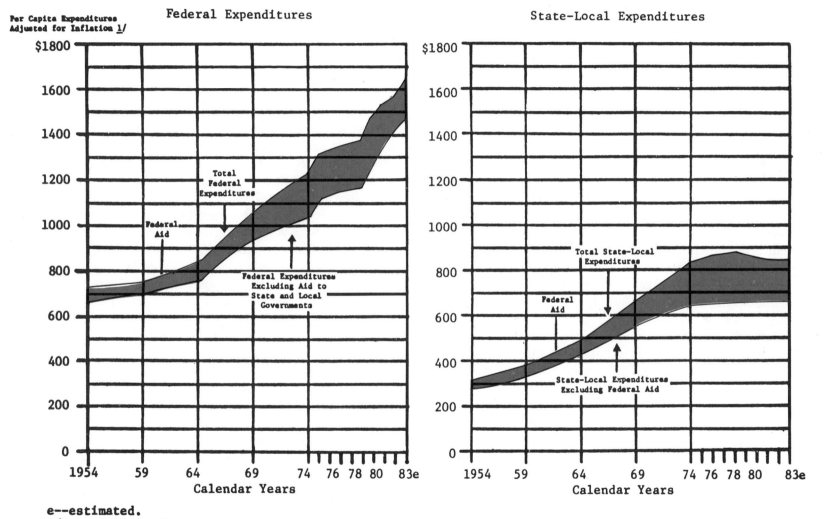

Per Capita Expenditures Adjusted for Inflation 1/

Federal Expenditures

State-Local Expenditures

177

Total Federal Expenditures

Federal Aid

Federal Expenditures Excluding Aid to State and Local Governments

Total State-Local Expenditures

Federal Aid

State-Local Expenditures Excluding Federal Aid

Calendar Years

Calendar Years

e--estimated.

1/ Inflation adjustment by GNP Implicit Price Deflator, 1972 = 100.

Source: ACIR computations based on U.S. Department of Commerce National Income, Advisory Commission on
    International Relations, Washington, D.C., 20575.

79
You Can't Put a Number on It

Ronald Reagan may be one of the greatest actors ever to be president. Good looks, clever phrases, and folksy charm aside, he is also lucky. By now you should have figured out that he didn't cause lower interest rates, as he wants you to believe; they have been falling together in lock-step throughout the world. He didn't make the long-sustained economic boom either; the economy has been booming worldwide. He has continued the explosion in federal spending, which is our biggest future problem. As shown in Chart 80, if federal spending keeps booming at the same rates relative to GNP, it will take only 100 years for Uncle Sam to take over the whole economy. What is bothersome is the way he justifies himself with overly simplistic economic theory.

It all started with this chart—the much-discussed, but seldom-seen Laffer curve, originally drawn on a restaurant napkin by economist Arthur Laffer to show that there are always two tax rates that yield the same total tax take. It was popularized by former *Wall Street Journal* editorialist Jude Wanniski in his modestly entitled book *The Way The World Works*. The chart plots tax rates against tax take (revenue). It shows that just as much can be collected by charging less—sometimes. Why? Because at very low tax rates, like point B, Uncle Sam can't collect much. And at high rates, like point A, folks feel overtaxed and won't work, so less is made and there's less to tax.

Obviously, there is an optimal rate for taxes—point E. There, the tax-take can't be boosted by raising tax rates, because folks will work less, but it can't be boosted by rate cuts, because further cuts won't generate harder workers—just less taxes.

Society wants to be taxed at rate E. Supply-siders leap from here to the assumption that tax-rate cuts create booming economies, which pay more total taxes and wipe out deficits. Talking about "supply-side economics" and tax cuts, Laffer became famous, Wanniski became rich (founding Poleconomics), and Reagan saw magically how to boost his popularity—and taxes. The 1986 tax bill was originally designed by Reagan and his advisors as a societal tax hike with the businesses we all own picking up the tab—all disguised by "rate cuts" tied to eliminating deductions. Disguised or no, it is actually a Keynesian strategy of "hit the rich who own the corporations, and save the low incomer."

But it's fiction. Notice that the chart has no numbers. No one really knows the ideal tax rate for trading off more governmental "gimmes" against the burden of higher taxes. Everyone is for lower taxes, but few want Uncle Sam to ease off on pet boondoggles A–Z. There are no free lunches, this chart included.

Supply-siders seem to think lower rates are always better, but they ignore that their chart also states clearly that at times rates may be too low. Lowering rates isn't always best. Laffer, Wanniski, and Co. cite cases of foreign tax cuts that were followed by economic booms, but ignore how the U.S. economy boomed back in the days of higher tax rates (see Chart 81)—like the 1950s, with its 90 percent maximum income tax rates. Supply-side economics is just another on-the-come tax-hike disguise, which has caused dreamers to seek something for nothing—reminiscent in some ways of the overly optimistic bubble-brained mentality of 1720 (see the discussion of Chart 36).

The Laffer Curve

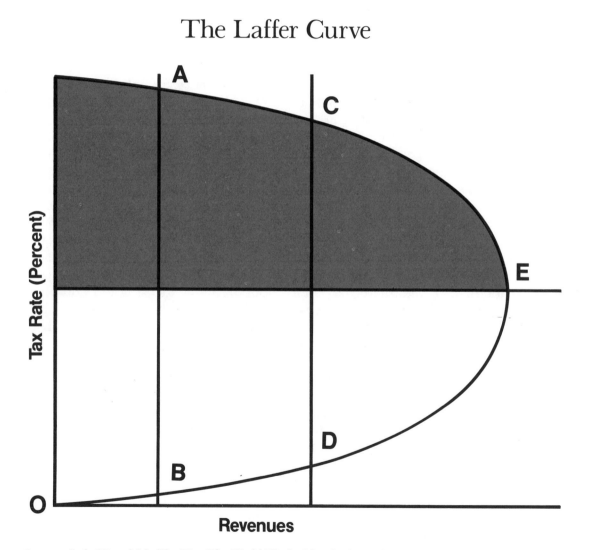

Source: Jude Wanniski, *The Way The World Works*, New York: Basic Books, 1978.

80
The Myth of Federal Taxes

Every time those Washington S.O.B.s jiggle taxes, folks have heart attacks. I've felt that way myself; it's only natural. But tax changes create less economic effect than most folks imagine, and you shouldn't overreact to the media's mumbo-jumbo tax sensationalism. Despite legislators, who in their never-ending pitch for votes rewrite the tax code every two years and promise everyone the sky, the total tax take has grown at an almost perfectly steady rate—almost forever.

This chart shows half the picture (the rest is in Chart 78), total federal taxes since 1965, as reported in Uncle Sam's budget. You also see total federal expenditures and those same expenditures as a percentage of GNP. Despite numerous major tax revisions, reforms, simplifications, and what-have-you, total federal taxes have grown at a whopping 10.25 percent per year—and in the entire period, despite numerous "tax cuts" there has been only one year in which the government's tax take actually declined.

Don't let the media's superficiality and the politicians' phony tax-cut claims take your eye off the real ball—which is government spending. Federal expenditures grew even faster than taxes, at 11.25 percent per year. While this includes inflation (about 4 percent per year), it's notably more than GNP's 9.4 percent nominal growth. The upshot? Government spending as a percentage of GNP has slowly grown over those years from 18 percent to a 1986 level of 24 percent of GNP.

Twenty years ago, that was referred to as "creeping socialism." At this rate of creep, my financial calculator says the government creeps will have expropriated *everything* in just 100 years. The relentless drain of increased and inefficient government spending as a percentage of total American spending (GNP) is at the core of why the U.S. economy's growth has slowed in recent years. With 25 percent of GNP going to the government, one-third of every productive worker's salary ends up, on average, going to foot the bill (25 percent divided by the 75 percent that is nongovernment).

So, don't let anyone fool you. When the government spends, the citizens will pay for it one way or the other. We might pay via higher taxes or via higher inflation. President Reagan, for example, has been extremely successful at maintaining his popularity by focusing folks on promised tax cuts. But despite all his hot air, government spending keeps rising. While the talk is about taxes (which come directly out of everyone's hide, and folks love to talk about what immediately affects them), the talk should be about spending.

Sadly enough, the situation is even worse. At the state and local level, spending has grown about 11 percent per year too (see Chart 77). Forget all the tax jiggling. The only societywide answer that makes any real economic sense is a constitutional limit on total government spending as a percentage of GNP. As an indivdual, your taxes may jiggle with the political gigolos, but as an investor you shouldn't let their shenanigans fool you either into panicking about the short term or into missing the longer-term economic risks.

Taxes and Spending and Their Relation to GNP, 1965–1987

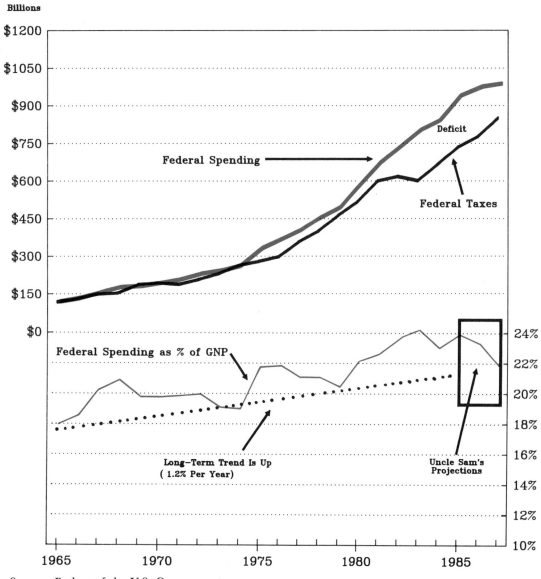

Source: Budget of the U.S. Government.

81
Balancing the Budget with Hot Air

The whole thing is nuts. I mean the 1986 tax hike, cleverly disguised as a tax-rate cut. Lower tax rates supposedly spur us to work harder in anticipation of keeping more of our earnings. Well, who knows, but if I work much harder, my wife is going to sue me for abandonment. Besides, it gripes me that all those government people, spurred on by supply-side economics (see text with Chart 79), want me to work harder so they can collect more to pay off a deficit that was created by them, spending money they didn't have on things I never wanted them to do.

I myself am opposed to federal spending, but if we must have it, instead of financing it through tax-rate cuts, I favor an ad valorum tax on hot air. There's certainly plenty of it around.

Besides, tax rates were great last year compared to the longer-term history of the United States. This 2-part chart shows maximum tax rates since the start of income taxes. The cameo shows the progressive taxation of one additional dollar of income. For example, between 1954 and 1967, if you earned $50,000, your next earned dollar would be taxed at 60 percent. (Remember, this has no inflation adjustment, so $50,000 then is like $200,000 now—see Chart 52).

Supply-side economists think tax-rate cuts generate booming economies and high tax rates are bad, bad, bad. So maybe they thought the booming 1920s resulted from Republican generated maximum tax cuts from 78 percent to 22 percent. Maybe it would have been a bigger boom still if corporate rates hadn't been rising. Of course, the market's second biggest rise started in 1932, as both corporate and personal maximum rates were steadily boosted. I guess the supply-siders forgot that one. Then there was the booming stock market and low inflation of the 1950s. Where are Ike and Give 'Em Hell Harry now that we really need them? While you may have forgotten it, they boosted personal and corporate tax rates. When somebody in the maximum tax bracket earned an extra buck, he lost 90 percent of it to Uncle Sam. So, I guess, according to the supply-siders, nobody's wife sued for abandonment back then, because nobody worked, because taxes were too high. Balderdash!

Almost no one has ever seen these charts. The interesting lesson is what very high tax rates U.S. taxpayers carried through some very prosperous years. Who would have thought top tax rates were higher going into the 1920s than into the 1930s? Who would have thought taxes were so high in the 1950s?

No one is for high tax rates, but rates are no more important than what you can deduct before calculating them. It really doesn't make much difference if there are lots of deductions and high tax rates or few deductions and low rates. While tax rates will fall in 1987, the actual tax take will rise as a percentage of GNP because the total reduced deductions are more than the combined personal and corporate tax-rate cuts.

Remember, it doesn't really matter how they constitute the tax code. If they spend money, taxpayers will pay for it through higher rates, lower deductions, or more inflation—it's really all the same. So don't be deceived by their devious smoke screens. When they promise you lower taxes, give 'em back what they give you: spare hot air.

Federal Income Tax Rates, 1909–1987

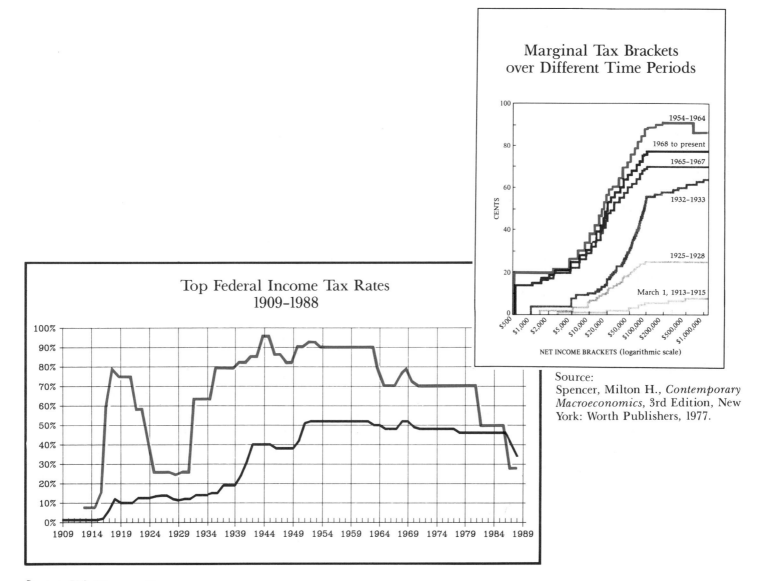

Marginal Tax Brackets over Different Time Periods

1954–1964
1968 to present
1965–1967
1932–1933
1925–1928
March 1, 1913–1915

CENTS

NET INCOME BRACKETS (logarithmic scale)

$500 · $1,000 · $2,000 · $5,000 · $10,000 · $20,000 · $50,000 · $100,000 · $200,000 · $500,000 · $1,000,000

Top Federal Income Tax Rates 1909–1988

1909 1914 1919 1924 1929 1934 1939 1944 1949 1954 1959 1964 1969 1974 1979 1984 1989

Source:
Spencer, Milton H., *Contemporary Macroeconomics*, 3rd Edition, New York: Worth Publishers, 1977.

Source: U.S. Treasury Department.

82
Uncle "Fat Cat" Sam's Real Estate Scam

So you accept that federal debt as a percentage of GNP isn't sky-high like the media and others have led you to believe. But if Uncle Sam is broke and so far in hock that he can't repay his debt, aren't we going to get stuck paying for it through higher taxes? Maybe not. As Chart 76 shows, Andy Jackson repaid the federal debt in 1836 by selling federal land to eager speculators.

Could the government do it again? Most folks can't conceive of it, but it's possible. This chart, which was completed in 1964 shortly after Alaska became a state, gives a visual glimpse of how much asset value Uncle Sam has tucked away. It shows total federal lands in millions of acres for each year from 1781 through 1964. Since then, total federal acreage hasn't changed much, so we can envision a relatively horizontal line extending from where this chart ends right up to 1986.

Before 1850, despite Andy Jackson's little sale and some earlier giveaways and sales, Uncle Sam added to his real estate portfolio in two big steps: the Lousiana Purchase (1803) and the Oregon and Mexican Territories (late 1840s). So, by 1850 federal lands totaled 1.2 billon acres, but some was in places like the Nevada desert and not worth much. Starting in 1850, Uncle Sam pared his portfolio, reducing total acreage by 66 percent (to 400 million acres) by 1930. The government pruned and cut its least worthy lands, keeping its most valuable urban tracts, the national park and forest system (most of which wasn't created until later), military bases, and the like.

Franklin Roosevelt slowed land sales to a trickle and even started buying land, so Uncle Sam's holdings stopped declining in the 1930s. Then, with Alaskan statehood in 1958, federal land almost doubled to 750 million acres, which is about what the federal government owns today—ranging from isolated military sites in places like Nevada to downtown office buildings in virtually every major city, to big chunks of Washington, D.C. Uncle Sam is by far the world's wealthiest real estate holder—all financed with borrowed money.

How wealthy? Well, national forest land, including mineral rights, may be worth only about $100 per acre. But the downtown land is worth oodles. If sold slowly, without flooding the market, Uncle Sam's Washington, D.C., land alone is worth $350 to $500 a square foot according to local investors—that's $15-20 million an acre for more than 15,000 acres. That comes to more than $300 billion, or 17 percent of the total federal debt. Add in Uncle Sam's other 750 million acres, and he almost certainly owns more land than he has debt—several times over.

Now, we shouldn't sell off everything to repay the debt. As you saw in Chart 74, the debt's not such a problem as long as it stays within its historical averages in relation to GNP. Besides, nobody wants to sell off the Lincoln Memorial. But if you worry that the debt is too high, and you don't believe all that GNP jazz, at least this chart lets you know that repaying the debt is merely a tradeoff between higher taxes and real estate sales. If the taxes get sky-high, we can pull an Andy Jackson. If the politicians suggest selling something we really want to keep, then we just dig into our pockets to keep it. The choice is yours.

P.S. Your state and county own a lot of land too.

Approximate Area of Federal Lands in the United States, 1781–1960

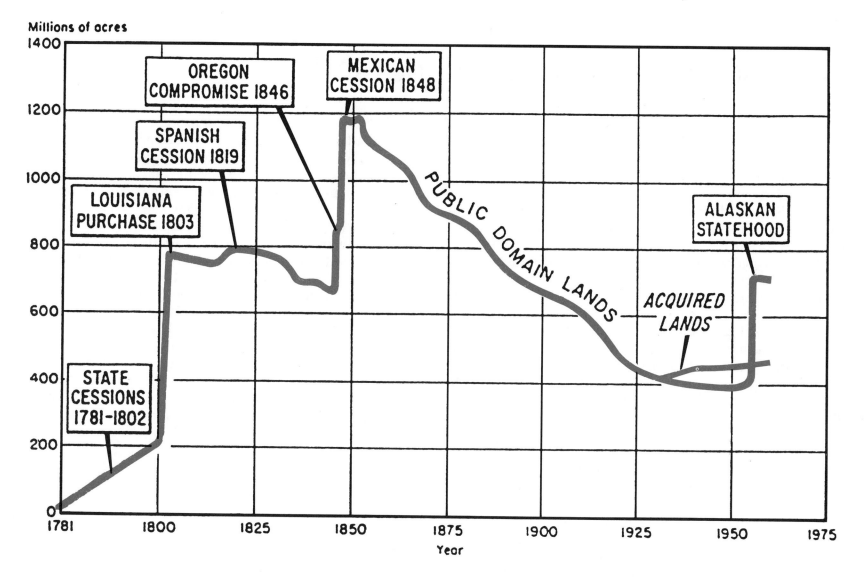

Source: Clawson, Marion, *Man and The Land Use*, University of Nebraska Press, 1964.

83
Defense Expenditures and the GNP

Worried that the recent rise in military spending will harm the economy? A look at this historical perspective of defense expenditures, showing military outlays relative to total gross national product, should allay your fears.

For several years we've been bombarded with media reports about the Reagan administration's massive military buildup and the astronomical sums being appropriated for defense. In fact, Uncle Sam spent more on the military from 1982 to 1985 than in any four-year period since World War II, including the Korean and Vietnam Wars. In dollar terms, this raised last year's total defense outlays to $254 billion, roughly twice what they were when Reagan took office in 1980.

With statistics like these being bandied about, you can see why folks conclude that defense expenditures have gotten dangerously out of hand. Then they wonder whether this military spendup will seriously undermine the nation's economic health. But if you examine the issue dispassionately, you'll discover that the economic impact of the current buildup isn't nearly as great as most critics claim. The adjacent chart provides the evidence.

Surprising as it may seem, there's been a dramatic downturn in the portion of the nation's total output devoted to the military. During the Korean conflict, the percentage of GNP spent on defense reached nearly 14 percent, but by 1986 it was only 6.4 percent, less than half. Furthermore, recent Defense Department estimates say that military spending will drop sharply again in 1987 to just under 6 percent. Even if you don't put much faith in Defense Department estimates, the Gramm-Rudman balanced-budget amendment and the current mood in Congress virtually assure smaller defense budgets for the balance of the decade.

When you examine the facts, the arguments that large defense expenditures are lowering the standard of living by crowding out private spending simply don't hold water. In truth, we've shown a growing preference to spend less on guns than on butter. In a way, you could say that private spending has been crowding out the military. As the chart shows, each previous surge in military spending (1951–1953, 1966–1968, and 1981–1985), however intense, was short-lived and led to a period of reduced growth, a pattern that seems to be repeating itself once more.

As is so often true with emotional issues, the facts differ from the perception. So you may not like military spending, but you have to base your view on something other than a misperception that military spending is about to cripple the economy. Clearly it isn't. We are spending a far smaller piece of the economy on it now than in the recent past.

Defense Budget as a Percentage of GNP, 1945–1986

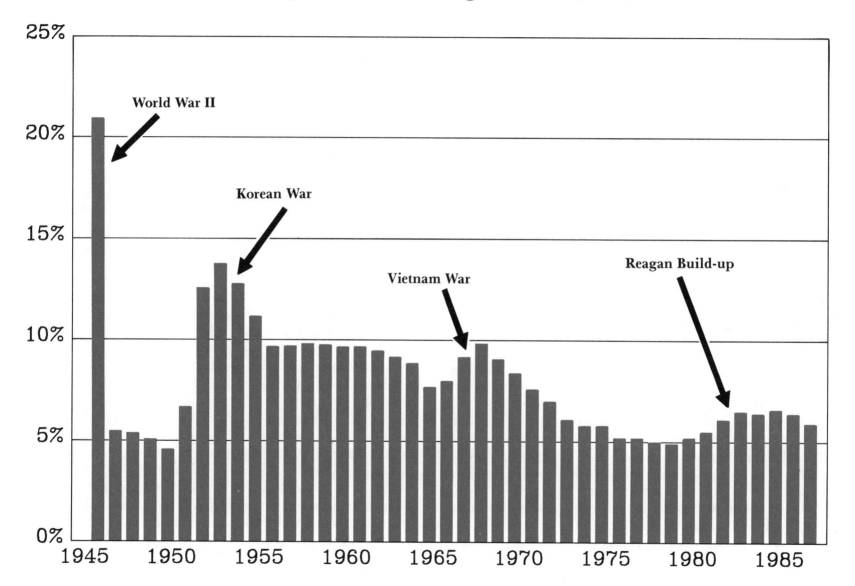

Source: *Statistical Abstract of the United States, 1986*, U.S. Bureau of the Census.

84
The Economic Cycle Economists Deny

The Kondratieff wave has forecasted booms and busts better than most economists—most of whom sneer at it. Kondratieff, a Russian, was exiled to Siberia in the 1920s for theorizing that capitalism had 55-year evolutionary cycles, which purged it of excesses. Soviet dogma held that capitalism was in a cycleless down-and-out spiral. But Kondratieff's fans roughly presaged the 1920s boom-bust cycle. Modern fans foresaw the vicious 1974 and 1982 recessions, and the speculative boom of the 1980s. Waves are baffling to understand; none recur just like the prior one, partially because just two cycles require 100-plus years—a tremendous expanse of evolution. *The Kondratieff Wave*, by Shuman and Rosenau, gives a too-simple but understandable script. Most accounts fail to note the complexities of the wave's coincident international existence.

The "idealized" wave of 50 to 55 years starts at the low stage, for example in 1935–1955. Interest and inflation rates and stock and real estate prices are very low. Politicians shift from antigovernment policy to federalism. Infrastructure is built: airports and freeway systems in the 1950s, railroads from 1880 to 1910, and canal systems in the 1830s and 1840s. Older business managers had their confidence shaken by the prolonged gloom and deflation of the recent depression (1930s, 1873–1888, and 1837–1843). Few expect inflation, and none conceive of expanding without existing orders in hand.

But there are always young turks. Some young managers expand aggressively. Society has fought deflation and depression for 20 years and has closed too much plant and capacity. Demand was pent up for too long. Folks are eager for houses and whatever they can afford. Government fiscal policies are expansive. Slowly the young turks get bailed out by mild inflation. Over and over again, the young turks bet and win and are continually promoted until they become the new top dogs.

A war starts (Vietnam, World War I, Civil War, 1812). Inflation soars for five to ten years after the war ends (see Chart 55), and interest rates trail a little behind, which stops the saving of money. Instead folks speculate against inflation with stocks and real estate—one of which is heavily financed by debt in each wave. In one 55-year wave, real estate takes center stage; the next time, stocks do. The now-older turks keep betting on inflation, adding capacity at a gallop. Finally, they've overbuilt. Interest rates soar to the highest levels most folks think have ever occurred. The worst recession in 40 years rocks business.

Now, five to ten years after the war, inflation dribbles to death. The old turks disbelieve it and keep building. They had bet on inflation their whole lives—and won. They were lucky, but think they were smart. To them deflation is impossible. Commodity prices and interest rates plummet. Low prices can't justify new plants, so a new breed of young turks start a merger mania. It is now cheaper to buy assets than to build them. As prices fall, managers cry for government trade barriers to block "predatory foreigners" who are "flooding our markets." Stock and real estate prices soar. Then, 1929, 1873, 1835, *or perhaps 1987* occur, all followed by 10 to 15 years of depression and deflation—and a new cycle's birth.

The Kondratieff Wave, 1780–1986 and Beyond

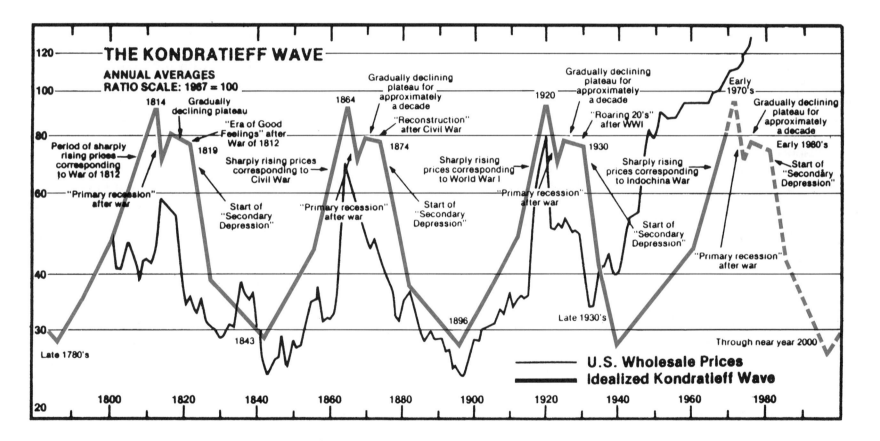

85
Sunspots

When I first encountered folks trying to predict future events based on sunspots, I thought they were nuts. I still do, but now I'm convinced that someday, when scientists know lots more than they do now, they will make amazing predictions with sunspots. I became convinced when I learned that the bulk of the crazies are serious NASA scientists. But let's start at the beginning.

Sunspots are visible blemishes on the sun's surface. Astronomers have recorded their number and size since the 1700s. They fashioned their findings into an index calibrating an overall sunpot "number." Interestingly, sunspots recur in rather regular 11-year cycles. This chart shows sunspot "numbers" from 1755 to 1978.

As science buffs passed the good word to investors, amazing coincidences were noticed. The three largest stock market disasters (1836–1843, 1872–1878, 1929–1932) were immediately preceded by peaks in sunspot activity. So were more minor, but still gut-wrenching drops like 1907 (see Chart 32), 1937, and 1969. So sunspots gained a following.

Of course, there have been many declines that didn't fit into the 11-year solar pattern and some significant sunspot peaks that weren't followed by a decline in stock prices. So sunspot worshipers were quickly labeled as freaks—as they probably deserved to be. Of course, the freaks continue, as measured by several recent books like Thomas Reider's *Sun Spots, Stars and the Stock Market*.

When modern scientists stepped into the picture, they found that sunspots are approximately predictable and correlate perfectly with fluctuations in emissions of differing types of solar radiation. Beta rays, gamma rays, cosmics, and the whole nine yards vary directly and predictably with sunspots. Why is that important? For example, when the sun emits a lot of ultraviolet radiation, the ionosphere ionizes and becomes like a tinfoil blanket around the earth, making it more difficult to transmit communications through the ionosphere to satellites and other receivers.

Enter NASA, which is seemingly an acronym for Need Another Sunspot Assessment. NASA has spent multimegabucks studying sunspots. They discovered amazing correlations, most of which are detailed in a book they published, *Sun, Weather and Climate* (available from the U.S. Government Printing Office), which is this chart's source. Tidal-height fluctuations, total ozone, atmospheric electricity, storm tracks, thunderstorm activity, rainfall and drought, X-rays, and alpha particles—all tie into those pesky little sunspots. Who would have thought it?

They've never really figured out what causes sunspots, so we're still largely in the Dark Ages on the subject. But with sunspots, or whatever causes them, controlling how many beta rays are bouncing around between our little brains and altering our radiowave capabilities and all these other freakish events, why are we so cocky as to assume that sunspots don't also affect our pyschology, individually and en masse, and thereby alter the course of our emotionally and psychologically driven financial markets (in ways we don't understand yet)? Who knows, someday scientists may even discover that the world is round.

Sunspots, 1755–1978

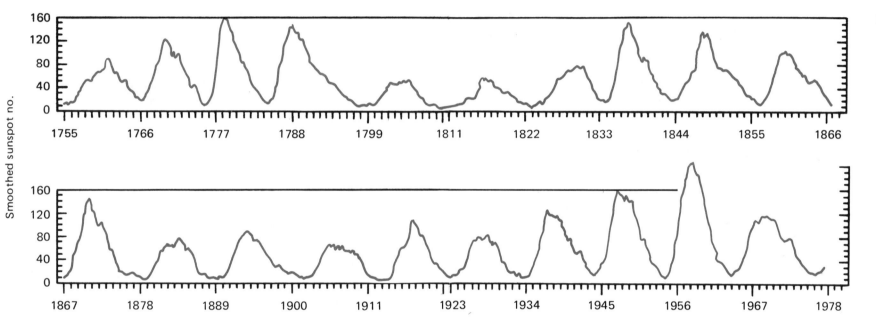

Source: John R. Herman and Richard A. Goldberg, *Sun, Weather, and Climate*, National Aeronautics and Space Administration, 1978.

86
Bear Markets Versus Bare Knees

Do you get a leg up on others by focusing on interest rates or by keeping your interest on rating girls' legs? Well, Wall Street may remain among the last bastions that feminists can't reform, and some Wall Streeters think girls' legs are a more telling indicator of future prices than more traditional measures displayed throughout this book and elsewhere. Enter the hemline indicator. Amazingly enough, it's taken quite seriously.

Its proponents argue that the same psychological forces that move investors to excessive swings of optimism and pessimism also dominate noninvestors and flow easily into fashions. This chart shows what they mean. Short and racy hemlines that expose lots of leg often have been associated with bull markets. Long Victorian-looking hemlines often have been associated with bear markets.

Take the pre–World War I period. As shown in Chart 27, stocks didn't do much for anyone then. Girl watchers didn't get much to cheer about either. Dresses were long, and so were bear markets. But the 1920s brought new enthusiasm to stocks and girl watchers. Hemlines shortened, and by 1929 fashionable flappers wore skirts that were daring—even by today's standards. As stock prices collapsed in the 1930s, so did hemlines, returning to cover all but the ankle. The market went nowhere in the 1940s, and neither did hemlines. But then with the rising markets of the 1950s, hemlines started moving back up. As girl watchers' spirits brightened, the market moved up more. The market exceeded 1929's level for the first time on an inflation-adjusted basis, and by the mid-1960s was at all-time highs. Enter the miniskirt.

Other folks think this indicator skirts the basic issue (sorry). They think hemlines react to more basic psychological and sociological forces. They'll note, for instance, that the mid-1960s was also when Carol Doda first unbared it all at the Condor in San Francisco and started a national trend. These social analysts believe that topless dancing was part of a psychological trend that pinpointed the market's top, too. But then the mid-1970s markets were bleak, particularly if you adjust for the ravages of inflation (see Chart 22). Skirt lengths plunged, too. Enter the maxiskirt.

The basic appeal of hemline watching is that they're all around you; you needn't get your investment data from some dusty library stack. But, of course, hemlines are impossible to quantify, much less study seriously. And, despite some amazing coincidences, you can't tell if hemlines predict the future or are a result of the past. Do short skirts mean the market will rise or that it already has? Technically hemlines have moved after the market; does that mean the market will then reverse course? Who knows? I don't. It seems like quackery to me. Perhaps the most notable bull markets, the ones coming after disastrous declines like the huge ones starting in 1932 and 1974, saw no hemline effect.

Where does this leave us today? One keen but skeptical observer wonders if indecision isn't what's wrong with the late 1986 stock market. She says, "Maybe the market is just like hemlines—anything goes these days."

The Hemline Indicator, 1897–1986

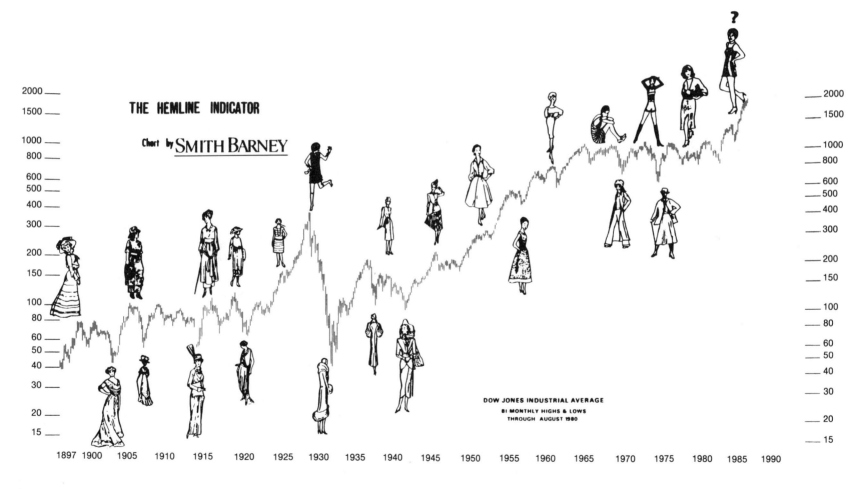

THE HEMLINE INDICATOR

Chart by SMITH BARNEY

DOW JONES INDUSTRIAL AVERAGE
BI MONTHLY HIGHS & LOWS
THROUGH AUGUST 1980

Source: Smith Barney Harris Upham, Incorporated.

87
Don't Buy Nuttin' What Eats

Early one morning, my wife noticed a man poking a 20-foot-long stick up a tree on the edge of our forest. It turned out to be our neighbor trying to get his $1,000 cat down from an oak tree. He was late for a flight east, but he was worried about his wife's prize feline and wanted to know if I had any suggestions. Scratching the cobwebs from my brain, I murmured the only thing that came to mind, which was a flash from my father's long-deceased Uncle Arthur, an old time investment junky, who babbled, "Don't buy nuttin' what eats."

Recently, for a hobby, I've raised some chicks and ducks. I like eating the fresh eggs and watching the ducks swim in our pond. It turns out the raccoons and coyotes like my fine feathered friends, too. Only two are left.

Some folks might get misled by this chart into believing that thoroughbred horses are good investments. According to the chart, yearling thoroughbreds increased in value from $7,676 to $30,000 in the decade ending 1980. I can see why. Ten-year-old yearlings are awfully rare critters. Of course, that's silly. But a horse's value does drop drastically with age, so these kinds of prices aren't really attainable over the long term. You certainly can't buy a horse the way Uncle Arthur owned stocks and real estate. When he died 15 years ago, he owned stocks he had bought in the 1930s. Then again, I guess a rare 40-year-old horse might be valuable as a curiosity.

Even worse, horses need care—rent, food, shoes, equipment, veterinary bills. A friend who quit the horse business in 1974 says it cost him about $1,100 per year per horse in direct costs to keep his 30 horses. Then, either you give up other activities (opportu-nity cost), or you pay a keeper to care for your critter. To sell your horse, you pay trainer's fees (brokerage), which average 15 percent.

Don't omit these ancillary costs as a discount in figuring an investment's real return by looking only at price the way the chart does. As shown in Chart 60, even property taxes can drop real estate's real return by a lot. Stocks and bonds have no operating costs. In fact, they may generate income, which should be added into your total return.

This chart says thoroughbreds did better than stocks. Did they? Deduct 10 years of $1,100 per year direct costs, adjusted for inflation, and you're reducing the $30,000 value by $12,750 to $17,250. Take out 15 percent for commissions, and you've got $14,662—less if you had to pay a keeper to care for the beast. The chart says the Dow rose from 600 to 1,000 in those 10 years, but the Dow also paid about a 5 percent dividend yield all those years. If that 5 percent were reinvested in the Dow each year, dividends compounding on top of price appreciation, the total 1980 value would have been about $15,910. Take out a 1 percent brokerage commission for selling, and you've got $15,750. Stocks win—in a decade that wasn't the greatest for stocks.

Stocks are liquid, too. Horses are liquid only as they enter the glue pot. And for $30,000, you could buy all 30 Dow Jones stocks instead of 8 to 12 legs. And stocks rarely die.

So whenever someone wants you to buy an investment requiring further postpurchase cash infusions and care, remember Uncle Arthur and "Don't buy nuttin' what eats."

Average Thoroughbred Yearling Prices Compared to Dow Jones Industrials Yearly Close, 1970–1980

195

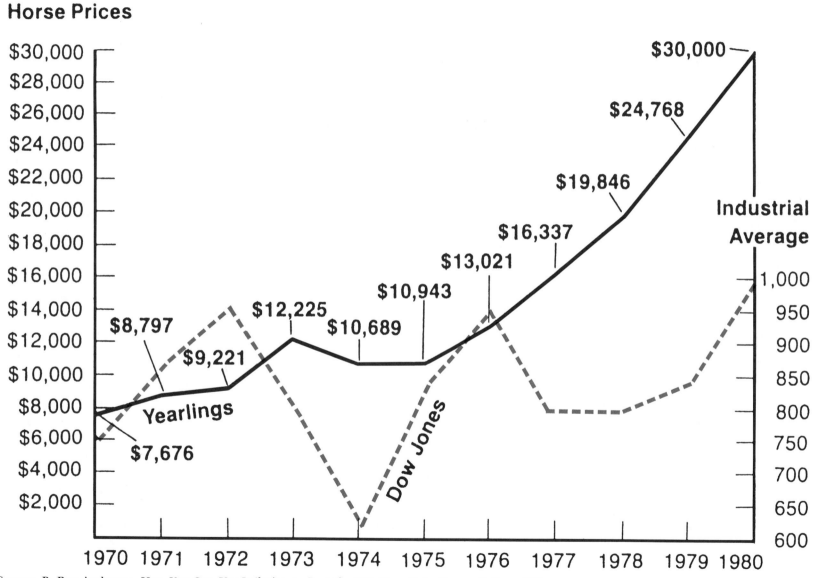

Source: B. Ray Anderson, *How You Can Use Inflation to Beat the IRS*, New York: Harper & Row, 1981.

88
Wall Street Witch Doctors

"Beware of false prophets" is always a wise warning with economic or financial forecasts. But when technical analysts, those veritable Wall Street witch doctors, start prophesying the future from past price action alone, watch out! Here is a good example of voodoo charting. This chart appeared in a 1964 book that argued that stocks obey the laws of physics. The argument ran about like this: Because the market had started an exponential growth curve, as the chart shows, and because the laws of physics indicate that exponential trends continue, stocks should proceed along this path indefinitely. If you take this to its illogical conclusion, stocks should have risen ever faster until, by now prices should have been skyrocketing at the orbital velocity of 1,000 percent a minute.

Common sense tells you this is nuts. It would have been better to observe the laws of gravity: What goes up, comes down. In fact, several years later, the market leaped off this "exponential curve" and lost more than 70 percent of its real purchasing power in the next 17 years (see Chart 22). In a bull market, folks believe anything bullish—even bullheadish.

The underlying fallacy is to assume that past price action alone, without other causes, can predict the future. Despite the plethora of books written to convince you of this, no solid academic, empirical, or theoretical evidence supporting this idea has been produced—ever. Past price action alone has zilch power in predicting future price action—maybe even less.

Anyone familiar with probability theory knows this. To convince yourself, try an experiment: Get some graph paper and make a dot on it. Now, flip a coin 50 or 100 times. If your first flip is heads, move one square to the right and up one square, and make another dot. If your flip is tails, move one square to the right, but down one square; then make your dot. Keep flipping and moving to the right. Before you've flipped your lid, envision that each square vertically represents $1 and each square horizontally represents 1 day. Connect the dots, and you get a chart identical to the price action of a typical stock, complete with extended trends up and down.

Few people expect such patterns; most think that several consecutive heads increase the chances that the next toss will be tails. But any statistics student knows that no matter how many tosses turn up heads, the odds of the next toss being tails is still exactly 50/50. In the same way, each change in stock prices has nothing to do with past price action alone.

This is not to say that all price charts lack predictive value. For example, turn to Chart 4, which shows the historic relationship between the earnings yields of stocks and bond yields. When stocks sell at P/Es of 20 (earnings yields of $\frac{1}{20}$, or 5 percent) and bond yields are 9 percent, an arbitrage spread exists (see text with Chart 4). If corporate earnings don't rise far and fast, you're better off with bonds—for the higher return—and probably better future prices. Similarly, other charts in this book have predictive value, because they illustrate a basic economic causal relationship. The important point is, don't be suckered by predictions based on price action alone. They don't work.

Exponential Upsweep of Dow Industrials, 1926–1962+

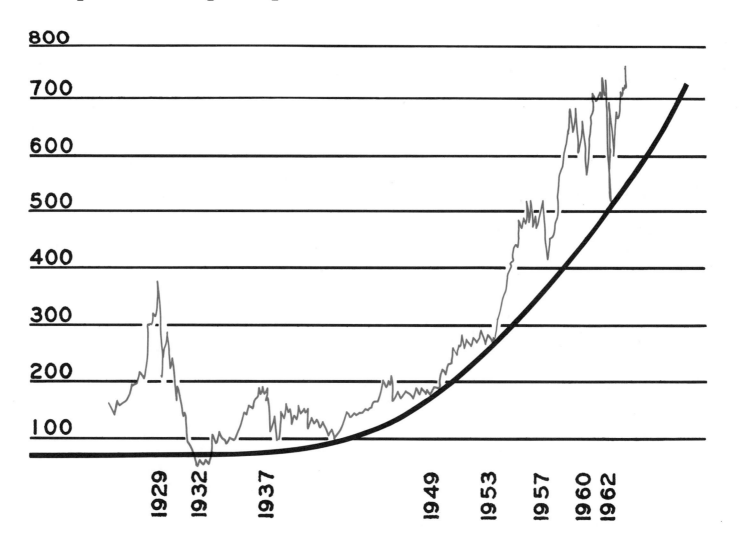

197

Source: Benton W. Davis, *Dow 1000: The Exponential Secret of the Great Bull Market*, Larchmont, New York: American Research Council, 1964.

89
Flukes of Nature and Finance

Some folks get too carried away with charts. They can be a good source of quick historical overview, so you can learn lots from them. But charts can lead to erroneous conclusions, too. There is a whole world of "technicians" who believe something's future can be predicted merely from its past price action. That is rarely, if ever, true. While charts can help you understand the environment—which may help you understand the future—there is no evidence whatsoever that prior price action alone is a positive predictor of future prices.

Most cyclical patterns, of any type, that fit into prolonged but neat zig-zag patterns tend to involve nature. Tree rings, population dynamics of Alaskan brown bears, populations of foxes versus rodents, solar radiation, the tides, all of these and more show signs of recurring, understandable, and rather predictable cycles. When people get involved, the understandable portion often gets messy, and the predictable portion becomes impossible. Yet it is here that folks get most carried away with wacko theories.

This chart shows the 9.6-year cycle in wheat harvests. As a partial phenomenon of nature, it has done well at seeming to have predictive qualities. Note that the peaks and troughs neatly fit a 9.6-year-long, almost perfect, zig-zag pattern. The periods represented by points A fit the mold. But there are some exceptions. The dates represented by points B are the few clear exceptions to this almost perfectly repeating pattern.

Are wheat harvests dominated by nature or humans? There is probably a big effect from both. But people surely have lots to do with it. Along the way, it isn't likely that this seemingly recurring pattern is as logical or as predictable as something perfectly natural—like tidal cycles.

Would you be willing to bet money that this pattern will recur perfectly? If so, you would bet that wheat harvests would be huge in 1986—and you would lose. You would also bet that when 1991 rolls around they won't be harvesting much wheat. Are you ready to make that bet? I wouldn't. It's just shooting blindly.

Probability theory dictates that some events that appear to be cycles are merely coincidences. If every American kept flipping coins, somebody somewhere would generate thousands of consecutive uninterrupted heads tosses. That wouldn't mean the person could keep generating heads or could have predicted the streak. It just means he or she had loads of luck. The same principle applies to the "chain letters" that make your friends oodles of money but break down just before you get yours. Some things are just luck.

Beware of chart patterns that look too perfectly recurring. If there isn't a perfectly natural explanation (spelled "nature"), the seemingly perfect cycle will probably break down just before you need it to work.

The 9.6-Year Cycle in Acreage of Wheat Harvested, 1860–1970

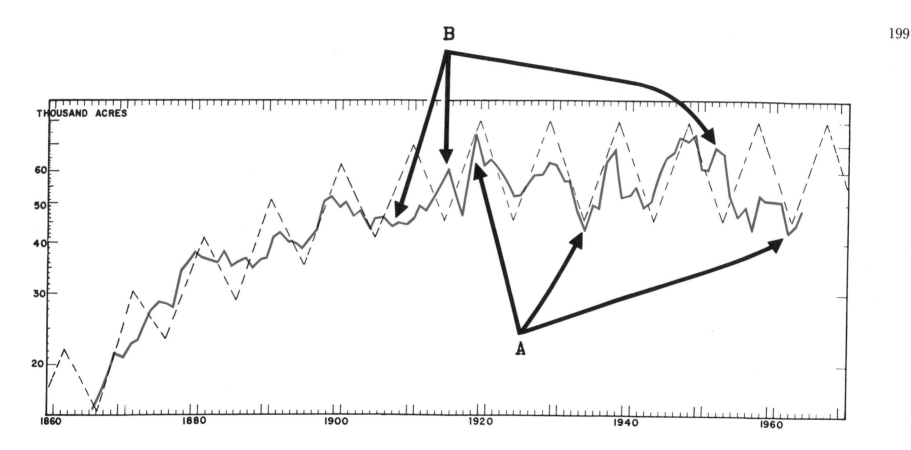

90
Don't Lose Your Hide in the Market

"Don't buy stocks now—the indicators are giving you a bum steer. They're breaking out of their range, and the bulls will end up having a cow. They're gonna get milked. The herd effect is just too strong. So don't lose your hide over it."

Vintage circa 1900! And it's all from this chart. As this century began, more folks still lived on farms than in the cities, and you could tell a lot about finance and business from looking at trends in the cattle industry—maybe a little like looking at autos or housing starts today.

This book presents charts and offers analysis, lessons, and predictions based on charts—many of which are quite old. But you can go much too far with parallelism from yesteryear. The key is to make sure that historic trends that once tied events together in tight-knit correlations were and are supported by valid causal relationships, so that the chart truly teaches a valid lesson for the future.

This chart is beautiful and fascinating, and it teaches a valid lesson even if you won't make a fortune outguessing the market based on cattle trends. It comes from the Brookmire Economic Chart series (see also Chart 33) and was state of the art for its day. It shows a lot more than you need to focus on here.

Look in the middle of the chart, where it shows hide prices, which range from a low in 1908 of 9 cents to a high in 1913 of 20 cents. (The scale is on the left.) If you flip back to Chart 33 and compare this chart to that one, you will see that movements in hide prices paralleled stock market fluctuations—particularly railroad prices. Because shipping cattle was a big part of the railroad business in those days, investors used hide prices as a coincident indicator of stock trends, by noticing any divergence between stock trends and hide trends. If hide prices were falling and stock prices rising, or vice versa, observers would look for signs that one of the two would soon reverse and point to a major trend for both.

So when Chart 33 was ending, in 1911 and 1912, investors would have looked to the 50 percent rise in hide prices as an indicator that stocks would likely rise, too. But they would have been wrong. As shown in Chart 27, stocks didn't exceed their old 1909 peak until 1917 and didn't exceed it by any significant amount until the mid-1920s. But the significance of farm activity on the economy had been rapidly fading for decades, and the old correlations were no longer valid.

The charts in this book are important, and their validity is strong. But just as it would be a mistake to forecast movements in stock prices today based on what had happened to hide prices, it is a mistake to base investment decisions on logical causal relationships that were once valid but no longer pertain. Be careful with any single relationship that seems to have historically strong powers for future prediction. Ironically, God seems to design life so that just about the time you locate and learn the relationship, it falls apart, and you lose your hide trying to navigate with bad instruments.

Cycles of Hide and Leather Prices

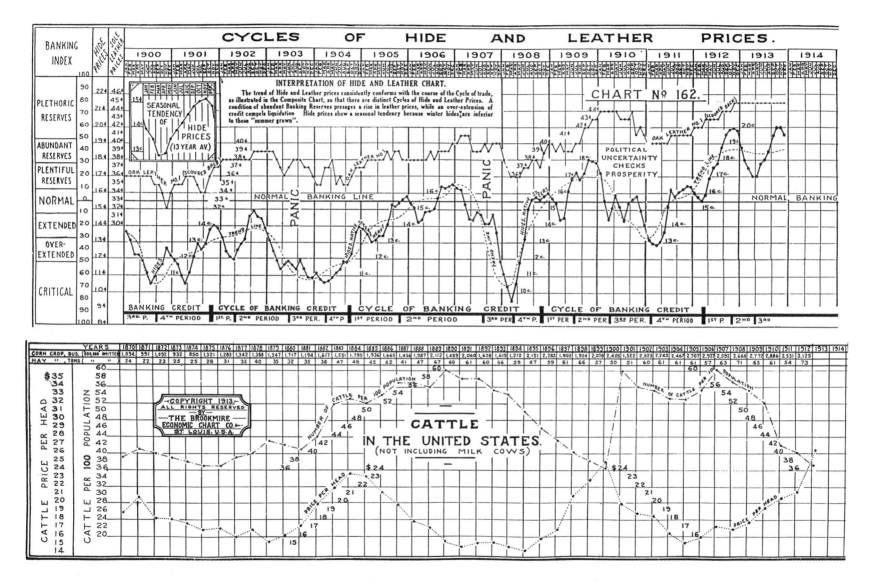

CONCLUSION

People are scared of lots of things—federal deficits, the drug crisis, wars, escalating crime rates, even Wall Street. You should know by now that not much of what scares people is really worthy of fear. The financial world won't come to an end soon due to factors like these or any others. There are real problems to face in life and always have been. But they are the kinds we've always faced and lived with.

You're not going to lose all your money in the market, for example, because of a financial crisis caused by the deficit. You're much more likely to lose money if you pay too dearly and then panic and sell out after the subsequent crash that always follows excessive optimism. People do that all the time without the aid of massive societal dislocations. Wall Street and your own hysteria are perfectly capable of providing you with all the dislocations imaginable, all of them based on myths and mirages.

The Wall Street Waltz has gone on for centuries, through wars, revolutions, famines, and inflations. It's gone on through explorations, scientific discoveries, communist and Nazi threats, depressions, and Great Depressions. It's gone on all around the world in boom-bust cycles and with a rhythm all its own. Wall Street doesn't dance for politicians or kings or journalists or you or me. It dances for itself. And it will keep going on dancing, largely as it has, for the foreseeable future. Your only real choices are whether or not you want to be part of the dance, and if you do, whether you want to make a fool of yourself or profitably have fun.

If you want to waltz, these 90 visualizations should provide you continued guidance on valuation, on how the market wiggles, and on what happens with interest rates, real estate, commodities, and inflation. And years from now when some seemingly new mania or hysteria is causing all those about you to lose their heads, you can look back at these visualizations to reacquaint yourself with a glimpse of financial history that will make you relatively secure as to what is unusual and what isn't.

Just as these charts don't need much introduction, they need little conclusion. They speak for themselves, and the main conclusions should be yours. When the markets sell at the high end of most valuation measures, is it worthwhile to hang on? You must judge that for yourself. Only tools are offered here—the dance steps—but only you can actually do it.

Is the federal debt too big? That, as you've learned here, is more a moral issue than an economic one at this point, and accordingly, only you can decide it. Would it be worthwhile to sell off federally owned real estate to pay down the debt? You decide. If you've looked at the charts, you've been forced either to accept my viewpoints or you've thought for yourself. Either way, you're much better off than if you had never been exposed to the charts.

Beating the Market

No one who tries to "out-time" the market ever succeeds. There are all kinds of seers who claim to call all the market's turns.

Some claim to do it precisely, and most of them sell newsletters. But I don't believe them. If such a person really existed, that person would have made so much money that he or she would be highly visible. If such a person existed, according to calculations I made in my last book, he or she would have generated average annual returns of about 50 percent—and that's a lot.

Starting with just $25,000, which this fictitious investor might have borrowed against his or her home, it would have taken only 21 years to make the Forbes 400 list of richest Americans. It would have taken only 26 years to be worth $1.5 billion. Where are all these great market timers hiding? Wake up! You can't find them because they don't exist.

Do people beat the market? Yes. There are lots of visible records of masters who have beaten the market handily for decades. And most of them had an amazing knack for having lots of cash at market tops and being heavily invested around market bottoms. What did they have in common? None of them tried to time the market per se. They focused elsewhere. They didn't try to say, "Today is the top, sell everything." They didn't pick "bottoms" either.

Instead they leaned on some fundamental value-oriented mechanism such as those I described in *Super Stocks*, and regularly describe in *Forbes*, which encouraged them to buy stocks when they could find ones meeting their standards for quality and price. When stocks got too high, and they couldn't find stocks to meet those standards, they didn't buy stocks. As a bull market continued further, lots of the stocks they had bought earlier in the market advance became too pricy, and these savvy pros sold. But unable to find more stocks that met their buying standards, their cash balances bulged ever bigger.

Getting the Facts

Of course, all that cash at the top of a market makes anybody a little goosey. How would you feel if it kept going up? And buying after a major decline makes the most sophisticated pro nervous. These guys knew their stuff. But ironically guys like Warren Buffet, John Templeton, Ben Graham, T. Rowe Price, and others often looked over their own shoulders to seek solace from facts. They got their facts in varying ways. But one of the ways they often employed was to consider what reality from the past had provided as a menu of alternatives. From that they made their choices. They don't need these kinds of chart-based visualizations; the raw input is etched in their brains. But you can use these charts to emulate them.

Don't use charts like these as input to try to call all the market's turns. No one can do that (because no one's ever done it—why try to play a game no one's ever won?). Instead, seek value in stocks, and buy quality stocks that fit within the common historical perspectives provided by this book's first few charts. When stocks are too pricy to provide you that opportunity, pull back. Use these charts as a kind of board of directors to keep you on an even keel and advise you the way the legendary investors used the data etched in their minds to advise them.

Use these charts when the market's dropped 25 percent and you're scared and you need comfort to reassure yourself that it's OK to buy the stocks because they're cheap on a value basis. Use them when everybody is talking about how much money they're making in the market, but you're scared because you can't find anything but absolute junk that is statistically cheap based on long-term history. Use them when everyone says interest rates are headed lower, and you suspect that whatever everyone says can't possibly work out to be true. Use them periodically to refresh your memory about everything you've learned initially from them.

Learning the Dance

What should you have learned from all these visualizations? Every picture tells a story, and it won't do to recount them all in a conclusion. Each section's introduction tells you what to look for in that section. They're all there for you. But there are two overarching points to learn. One of them is to get yourself a financial calculator, learn how to use it, and learn to think in terms of compound interest. It is the rhythm to which Wall Street waltzes. That one simple lesson will place you so far ahead of most who approach Wall Street that you will see notable improvement in your financial results and your comfort level almost immediately.

The other lesson is what this whole book is about—why it was written: so that you will enjoy looking for facts rather than acting based on fantasies. I would be so happy if from now on you look for charts on your own and use them to make your own visualizations that lead you to investment conclusions based on facts rather than what everybody else is saying. If you're considering some investment choice, whatever it is, the major libraries have charts that pertain to the subject. For example, while it was too narrow for inclusion in this book, if you become interested in Australian investments, you could benefit by the outstanding charts in A. L. Lougheed's *The Brisbane Stock Exchange, 1884-1984*. You could even get good economic charts from countries like Malaysia, or even Kiribati or Maldives—all which are in *Key Indicators of Developing Member Countries of the Asian Development Bank*.

There is so much more, that you can never exhaust it all—and you needn't. Just take what you can use, and leave the rest on the shelf. If a simple picture is worth a thousand words, then learning to visualize reality from financial history is worth vastly more. If you have learned to visualize from facts, rather than fantasies, and use fact-based charts like these to steer you clear of hysteria, you will never ever watch Wall Street waltz the same way again.

APPENDIX:
MYTHS TO FRIGHTEN CHILDREN

When the market fluctuates 100 points a day or more, as it has lately, people begin to panic. But don't let mass hysteria throw you off course from a sound long-term investment program. The most severe and real problem for most investors should be finding stocks with real value—particularly so in a market that is up 130% in four years. Stick to unpopular stocks of good companies.

But—some people say—isn't the federal deficit so bad that it threatens the entire economy, unpopular stocks included? Not so. While you read lots of media hype about the deficit, and politicians babble about it to no end, the deficit/federal debt hysteria is just one many scarecrows needlessly frightening folks from sound investment policies.

The crucial issue isn't the deficit's size or total federal debt, but our ability to service that debt. The fact is, total federal debt is a smaller percentage of GNP than it was in mid-1960s, and lots lower than the 1950s. Public debt as a percentage of GNP reached a peak of about 120% during World War II. For the next 30 years we shrank that ratio. Even in years when we ran budget deficits, debt shrank relative to GNP because real growth and inflation raised the ratio's denominator more than the deficits raised its numerator. Inflation was a big force, boosting our repayment power by lowering the debt's value.

By 1955 the 120% had dropped to 58%. By 1965 it was 42%, and by 1975 it reached a 40-year low of 25%. Since then, things have worsened. Yes. That much is true. The deficits have grown, and the ratio has risen. Risen to where? Only to the low 40s. Nothing like what we lived with years ago.

Another way to look at the deficit is to compare it with those of other countries. Over the last five years our deficit has averaged about 3% of GNP. Other countries? In Japan it's 7.4%; in Germany, 2.5%; in France, 2.6%; in England, 3.5%; in Canada, 5%. But the worriers say the deficit and debt load are worse for us because our savings rate is lower. That, too, is exaggerated. As Susan Lee demonstrated in a compelling article (FORBES Dec. 16, 1985), the differences are mainly in accounting and how we do our savings now—like pension plans.

It isn't clear to me that the much heralded deficit even exists—if you account for it right. If Du Pont kept its books the way Uncle Sam does, that stalwart chemical giant would have run deficits virtually nonstop for decades. But Du Pont rolls right along, and with good company. Why? When a business builds a plant, buys a car or a computer, it capitalizes the item on its balance sheet and slowly counts it as expense over the asset's estimated life. But Uncle Sam doesn't keep a balance sheet. When it buys those same items, it expenses them immediately. A major portion of the companies in The Forbes 500s would run deficits if their books were kept via the government's ultraconservative cash basis.

Our major airports are worth a few billion bucks each. Ditto for the highway system. The military system. The Postal Service. The parks and forest lands. There's also the small stuff, like computers and trucks. The government is, by far, the largest buyer in every major category of big-ticket items, but these purchases are all expensed immediately—even raw land.

Then there are the huge budget surpluses generated by states and municipalities—which total almost half of the official federal deficit, but are financed by federal government transfer payments of $100 billion-plus. The states and municipalities also understate their surpluses, because they don't capitalize their asset purchases either.

So if you lumped the federal government, states and municipalities together, and treated all their asset purchases the way corporations do, you would either have vaporized the government "deficit" or come damn close. As a percentage of GNP? It would be so small, it wouldn't be worth mentioning.

Don't get me wrong. There are real problems—like the growth in government spending. Since 1965 federal spending has risen 11% per year. Worse, it grew from about 18% of GNP to 24% now. If those relative growth rates continue, it would take only a shocking 96 years for the government to take over the whole GNP—everything. And President Reagan's 11% annual profligacy is even higher than Carter's was, once you adjust for the lower inflation during Reagan's terms.

If you want to worry, then, worry about the trend in government spending. But despite a frightening-sounding federal deficit and scary air pockets in the stock market, our world is not coming to an end. It will continue to reward folks who buy good stocks when they are cheap and hold them until the market recognizes their merits.

Reprinted from Mr. Fisher's 10/6/86 FORBES column.

Index

Acquisitions, 54-55, 72-73
Agricultural land values, 134-37
Alternatives, stocks *vs.*, 52-53
Animals for investment, 194-95
Annual sales, stock prices and, 28
Antibusiness attitudes, 141
Art, investing in, 52
Assets, replacement cost of, 54
Auto sales, 150-51

Bank of England, 82-85
Bear market trends, 64-65
Bonds
    AA, 103
    earnings and, 20-21
    foreign, 100-101
    interest rates and, 30
    prices of, 1896-1912, 78-79
    railroad, 30, 78-81
    vs. stocks, 20-21, 36, 102-3
Book value, 24
Britain. *See* England
Budget, federal, 182
Bull market trends, 64-65
Business activity, 1790-1986, 144-45
Business cycles, 1790-1925

Calculator, electronic, 7
Canadian market, 40-43
Capital expenditures, 26
Capital gains tax, 20
Capital spending, 156-57
Car sales, 150-51
Cash flow, 26
Cattle industry cycles, 200-201
Chapter 11, preferred stock and, 74
Charts, use of, 5-6, 202-4
Commercial paper, prime, 32, 106-7
Commodities, 93-95
    gold and, 122-23
    prices of, 1982-1986, 128-29
    wholesale prices of, 118-19
Common stocks
    foreign, 100-101
    rate of return on, 88-89
    vs. preferred, 74-75
Compound interest rates, 90-91
Consols, 108-9
Consumer Price Index, 120-21
Cowles Commission data, 16
Crash of 1929, 11
    P/E ratio and, 14, 68-69
    warnings of, 70

Crude oil
    prices of, 104-5
    supply, 164-65
Cycles, 132
    business, 1790-1925, 146-47
    hemlines and, 192-93
    hide and leather, 200-201
    Kondratieff Wave and, 188-89
    stock market, 64-65
    sunspots and, 190-91
    wheat harvests and, 198-99

Debt
    federal, 140
    public, 168-69
Defense expenditures, 186-87
Deficit, federal, 140
Depreciation, 26
Depression, 11
    P/E ratio and, 14
Discount rate, 30
Dividends, 22
    of common stocks, 74
Domestic car sales, 150-51
Dow Jones Industrials, 24
    GNP and, 44
    inflation and, 56
    interest rates and, 32-33

moving average of, 58-59
    1920s *vs.* 1980s, 66-67
    1926-1962, 196-97

Earnings
    on bonds, 20-21
    on stocks, 10, 18-21
        Depression and, 14
        Panic of 1893 and, 16
        See also Price/earnings ratio
    price-to-book ratio and, 24
Economic forecasting, 142
Economic growth and electricity use, 162-63
Economy, stocks and, 62
Electric utility industry, 166-67
Electricity use, 162-63
England
    Bank of, 82-85
    interest rates in, 110-11
    prices in
        retail, 124-25
        wholesale, 114-15
    Southern, prices in, 116-17
    stocks in, 38-43, 82-85
        1860-1980, 108-9
    unemployment in, 154-55
E/P ratio, 10

208

Equipment expenditures, 156–57
European stock market. *See* Overseas stocks
Exponential rise of stock prices, 196

Farm real estate, 134–37
Fashion, economic cycles and, 192–93
Federal budget, 182
Federal debt, 140, 168
Federal deficit, 140
Federal expenditures, 176–77
  taxes and, 180–81
Federal lands, 184–85
Federal revenue, 170–71. *See also* Taxes
Forecasting, economic, 142
Foreign business cycles, 146–47
Foreign GNP, 44–45
Foreign investing, 11, 38–43, 82–85
  crash of 1929 and, 70
  interest rates and, 98–99
  1955–1965, 100–101
Foreign labor, 160–61
Fundamental investment analysis, 58

Germany, retail prices in, 124–25
GNP, 44–45
  defense spending and, 186–87

electricity use and, 162–63
plant and equipment expenditures and, 156–57
public debt and, 168–69
Gold
  commodity prices and, 122–23
  inflation and, 95
  price of, 130–31
  production of, 158–59
  South Africa and, 158–59
  vs. stocks, 52
Government growth, 172–73
Government policies, 140–43
  Laffer curve and, 178
  oil supply and, 164
Growth stocks, 12
  P/E multiples of, 46–49

Hambrecht & Quist Growth Index, 48–49
Harvests, economic cycles and, 198–99
Headlines, stocks and, 60–61
Hemlines, 192–93
Hide prices, 200–201
Horses for investment, 194–95
Housing prices, 138–39
Housing starts, 152–53

Income tax, 20, 170, 174
  rates for, 182–83
Industrial Composite, Value Line, 34–35

Industrial Revolution, labor costs and, 160
Inflation
  Dow Jones average and, 56–57
  GNP and, 44
  interest rates and, 93–95
  Kondratieff Wave and, 188
  price-to-book ratio and, 24
  prices in Southern England and, 116–17
  1790–1985, 120–21
  wholesale, 118–19
Initial public offerings (IPOs), 12, 50–51
Interest rates, 92–93, 108, 112–13
  bonds and, 20–21, 30
  foreign, 100–101
  compound, 90–91
  1841–1918, 106–7
  long-term, 10, 30–31, 96–97
    British, 110–11
    foreign, 98–99
  P/E ratio and, 18
  1790–1980, 112–13
  short-term, 11, 32–33, 96–97
  stocks and, 32–33
Investment alternatives, stocks *vs.*, 52–53
Investment analysis, 58
IPOs (initial public offerings), 12, 50–51
IRA investments, 90–91

Kitchen cycles, 132
Knowledge, accumulation of, 167
Kondratieff wave, 108–9, 188–89

Labor costs, 142, 160–61
Laffer curve, 178–79
Land. *See* Real estate
Learning curve, 166
Leather prices, 200–201
Local expenditures, 176–77
Local taxes, 174–75
London market, 38, 82–85
Long cycles, 132
Long-term interest rates, 10, 30–31, 96–97
  British, 110–11
  foreign, 98–99

Market, stock. *See* Stocks
Mergers, 54–55, 72–73
Military spending, 186–87
Mining, gold, 158
Monthly railroad prices, 1843–1862, 80–81
Moving average of Dow Jones, 58–59

National debt, 172–73
News headlines, stocks and, 60–61

Oil
  prices of, 104–5
  supply of, 164–65
1 percent rule, 148
OPEC, oil supply and, 164
Overpriced stocks, 10
Overseas GNP, 44–45
Overseas stocks, 11, 38–43,
    82–85
  crash of 1929 and, 70
  interest rates and, 98–99
  1955–1965, 100–101

Panic of 1893, 16
Panic of 1907, 76–79
Panic of 1903, 78–79
Paper, prime commercial, 32,
    106–7

P/E. See Price/earnings ratio
Physics, stock prices and, 196
Plant expenditures, 156–57
Preferred stocks, 12, 74–75
Price/cash flow ratio, 26–27
Price/dividend ratio, 22–23

Price/earnings ratio (P/E), 10,
    14–17
  bonds and, 20–21
  business conditions and, 18
  Cowles Commission data
      and, 16
  growth stocks and, 12, 46–49
  interest rates and, 18
  1928–1929, 68–69
Price/sales ratio (PSR), 28

Prices
  of commodities. See
      Commodities
  gold and, 122–23
  of gold, 130–31
  housing, 138–39
  real estate. See Real estate
  retail, 124–25
  of stocks. See Stocks
  wholesale, 114–15
  war and, 126–27
Price-to-book ratio, 24–25
Prime commercial paper, 32,
    106–7
Public debt, 168–69
Public finance, 172–73

Railroad stocks and bonds,
    30–31
  consols vs., 108–9
  prices of
      1843–1862, 80–81
      1896–1912, 78–79
Real estate, 93–95, 132–33
  federal, 184–85
  rural, 134–37
Real interest rates, 112–13
Real residential fixed
    investment, 152–53
Recessions
  unemployment and, 148–49
  stocks and, 62–63
Replacement cost of assets, 54
Retail prices, 124–25
Revenue, federal, 170–71

Rich Man's Panic of 1903,
    78–79

Sales, stock prices and, 28
Sears, 28–29
Short-term interest rates, 11,
    32–33, 96–97
Single family house prices, 139
Skirt hemlines, 192–93
Small stocks, 36
"Snake," 102–3
South Africa
  gold and, 158–59
  investment in, 142
South Seas Company, 84–85
Southern England, prices in,
    116–17
Stagflation, 152
State expenditures, 176–77
State taxes, 174–75
Stocks
  common
      foreign, 100–101
      rate of return on, 88–89
      vs. preferred, 74–75
  cycles in, 64–65. See also
      Cycles
  dividends and, 22
  growth, 12, 46–49
  interest rates and, 32–33
  news headlines and, 60–61
  overpriced, 10, 26
  overseas and foreign, 11,
      38–43, 70, 82–85,
      100–101

performance of, 11
preferred, 12, 74–75
prices of
    1896–1912, 78–79
    1927–1929, 70–71
    1790–1980, 86–87
  railroad, 30, 78–81
  recessions and, 62–63
  replacement cost of assets
      and, 54
  small, 36
  vs. alternative investments,
      52–53
  vs. bonds, 20–21, 36, 102–3
  vs. GNP, 44–45
Sunspots, 190–91

Takeovers, 54–55, 72–73
Tax revolts, 176
Taxes, 170–71
  capital gains, 20
  Laffer curve and, 178
  rates for, 182–83
  spending and, 180–81
  state and local, 174–75
Technical investment analysis,
    58
Technology index, 48–49
Thoroughbreds for investment,
    194–95
Treasury notes, oil and, 104–5
2 percent rule, 76

Unemployment, 148–49
  British, 154–55

Utility industry, 166–67

Value Line Industrial
    Composite (VIC), 34–35

War, wholesale prices and,
    126–27
Wealth indexes of investments,
    36–37
Wheat harvests, economic
    cycles and, 198–99
Wholesale inflation, 118–19
Wholesale prices, 114–15
    war and, 126–27

210

While its appearance has changed over the years, Wall Street waltzs much the same today as it did at the turn of the century.

Photo by Peter Simon